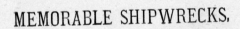

MEMORABLE SHIPWRECKS,

MEMORABLE SHIPWRECKS

AND

SEAFARING ADVENTURES

OF THE NINETEENTH CENTURY.

BY

J. F. LAYSON

———•———

PRESTON:

JAMES ASKEW, 30 GRAFTON STREET.

1884.

Preface.

TO the people of a maritime country, stories of the perils and providences endured and experienced by those who have had "their path in the great waters," must always present points of interest peculiarly their own. Nor will such narratives to any extent be otherwise than attractive to the reader when the eye-witnesses of the scenes are allowed to describe these, as far as practicable, in their own way. In compiling the following pages a preference has been shown towards personal descriptions by the ship-wrecked seaman, the passenger, and the adventurer, when bearing the marks of authenticity. Most of the tales of the sea now re-told have been re-written or condensed, so as to give all the main facts of each, but without unnecessary iteration.

CONTENTS.

Memorable Shipwrecks of the XIXth Century.

THE LADY HOBART.

THE English Mail Packet, *Lady Hobart*, sailed from Halifax, Nova Scotia, on the 22d of June 1803, steering a course to the southward and eastward, to clear Sable Island. On the 24th the vessel hauled to the northward, in order to pass over the northern part of the Bank of Newfoundland, and thus avoid contact with the French ships of war that were known to be cruising a little to the southward of the Bank. On the morning of the 25th a large schooner, with her deck full of men, was discovered bearing down upon the packet. The stranger displayed the French tri-coloured flag, and otherwise indicated that she took the English ship for an unarmed merchantman, that would fall as an easy prey to the prowess of her crew. In that surmise, however, the French captain was mistaken, for when within range of the *Lady Hobart's* guns, a shot from the latter speedily dispelled the illusion, and urged him to strike his colours, and quietly submit to be boarded by a party from the English ship, sent to take possession of the prize.

The French schooner was found to be *l'Amiable Julie*, of eighty tons, hailing from Port Liberté and bound for St.

Pierre, whither she was taking a cargo of salted fish, under the charge of her master, Citizen Charles Rossé. After the commander and his crew had been removed, the *Julie* was taken into the charge of two officers of the English Royal Navy, who were passengers in the *Lady Hobart*, and who volunteered their services in the emergency. To assist in navigating the prize, two of the English seamen and two prisoners also went on board the schooner.

On the morning after the capture of the Frenchman a strong gale blew from the westward. There was a heavy sea, with hazy weather and dense fogs at intervals. About one o'clock the *Lady Hobart* was going at the rate of seven miles an hour, when she struck against an island of ice with such force as to pitch several of the crew out of their hammocks. The suddenness of the shock also aroused the captain, and he instantly ran upon deck. The helm being instantly put hard-a-port, the vessel again struck about the chess-tree, and then swung round on her keel; the stern-post being stove in and the rudder carried away, before the crew could succeed in their attempts to haul her off the iceberg, which now appeared to hang over the ship, menacing her with instant destruction. The length of the berg was calculated to be nearly half-a-mile, and it formed a peak about twice the height of the masthead. The sea was now furiously breaking over the ice, and the water rushed in so fast as in a few minutes to fill the hold of the vessel.

Orders were now given to heave the guns overboard, to cut away the anchors from the bows, and to get two sails under the bottom of the ship, while both of the pumps were kept a-going, and some of the crew baled the hold by means of buckets from the main hatchway, in the hope of preventing the sinking of the vessel. In less than a quarter of an hour, however, she settled down to her forechains in the water. The situation had now become most perilous, and the captain took counsel with an officer of the Royal Navy, who was a passenger on board, and also with Mr. Bargus the sailing-master, as to the propriety of making any further efforts to save the ship, as well as the likelihood of being able to preserve the mails, by embarking these in the boats from over the ship's side.

After a hurried consultation, it was agreed that no time should be lost in hoisting out the boats, and as the vessel was fast sinking, that the first and only consideration was to endeavour to save the passengers and crew. Accordingly the cutter and jolly-boat were launched upon a sea that was running high, while all on board seemed animated by a desire to face the dangers of the hour with composure and self-possession. Indeed, from the first moment of striking the iceberg, not a word was uttered by any one expressive of a wish to ensure personal safety by leaving the wreck, and the captain's orders were promptly obeyed by the crew without the slightest manifestation of panic or fear, and with that remarkable attention to the claims of good discipline which is one of the most prominent traits of the British seaman when in the presence of danger.

In the cutter three ladies were placed, though one of them was so terrified that she leaped from the gunwale of the ship, and was pitched into the bottom of the boat with considerable violence. But, happily, no fatal consequences ensued. The safety of the only females on board having thus been primarily attended to, the few provisions that had been secured from the men's berths were next put into the boats, which were quickly veered astern. By this time the main-deck forward was under water, and nothing but the quarter-deck was visible. The captain then ordered the men into the boats, and after heavy weights had been lashed to the mails, that portion of the freight was thrown overboard. It was perceived that the vessel was speedily settling down, and only two persons now remained upon the doomed mail packet — namely, the captain and the

sailing-master. The former urged the latter officer to take
his place in one of the boats; but Bargus replied, with a
generosity characteristic of his class, that he would see his
commander safely embarked before quitting his own post; an
arrangement to which the captain of the *Lady Hobart* was
at length reluctantly obliged to consent.

When the boats were launched, the sea was running so
high that but little hope was entertained of ever reaching
land in safety, and nothing but the most orderly conduct of
the crew could have enabled voyagers, under such adverse
circumstances, to accomplish such a hazardous undertaking.
Not a man had even attempted to make use of a portion of
the abundant supply of liquor on board the vessel. The
remainder of the captain's story may best be narrated in his
own words :—

While the cutter was getting out, I perceived John
Tipper, one of the seamen, emptying a five-gallon bottle,
and on inquiry found the contents had been rum. He said
he was doing so for the purpose of filling it with water from
the scuttle-cask on the quarter-deck, which had generally
been filled over night, and which was then the only fresh
water that could be got at. It afterwards became our
principal supply. This circumstance I relate as being so
highly creditable to the character of a British sailor.

We had scarce quitted the ship when she gave a heavy
lurch to port, and went down head foremost. I had ordered
the colours to be hoisted at the main-topgallant masthead,
with the union downwards, as a signal of distress, that if
any vessel should happen to be near us at the dawn of day,
our calamitous situation might attract observation and
afford us relief. I cannot attempt to describe my own feelings, or the sensations of my people. Exposed as we were
in two open boats in the great Atlantic, bereft of all assistance but that which our own exertions under Providence
could afford us, we narrowly escaped being swallowed up in

the vortex. Men accustomed to vicissitudes are not easily
dejected, but there are trials that human nature alone
cannot surmount. The consciousness of having done our
duty, however, and reliance on a good Providence, enabled
us to endure the calamity that had befallen us, and we
reanimated each other with the hope of a better fate.

While we were employed in deliberating concerning our
future arrangements, a singular incident occurred, which
occasioned considerable uneasiness amongst us At the
moment the ship was sinking, she was surrounded by what
seamen call "a school," or an incalculable number of whales,
which could only be accounted for by our knowing that at
this particular season they take a direction for the coast
of Newfoundland, in quest of a small fish called capelard,
which they devour.   From their near approach, we were
extremely apprehensive that they might strike the boats
and materially damage them, frequent instances having
occurred in the fishery of boats being cut in twain by the
force of a single blow from a whale.   We therefore shouted
and used every effort to drive them away, but without
effect.   As it seemed, the whales continued to pursue us,
and remained about the boats for half-an-hour, when they
disappeared without having done us any injury.

When the ship foundered, an hour had scarcely elapsed
from the moment of her striking the iceberg.   The crew
were distributed in the following order.   In the cutter,
which was twenty feet long, six feet four inches broad, and
two feet six inches deep, were embarked three ladies and
myself, Captain Richard Thomas of the Navy, the French
commander of the schooner, the master's mate, gunner,
steward, carpenter, and eight seamen—in all eighteen people.
These, together with the provisions, brought the boat's gunwale down to within six or seven inches of the water.
Some idea of our crowded state may be formed from this ;
but it is scarcely possible for the imagination to conceive

the extent of our sufferings. In the jolly-boat, which was fourteen feet from stem to stern, five feet three inches broad, and two feet deep, were embarked Mr. Bargus the master, Lieut.-Col. Cook of the Guards, the boatswain, sail-maker, and seven seamen—in all eleven persons.

The only provisions we were able to save consisted of between forty and fifty pounds of biscuits, a vessel containing five gallons of water, as also a small jug, and part of a barrel of spruce beer, five gallons of rum, a few bottles of port, with two compasses, a quadrant, a spy-glass, and a small tin mug. The deck-lantern, which had a few candles in it, had also been thrown into the boat; and the cook having taken the precaution to secure his tinder-box and some matches that were kept in a bladder, we were enabled to steer by night.

The wind was now blowing strongly from the west-ward, with a heavy sea, and another day had just dawned. Estimating ourselves 350 miles distant from St. John's, Newfoundland, with the prospect of westerly winds continuing, I found it necessary at once to use the strictest economy. This I represented to my companions in distress, and also that our resolution should on no account be changed, but that we should begin by suffering privations, which I foresaw would be greater than I ventured to explain. To each person, therefore, we served out half-a-biscuit and a glass of wine, which was the only allowance for the ensuing twenty-four hours. We all agreed to leave the water untouched as long as possible.

Soon after daylight we made sail, with the jolly-boat in tow, and stood close-hauled to the northward and westward, in the hope of reaching the coast of Newfoundland, or of being picked up by some vessel. We sailed past two islands of ice nearly as large as the first, and returned thanks to God for our deliverance.

Wednesday, the 29th of June, was ushered in with light

variable winds from the southward and eastward. We had passed a long and sleepless night, and I found myself, at dawn of day, with twenty-eight persons anxiously looking up to me for the direction of our course, as well as for the distribution of their scanty allowance. On examining our provisions, we found the bag of biscuits much damaged by salt water, on which account it became necessary to curtail the allowance. All cheerfully acquiesced in this precaution. A thick fog soon after came on, which continued during the day, with heavy rain ; but now being destitute of any means of collecting, the rain afforded us no relief. Our crowded and exposed condition was now rendered even more distressing by each of us being thoroughly wet, for no one had been permitted to take more clothing than they wore, with the exception of a greatcoat or a blanket.

The oars of both boats were kept constantly going, and we steered a N.N.W. course. All hands were anxiously looking out for a strange sail. At noon, a quarter of a biscuit and a glass of rum were served to each person. St. John's bore 310 miles distant, but we made no observation. One of the ladies again read prayers for us, particularly those for delivery after a storm, and those for safety at sea.

At daybreak next morning we were all so benumbed with wet and extreme cold, that half-a-glass of rum and a mouthful of biscuit were served out to each person. The ladies, who had hitherto refused the spirits, were now prevailed upon to take the stated allowance, which afforded them immediate relief, and enabled them the better to resist the severity of the weather. The sea was mostly calm, with thick fog and sleet ; the air raw and cold. We had kept at our oars all night, and we continued to row the whole of this day. The jolly-boat having unfortunately put off from the ship with only three oars and a small sail, converted into a foresail from a topgallant steering-sail without needles

or twine, we were obliged to keep her constantly in tow
The cutter also having lost two of her oars in hoisting out,
was now so deep in the water that with the least sea she
made but little way, so that we were not enabled to profit
much by the light winds.

Friday, 1st July. During the greater part of the last
twenty-four hours it had blown a hard gale from W.S.W.,
with a heavy, confused sea from the same quarter. Throughout there were thick fog and sleet, with excessive cold;
while the spray of the sea, freezing as it flew over the
boats, rendered our situation really deplorable. We now
felt a most painful depression of spirits, as the want of
nourishment, added to the continued cold and wet, had
made us almost incapable of exertion. The very confined
space in the boats would not admit of our stretching our
limbs, and several of the men, whose feet were considerably
swelled, repeatedly called out for water. But on reminding
them of the resolution we had made, and of the absolute
necessity of preserving it, they acknowledged the justice
and propriety of my refusal to comply with their desire,
and the water remained untouched. We had stood to the
northward and westward at the commencement of the gale,
but the cutter was so slow in the water, and had shipped so
much sea, that we were obliged to cast off the tow-rope, and
the jolly-boat was very soon lost sight of in the fog.

During this day there were repeated exclamations of a
strange sail, although I knew that it was next to an impossibility to discover anything, owing to the thickness of
the atmosphere.   Yet these exclamations escaped from
several seamen, and with such apparent certainty of the
object being there, that I was induced to put the boat before
the wind to convince them of their error. As I then saw
the consequences that might arise from such a deviation of
our course, I remonstrated with the men, and represented,
with all the persuasion at my command, that the depression

arising from disappointment infinitely overbalanced the momentary relief proceeding from such delusive expectations, and I exhorted them not to allow such fancies to break out into expression. Under all these trying circumstances, the ladies, with a heroism which no words can describe, afforded to us the best examples of patience and fortitude. Joining in prayer tranquilised our minds and inspired the consolatory hope of bettering our condition. On such occasions we were all bareheaded, notwithstanding the incessant showers.

At half-past eleven in the forenoon a sail was discovered in the eastward. Our joy at such a sight, with the immediate hope of deliverance, gave to us all new life. I immediately ordered the people to sit as close as possible, to prevent our having the appearance of an armed boat, and having tied a lady's shawl to the boat-hook, I raised myself as well as I could, and from the bow waved it as long as my strength would permit. Having hauled close to the wind we neared each other fast, until we perceived that the supposed stranger was our own jolly-boat.

The cold, wet, and hunger that we experienced upon the following day are not to be described. Our condition was now extremely desperate. At eight in the evening, having a strong breeze from the southward, we stood on under all the canvas we could spread, with the jolly-boat following in our wake, and rowing to keep up with us. The French captain, who had for some days laboured under a despondency which admitted no consolation, leapt overboard in a fit of delirium, and instantly sank. The cutter was at this time going very fast, and the oars being lashed to the gunwale, it would have been impossible to save him had he floated. One of the other prisoners in the jolly-boat became also so outrageous that it was necessary to tie him to the bottom of the craft. The melancholy fate of the poor captain, whom I had learned to esteem, perhaps affected me more at first

2

than it did any other person, for on the day of our disaster,
when I was making the distribution in the boats and considering in which I was to place him, he came to me with
tears in his eyes, imploring me not to leave him to perish
with the wreck. I assured him that I had never entertained such an idea; that as I had been the accidental
cause of his misfortunes, I should endeavour to make his
situation as easy as I could ; and that as we were all exposed
to the same danger, we should survive or perish together.
That assurance, with the hope of being speedily exchanged
if ever we reached land, operated for a time in quieting his
mind ; but fortitude soon forsook him, and the raw spirits,
to the taking of which he had not been accustomed, produced the most dreadfully intoxicating effects, and hurried
on the fatal catastrophe. The sea continued to break so
much over the boats, that those who had strength enough
were obliged to bale without intermission ; while those who
sat in the stern of the cutter were so confined that it was
difficult for any one to put his hand into his pocket, and
the greater part of the crew lay in water at the bottom of
the boat.

The next day a very heavy gale arose from the southward, accompanied with so tremendous a sea, that the
greatest vigilance was necessary in managing the helm, for
the boats would have broached-to from the slightest deviation, and occasioned our inevitable destruction. As we
scudded before the wind, we expected every returning wave
to overwhelm us; but through the providence of God we
weathered the storm, which towards night began to abate.
In the evening we passed several pieces of rock-weed, and
soon after Captain Thomas saw the wing of a hackdown, an
aquatic bird that frequents the coast of Newfoundland, and
is often eaten by the fishermen. This afforded us great
hopes of our reaching the land, and all eyes were now
eagerly occupied in observing what passed the boat. About

this time a beautiful white bird, web-footed, and not unlike a dove in size and plumage, hovered over the masthead of the cutter, and, notwithstanding the pitching of the boat, frequently attempted to perch thereon. The bird continued to flutter over and around us until darkness set in, and trifling as such an incident may appear, we all considered it a propitious omen. The impressive manner in which the bird left us, and then returned to gladden us with its presence, awakened that superstition in our minds to which sailors are said to be at all times prone. We therefore indulged in the most consolatory assurances, that the same Hand which had provided this solace to our distresses would extricate us from the surrounding dangers.

We had been six days and nights constantly wet and cold, and without any other sustenance than a quarter of a biscuit and one wine-glass of liquid for twenty-four hours. But now the men who had appeared totally indifferent as to their fate summoned resolution, and as many as were capable of moving from the bottom of the boats betook themselves to the oars.

As the morning of Monday dawned, the fog became so thick that we could not see very far from the boat. During the night we had been under the necessity of again casting off the tow-rope, so as to induce the crew of the jolly-boat to exert themselves by rowing. We again lost sight of our companions, and I perceived that this unlucky accident was beginning to excite great uneasiness among the occupants of the cutter. We were so much reduced in strength that the most trifling remark or exclamation agitated us greatly. I therefore found it necessary to caution the people against being deceived by the appearance of land, or calling out until we were quite assured of its reality ; more especially as fog-banks are often mistaken for a coast. Nevertheless, several of the poor fellows repeatedly exclaimed that they heard breakers, and some the firing of guns. To own the truth, the sounds bore such a resemblance to the noise of artillery that I concluded some vessels had got on shore, and were making signals of distress. The sounds were afterwards proved, however, to proceed from the blowing of whales, of which we saw a great number.

Soon after daybreak the sun rose to our view for the second time since we had quitted the wreck. While we had been in the boats, during a period of seven days, we never had an opportunity of taking an observation either of the sun, moon, or stars; neither could we once dry our clothes. At length the fog began to be dispelled, and we instantly caught a glimpse of the land within a mile's distance, between Kettle Cove and Island Cove, in Conception Bay, fourteen leagues from the harbour of St. John's. Almost at the same moment we had the inexpressible satisfaction of discovering the jolly-boat and a schooner near the shore standing off towards us. I wish that it were possible for me to describe our sensations. From the constant watching and fatigue, and also from the languor and depression produced by our exhausted state, such accumulated irritability was brought on, that the joy at a speedy relief affected us all in a remarkable manner. Many burst into tears; some looked at each other with a stupid stare, as if doubtful of the reality of what they saw; while others were in such a lethargic condition that no consolation, no animating words, could rouse them to exertion.

At this affecting moment, though overpowered by my own feelings, and impressed with the recollection of our sufferings, as well as the sight of so many deplorable objects, I proposed offering up our solemn thanks to heaven for our remarkable deliverance. Every one cheerfully assented, and as soon as I opened the prayer-book, which I secured the last time I went down to my cabin, a general silence prevailed. Indeed, a spirit of devotion was so singularly manifested on the occasion, that to the benefits springing from a sense of religion in uncultivated minds must be ascribed that discipline, good order, and exertion which even the sight of land would now have failed to produce.

The schooner being within hail, when our situation was made known she hove-to and received us on board, while our boats were taken in tow. My men could now with difficulty be restrained from taking large and repeated draughts of water, and in consequence of their intemperate indulgence in this way several suffered much inconvenience; but by the exercise of greater caution afterwards, no other sinister effects followed.

It was most fortunate that we fell in with the land about Island Cove. A very few miles to the northward the coast is inaccessible, and with dangerous reefs of rocks, which we should have pushed for in the night had we seen them. Our situation had become so desperate that I had resolved to land at the first place we could make, and in that case we must all have inevitably perished. Mr. Lilly, a planter, received us with much humanity, and I hired a small schooner for St. John's, where we at length arrived in safety.

THE DUKE OF CUMBERLAND.

ON the 3rd of September 1804, the packet-ship *Duke of Cumberland*, Captain Lawrence, was lying at anchor in the roadstead of St. John's, Newfoundland, waiting for the mails that were expected to come on board that day. His Majesty's ship the *Seraphis*, of forty-four guns, lay about two miles further out, for the purpose of conveying the packet down to Tortola. During the previous night the wind had been blowing very fresh from the north, and at noon the breeze had considerably increased. Another British man-of-war, the *De Ruyter*, an old seventy-four, lay in Deep Bay. The latter vessel had lately been taken thither to be fitted as a prison-ship, and she had a very weak crew on board. When the gale came down upon her she made signals of distress to the *Seraphis*, and also sent a boat alongside the *Duke of Cumberland*, requesting the aid of some men with a view to relieve the *De Ruyter* from the position in which she had been anchored, and which promised to be a perilous one, short-handed as she was then. Captain Lawrence felt that he could not with propriety comply with that request, as the gale gave signs of soon merging into a hurricane, and the commander of the *Duke of Cumberland* ordered topgallant-masts to be struck, and another anchor to be let go, so as to ensure if possible the safety of his vessel. But the hurricane soon burst upon the coast with destructive fury, and the incidents of the wreck which ensued were recorded by one of the officers.

The gale continued to increase, says the narrator, and at six in the evening it blew a perfect storm from the N.W. by W., when we struck our yards and top-masts. The men had scarcely finished this work when it was discovered that the vessel had parted her best bower-cable. This surprised and alarmed us exceedingly, as the rope was nearly new, and we had been assured that the bottom of the roadstead was a hard sand; but the rope must have been cut upon a ship's anchor or on a bed of coral. We immediately bent the remaining part of the broken cable to the stream-anchor, and the stream-cable to the kedge. The wind continued to rage with unabated violence, which caused the ship to pitch immoderately, and dreading lest the cable should give way, at ten o'clock we let go the two remaining anchors.

Everything had now been done for the safety of the ship that was in the power of the crew to accomplish; the rest we confided to Providence, and having recommended ourselves to the protection of the Almighty, we remained idle but anxious spectators of the scene before us, and awaited the event in silent dread. To men who were so deeply interested in the effects of the storm, no scene could be so truly awful. The wind raged with a violence known only in tropical climates, the rain fell like a deluge, the waves rose to a stupendous height, the ship was pitching her forecastle under water, our best cable was gone, and we every moment expected to part the others. To add to the horrors of our situation, the lightning flashing now and then discovered to us, amidst the extreme darkness of the night, that as soon as we should part or drive away from our moorings, a reef of horrid rocks lay to leeward ready to receive us. Thus situated, every man was sensible that it was absolutely impossible to combat singly the terrible agitation of the elements; and the feeble expectation of saving our lives rested solely on the frail hope of the ship riding out the tempest.

The masts of the *De Ruyter* had been frequently shewn to us by the glare of the lightning, and we could perceive that she was driving from her moorings. Suddenly disappearing, however, we concluded that she had foundered. We also supposed that the *Seraphis* had shared the same fate. About eleven o'clock the windlass gave way with a tremendous noise. The sailors immediately clapped stops upon the cables, and secured them by means of ring-bolts on the decks, but these were continually breaking, and were as often replaced.

The cable had now held so long that we began to entertain some faint hopes of riding out the gale, and we dared for a moment to quit the deck for the purpose of getting some refreshment; but no sooner had the officers sat down than a loud groan from the crew summoned us on deck. We had dreaded the worst, and the captain, running forward, soon put an end to our doubts by exclaiming:—"All's now over! Lord have mercy upon us!" The cable had parted, and the ship, after hanging for about two minutes by the stream and kedge, began to drive broadside-on, and dragging the anchors with her.

Our feelings at this moment are not to be described. While some of the seamen appeared to become oblivious to the perilous nature of their situation, the cries of others for their homes, their wives, and their children, resounded through the ship; but they soon became sensible of their folly, and resumed their usual firmness and self-possession.

As soon as the ship parted, which was about midnight, every man clung to a rope, and determined to stick to it as long as the vessel remained entire. The wind had veered somewhat to the west, which prevented her from striking on the reef of rocks that we so much dreaded. It was one o'clock, and we had drifted for an hour without knowing whither. We continued holding fast by the rigging ; our bodies beaten by the heaviest rain, and lashed by each successive wave. A dreadful silence reigned among the men, every one being too intent upon his own approaching end to be able to communicate his thoughts or feelings to another. Nothing could be heard but the horrible howling of the storm.

A little after one in the morning we struck, but instantly went off again. This incident, together with the appearance of several lights at a distance before us, led us to conclude that we were driving towards the harbour of St. John's, and that we had struck on the bar. In the direction of the land loomed a large object, which we dreaded was Rat Island, a perpendicular rock in the centre of the harbour, upon which stood a fort. We were fast approaching it, and we surmised that the garrison might be spectators of our fate ; for it was vain to think that assistance could be tendered to us in such circumstances and at such an hour. Two alarm-guns were fired from the ship, but we doubted if the reports could be heard amidst the tremendous noise of the wind and waves. We soon found, however, that what we took to be a rock in the harbour was a large vessel, on which we were driving with the utmost speed. But when we came up to her our ship went close under her stern, and so a collision was narrowly avoided.

Some faint hopes began now to be entertained of our being stranded on a sandy beach ; for we knew that although the harbour is chiefly bounded with rocks, yet there were a few banks of mud and sand, and our wishes led us to hope for the best. The captain therefore ordered the carpenter to get the hatchets all ready to cut away the masts, in order to construct a raft for those who might venture to seek safety thereon. We could now plainly perceive land not far distant, on which we were driving, and as we knew it to be a huge rock, we ran up the fore and mizzen-staysails; thinking by these means to divert the course of the ship. But while we were thus employed, the wind chopped from N.N.W. to west, being not less than six points, while the hurricane continued with unabated fury. This kept us clear of the projecting land, and drove us a short distance beyond it, when the ship again struck. The first stroke of the keel was apparently upon a sandy beach, and we could plainly discern two large ships that were stranded just abreast of us.

We now fondly imagined that we should be driven on these ships, but in this we were disappointed, for we drove past, beating with violence at every wave, and in a few seconds found the ship brought up on some dangerous rocks at the foot of a stupendous precipice. Every hope now vanished, and we began already to consider ourselves as beings of another world. The vessel was dashed with extreme force upon the rocks, and we could distinctly hear from below the cracking of her timbers. In order to ease the ship, and if possible to prevent her from parting, we immediately cut away the mizzen-mast, and shortly afterwards the fore-mast. The main-mast we allowed to remain, in order to steady the vessel, and with a view to prevent her from canting to windward, which would inevitably have caused us all to be drowned.

The *Duke of Cumberland* had struck about two in the morning, and in half-an-hour afterwards we found that the water in the hull was up to her lower-deck. Never was daylight more anxiously wished for than by the unfortunate crew. After having held so long by the shrouds, we were forced to cling for three hours longer before the day dawned, during which time we were under a continual dread of the parting of the ship, and our being launched into eternity. As she lay on her beam-ends the sea was making a complete breach over her, and stiff and benumbed as we were, it was with the utmost difficulty that we could preserve our hold against the force of the waves.

The break of day discovered to us all the horrors of our situation. The vessel was lying upon large rocks at the foot of a craggy, overhanging precipice, twice as high as our main-mast. Although cut away, the mizzen-mast still hung in a diagonal direction, supported by some ropes, and reached within about four fathoms of the rock. Forming a sort of bay around us, the land also approached us a-head, and a portion thereof lay not far from the extremity of our jib-boom. In various parts of the harbour might be seen several ships on shore, while the wind and rain continued to beat upon us with unabated violence.

Our vessel now lay a miserable wreck. One wave had carried away her stern-boat, unstripped her rudder, and washed overboard the quarter-boards, binnacle, and round-house. The fore and mizzen-masts lay alongside, supported by small ropes, and the ship had bilged her larboard side. After the appearance of the dawn, our first thoughts were naturally directed to the possibility of saving our lives, and we all agreed that the only hope of effecting this was by means of the mizzen-mast. We therefore immediately got the top and topgallant-masts launched out on the mizzen, which enabled us to reach within a few feet of the rock; but the part of the precipice that we approached was so perpendicular as to afford us but a faint expectation of relief, unless our safety might be secured by the means of some bushes which grew upon the brow of the rock.

One of the sailors soon proved the fallacy of the rising hopes which we had entertained of effecting a rescue from our perilous position in the manner suggested. To the great mortification of all on board the wreck, we saw the man heave a rope, on the end of which was a running-noose that caught hold of the largest bushes ; but these came away in an instant, and discovered to us that the roots of the shrubs had no secure hold of the ground, as their position was upon a much-decayed and weather-beaten rock, incapable of affording them support sufficient to withstand the smallest weight. Despair at the failure of this attempt at rescue gave an extraordinary degree of courage to another seaman, who speedily followed his shipmate out on the mast, with the intention of throwing himself upon the rock from the end of the spar. He had proceeded to the extremity of the topgallant-mast, and was upon the point of leaping among the bushes, when the pole of the mast, unable to sustain his weight, gave way, and he was pre-cipitated into the bosom of the waves. As the fall was at least forty feet, it was some time before he made his appearance above the surface of the water, and when he did, every one expected to see him dashed to pieces among the rocks ; but the man had fortunately carried down with him the piece of the broken spar, to which were fastened some small ropes, and by clinging fast to these lines he preserved his head above water, at the intervals of the receding waves, until a tackle was fixed wherewith to hoist him upon deck.

All our hopes of being saved by means of the mizzen-mast were now blasted, yet some decisive measure seemed absolutely necessary to further our escape from our dreadful situation. As the storm did not in the smallest degree abate, we suffered an increased dread that the ship would part, as she had already bilged on the larboard side ; while the whole crew had now become so fatigued, benumbed, and dispirited, that they were scarcely able to hold out any longer. It was in vain to expect any outward assistance, as we were not seen from the town, and the ships that were not in sight of us could not have it in their power to render the

slightest aid. Some negroes indeed made their appearance on
the top of the rock, and we requested them to descend a
little way in order to receive the end of a rope; but
whether from fear or stupidity, and in spite of all our
entreaties, promises, and threats, these creatures stood
gaping in the most idiotic manner, sometimes at us, sometimes at each other, but without making the least effort to
approach or assist us.

While we were meditating on our situation in sullen
silence, Mr. Doncaster, the chief mate, unobserved by
any one on board, went out on the bowsprit, and having
reached the end of the jib-boom, was suddenly seen to throw
himself headlong into the water. So soon as he had touched
the surface, a tremendous wave threw him upon the rock,
and left him dry. There he remained a few moments,
without motion, until a second wave washed him farther
up the precipice, where, clinging to a projection of the cliff,
he effectually secured his hold. Thus he lay for a few
minutes to recruit his strength, when he began to scramble
up the rock. Mr. Doncaster's preservation was most
miraculous. All the ship's company were unanimous in
declaring it to be next to an impossibility, and it indeed
seemed to be a most singular interposition of Providence in
our behalf. In about half-an-hour he had, with infinite
difficulty, reached the summit of the cliff.

Most anxiously had we been watching every step that the
mate had taken in his perilous ascent, while conscious that
the preservation of all our lives depended solely upon the
successful accomplishment of his task. He immediately
came round to that part of the precipice which was over our
quarter. Descending a little way he got hold of a rope
which was thrown to him from the maintop; this he
fastened to some trees upon the summit of the rock, and we
passed the end of the rope to the head of the mizzentop-mast.
This being done, a few of the most expert seamen warped

themselves up the rope, carrying with them the end of another, upon which a tackle was bent, and the second rope they also fastened to the trees. The other end of the tackle was then made fast to the mizzen-mast, and the fold of it passed to the remainder of the crew upon deck. By means of these ropes—one of which we fastened successively to our waists, while with the other we supported ourselves as we warped along with our hands—we were all in the space of three hours safely hoisted to the top of the cliff, with the exception of some of the most active of the crew, who were left to the last, and were compelled to warp themselves up, as the first sailor had done, without the assistance of a second rope.

The whole ship's company—comprising Captain Lawrence, Mr. Lawrence the master, Mr. Doncaster the chief mate, Mr. Lowrie the surgeon, with twenty-four seamen and petty-officers, and three passengers, Mr. Verchild, Mr. Wood, and Lieut. Webber of the Royal Artillery—having now safely assembled on the rock, we took leave of our unfortunate vessel, and bent our way towards the town of St. John's. But our difficulties had not yet ended. In consequence of the rain which had fallen, and was still pouring down without intermission, the whole plain before us presented the appearance of a large lake, through which we made our way with much difficulty. In those places where roads or furrows had been made, we frequently plunged up to the neck, and were in danger of being carried down by the stream.

After wading about three miles through fields of canes, the tops of which could scarcely be discerned above the water, we reached the town, where we were so inhospitably received that I believe we would have died for want of food and necessaries had it not been for the kind offices of a mulatto tailor, to whom we sent for clothes, and who carried us to a house, where we were furnished with beds and provisions. In a few hours after our arrival at St. John's the wind chopped round to the south, from which quarter it blew with continued violence during the next twenty-four hours. The hurricane lasted in all about forty-eight hours, during which time it made a complete sweep of half the compass. The favourable change that now ensued, however, saved the ship from breaking-up, and we found her, after the storm had been allayed, lying nearly dry among the rocks, but with five large holes in her larboard side.   All that we were able to save of our effects from the wreck were some articles of wearing apparel which we found floating in the hold.

THE NAUTILUS.

THE British war-sloop *Nautilus*, Commander Palmer, sailed from the Dardanelles on the 30th of January 1807, bearing important despatches for the Government in England. Making her way through the numerous islands of the Greek Archipelago, she neared the Negropont just as the night set in, with every promise of a squall. The navigation of the vessel having become dangerous in the darkness, the Greek pilot on board recommended the commander to lay-to until daylight, and the advice was followed. At the breaking of day the sloop again proceeded on her course, and by evening she had passed Falconera and Anti-Milo. Now the pilot gave up his charge to the captain, who, knowing that the despatches he carried were of considerable moment, resolved to continue his voyage during the night, so as to clear the Archipelago with as little delay as possible. After pricking out on the chart the course he desired to steer, Captain Palmer retired to his cabin, in order to obtain the rest of a few hours.

The wind had been blowing high all day, and the night was exceedingly dark, while the wind increased in violence until a storm of an awe-inspiring character broke over the vessel, and rendered her situation perilous to a degree. Frequent and vivid flashes of lightning darted from the rolling clouds overhead, and the ship was borne on her way by a high sea, that ever and anon threatened to engulph her in its angry waves. At the rate of nine miles an hour the *Nautilus* was carried by the gale, until at half-past two in the morning a rising land was seen, and as this was taken to be the island of Cerigotto, all danger was supposed to be passed, and the navigation of the sloop proceeded with greater confidence on the part of her officers and men. The favourable expectations which had thus been excited in the breasts of those on watch were but short-lived, however, for at half-past four the man on the look-out cried, " Breakers ahead," and without further warning of the danger that menaced all on board, the ship struck upon a reef of rocks with a terrific crash, and alarm and confusion reigned supremely over the doomed vessel.

By the violence of the shock all below were thrown from their berths and hammocks, and now rushed on deck, but those who arrived there were compelled to cling to the gun-wale and cordage, in order to ensure for the moment their personal safety. Scarcely had part of the crew hurried from below when the ladder leading from the lower-deck gave way, and left numbers of the seamen to struggle with the water that now rushed into the hull with ominous force. The captain and first-lieutenant promptly endeavoured to quell the fears of the crew, and to restore that order and discipline which the disaster had for the time injuriously affected. Their efforts to that end having been in a great measure successful, they next proceeded below to consider the extent of the damage which had been sustained by the sloop, and any likelihood that might exist of their ever being able to deliver the despatches with which the commander had been entrusted. Finding that the vessel must become a total wreck, and that the papers and signals might fall

3

into hostile hands, the despatches and signals were at once committed to the flames, and the two officers then went upon deck to devise means for the rescue of their men.

Meanwhile, the *Nautilus* continued to be dashed against the rocks by each successive sea, and the officers and seamen were obliged to climb the rigging, where they remained for an hour, with the surge breaking over them without intermission. The lightning had now ceased, but the darkness was such as to prevent them from perceiving any object that might be a-head at the distance of the ship's length. A small rock lay very near, and the commander's only hope of establishing a communication with the shore lay in the possibility of the main-mast giving way under the excessive strain, and falling towards the rock in question. About half-an-hour before daybreak Captain Palmer's wishes in that respect were providentially gratified; for, the mast breaking, the spar fell towards the reef, and the surviving officers and seamen were by this means enabled to reach the land.

In the hasty struggle to obtain a footing upon the rock many accidents occurred. While passing along the mast some of the seamen fell into the sea and were drowned. One man had his arm broken, and several were otherwise severely injured. Commander Palmer was the last to leave the ship, as he refused to quit his post thereon until all his remaining officers and men had gained the reef. With the exception of one, all the boats had been driven in pieces. The jolly-boat alone remained, but it could not be hauled in, and it was consequently unavailable for their present great emergency.

The survivors were now huddled upon a strange and inhospitable shore, and were in a most sad and pitiable condition. The majority of the men had lost their shoes, and the loss was felt to be a grievous one, for their feet were cut by the sharp rocks, and blood flowed from the wounds thus received, as well as from others that had been sustained in their efforts to get on to the reef. For a time shelter from the violence of the surf was afforded to the unfortunate company by the hull of the wreck; but the *Nautilus* speedily broke up, and it then became necessary to abandon their position, by wading to a somewhat larger rock than that upon which they had landed. In crossing the channel between these two points of the reef many floating spars were encountered by the men, who in several instances were hurt by the heavy pieces of wood being dashed against their bodies by the waves. Such was their situation shortly after daybreak, and as the day advanced the sea around the reef was covered by fragments of the wreck, while many of their shipmates could be observed floating about on spars and timbers of the sloop, and pleading for that assistance which it was now utterly impossible for the more fortunate of the crew to render.

A survey of their situation disclosed the fact that the company saved from a watery grave had found a temporary asylum upon a coral island, which was nearly level with the ocean. The coral rock was about four hundred yards long, with a breadth of about three hundred yards, and as nearly as could be computed, was at least twelve miles from the islands of Pera and Cerigotta. In the hope of attracting the notice of any passing vessel, a signal of distress was hoisted upon a high pole. The previous day had been an exceedingly cold one, the deck of the *Nautilus* having then been covered with ice, and the temperature now experienced was piercing in the extreme. By means of a flint and powder, and after much difficulty, a fire was kindled, and around the smouldering wood the men clustered, in the hope of getting rid of some of the soaking moisture their clothing had absorbed during the storm. When evening came, a small tent had been erected of boards and pieces of sails, and into this shelter the men crowded, while their clothes were hung near the fire outside in order to be dried. The night was passed in a manner comfortless and dreary, but the hope that the fire might be descried in the darkness by a friendly ship, and adjudged to be a signal of distress, lent consolation to the shipwrecked crew in their awful solitude and distress.

Upon the following day considerable delight was experienced at the approach of a small whaling-boat, manned by some of their shipmates. When the sloop had struck, these men had lowered themselves over the side into one of the boats, and had reached, after much exertion, the island of Pera. Finding no fresh water there, however, the seamen had again embarked, and had rowed for some hours when the appearance of the fire attracted their attention in the night, and they made for the beacon which they supposed must have been ignited by their comrades. On nearing the coral island, it was found to be dangerous to attempt to land, owing to the waves running so high, and in the emergency some of those on the shore endeavoured to reach the boat by swimming. One of the sailors on board, desirous of saving the life of his captain, invited that officer to come out to the craft; but the commander steadfastly refused to do so, saying, " No, Smith, never mind me, but save your unfortunate shipmates."

Information having been volunteered by the Greek pilot to the effect that there were a few families of fishermen upon the island of Cerigotto who might probably be able to afford relief to distressed mariners, the boat's crew turned the head of their craft in that direction, after having taken the pilot on board. After the departure of their comrades, the survivors left upon the desolate rock were a prey to sufferings of the most acute nature, for the wind again rose with considerable force, and increased in violence until a second storm burst upon the hapless men with appalling fury. The waves now washed over the greater portion of the rock, extinguishing in their progress the embers of the fire which had proved of so much advantage to the chilled and dispirited seamen, who were now compelled to seek for safety by clustering near the higher part of the rock, around which a rope had been fastened to support the men in their fearful position. Thus did nearly ninety human beings pass a night of fearful suspense and horror—each man with one hand grasping the rope, while with the other he embraced the form that stood nearest to him upon the treacherous ledge.

Wearied out by their exertions and sufferings several of the seamen became delirious, and, losing their hold, were swept away by the remorseless waves; while those who still retained their reason were in constant terror of their position becoming wholly submerged—a contingency that was highly probable in the event of the wind veering a little to the north. As daylight again broke it was found that many more had begun to sink under their sufferings, while all were in a deplorable condition. During the night one had been so dashed against the rocks as to present a terrible spectacle; the poor fellow being nearly scalped and at the point of death. They had been ill-prepared for a long continuance of starvation, and now famine was upon them in all its horrible intensity. Escape seemed hopeless, for to their terrible bodily hardships was added the mental anguish induced by the thought that, in all probability, the storm had overtaken their friends ere the boat had reached Cerigotto, and the rescue of the party on the rock depended, as it was imagined, upon the safety of the boat and its getting to the land for which it had started. The position of those upon the island was rendered all the more unendurable by the sight of so many lifeless bodies of their shipmates being lashed by the seething surf; while the forms of some of their companions in misfortune were still writhing in the agonies of dissolution.

Shortly after daybreak a vessel was seen approaching, and the hearts of all on the rock beat high in expectation of a near deliverance. All the stranger's sails were set, and she came down before the wind, steering directly for the coral island. After repeated signals of distress the ship hove-to, and hoisted out one of her boats. The survivors, confident that the boat would be provided with the means for their relief, hastily prepared rafts to carry them through the surf. When the boat had arrived within pistol-shot, it was observed to be filled with men dressed in the costume of European seamen, but after having taken a survey of the famishing men, the steersman waved his hat, and his companions rowed off with all possible speed to their ship. The increased misery which such heartless conduct occasioned to the sufferers became still further augmented by parties from the vessel being employed all day in collecting the floating fragments of the *Nautilus.*

After this terrible disappointment, the only hope of a release was centred in the return of the whaling-boat, and many anxious eyes gazed across the broad expanse of water in the expectation of finding their friends bearing down towards them. All upon that bleak and barren rock were now tormented by a raging thirst, which was even more consuming than the famine that had wasted away many of their number. In spite of warnings, some drank of the salt water until madness ensued and their agonies were terminated by death. Another night of awful suffering and horror was passed by the occupants of the coral reef, who huddled closely, and covered themselves with their few remaining rags, in order to screen their pinched and lacerated bodies from the biting wind. About midnight they were hailed by the crew of the whale-boat, which had returned from Cerigotto ; but the fresh water which had been brought in the craft was carried in earthen vessels that could not safely be conveyed through the surf, and the sufferers were fain to console themselves with an assurance that had been given by their comrades, that all would be taken off the rock by a fishing-vessel next day. There seemed, however, to be but little probability of many surviving until the hour of their release arrived, and all night long those who had not been bereft of reason were haunted by the mad ravings of their insane companions in misery.

On the fourth morning after the wreck the sun shone upon the survivors for the first time since the calamity, but the day wore away without the promised succour having reached them. Hour after hour passed, but neither the whale-boat nor the promised vessel appeared, to mitigate the sufferings of famishing men, who were now glaring with greedy eyes upon the lifeless bodies of their shipmates as the only means of satisfying the cravings of inordinate hunger. As the day advanced, famine overcame their natural repugnance to the loathsome diet, and after a prayer to heaven for forgiveness of the act, the party made a meal of human flesh. Towards the evening death terminated the physical and mental anguish of the commander and his first-lieutenant, and several of the seamen also succumbed to the destroyer.

During the night some one thought of constructing a raft that might carry the survivors to Cerigotto, and as the wind seemed favourable for the attainment of that object, the suggestion was hailed by the others as the only remaining chance of release. Even if they failed in their effort to reach the island, it were better to perish in the ocean, it was thought, than to die a lingering death from hunger and thirst. Accordingly, at daybreak preparations were made to put the scheme into execution. As fast as the feebleness of the workers permitted, a number of the larger spars were lashed together, and at length the raft was launched; but scarcely had the structure been fairly floated upon the water than the lashings became loose, and the raft went asunder, to the bitter disappointment of the onlookers. Driven to desperation by the failure of a plan which had for some hours given renewed hope to all, five of the men hastily put together a few spars, and at once embarked upon the raft thus formed; but the small dimensions of the platform now launched upon the sea gave the occupants but a narrow space whereon to stand, and the raft being carried away by the treacherous currents of the ocean, the unfortunate seamen, who had trusted their lives to its keeping, were heard of no more.

As the day again wore on towards evening, the whaling-boat came in sight, and on its arrival at the rock the crew explained the cause of their prolonged detention. They had experienced much difficulty in their endeavours to persuade the fishermen of Cerigotto to venture to sea during the stormy weather that had prevailed. However, the fishermen had held out promises that as soon as the weather moderated they would proceed to the relief of the survivors. During the time that this explanation was being given, twelve of the men upon the rock plunged into the sea and made determined efforts to reach the boat. Two of the swimmers were at length taken into the craft, which was now considered to be dangerously overladen; while one of the men was drowned, and the remainder were reluctantly compelled again to seek a refuge upon the coral reef.

The weakness of the men had now reached the limit of endurance. One of the survivors afterwards described his sensations at the time. He felt the gradual but sure approach of annihilation; his sight failed; his senses were confused; his strength was exhausted; and he looked towards the setting sun in the expectation that he would never again behold the great luminary of the heavens. But suddenly was announced the coming of the boats from Cerigotto, and from the depths of dire despair the hearts of the survivors arose to the summit of exuberant joyfulness.

When the *Nautilus* struck she had one hundred and twenty-two persons on board, and of these fifty-eight had perished. Eighteen were drowned at the time of the wreck, five were lost in the small boat, and thirty-four died of famine. Including those saved in the whaling-boat, sixty-four had survived out of the whole of the ship's company, and about fifty now embarked in the four small vessels which had been humanely brought by Greek fishermen for their rescue. During the six days spent upon the coral island, the men had eaten nothing save the flesh of their dead shipmates.

Upon the evening of their rescue the survivors landed at a small creek on the coast of Cerigotto, where they were hospitably entertained by fishermen, whose only failing appeared to be a lack of sufficient surgical knowledge to enable them to dress the wounds of their maimed and famished guests. Having no other material for bandages, the Greeks readily tore up their own underclothing for that purpose, but it was soon found that experienced medical aid must be obtained, otherwise more lives would be sacrificed. Accordingly, after a sojourn of fourteen days with their preservers, the survivors set sail for the island of Cerigo, twenty-five miles distant from Cerigotto. Landing at their destination, the men applied to the English vice-consul, who afforded them all possible help in their necessitous condition, procured for them the needful medical assistance, and finally made arrangements with the captain of a Russian vessel to convey them to Corfu, where they arrived on the 2d of March 1807, about two months after the wreck of the *Nautilus.*

THE SEAFORD WRECKS.

ON Tuesday, December the 5th, 1809, a fleet of merchantmen, destined for the Downs, sailed from Plymouth, under the protection of a hired armed sloop, the *Harlequin*, of eighteen guns, employed as a convoy. At about three P.M., the signal for sailing having been given by the *Harlequin*, the sails of the respective vessels were unfurled, and speedily the whole, twenty-three in number, quitted the port with a fair leading wind. During the night, unhappily, the weather became turbulent, and as the wind repeatedly shifted to various points, the more heavily-laden ships were prevented from making much way. The convoy did not desert these, however, but fired signal-guns for the faster-sailing vessels to drop astern and keep in her wake as closely as possible, so as to protect themselves, if need be, from the attack of a hostile cruiser.

In the morning the sky brightened, and the promise was held out of a steadier wind and finer weather. The fleet now kept a fair and easy course until towards sunset on the day after sailing, when the general expectations of favourable weather, that had been cherished, were superseded by apprehensions of a gloomy complexion. Black clouds began

to congregate in the north-east, the atmosphere became dark
and hazy, and the wind from the south-west blew in sudden
blasts and squalls. Fears were now entertained of a storm
of considerable severity, and these were shortly to be completely verified. By eleven at night the gale had acquired
great power, and at midnight it blew a hurricane; but the
extreme violence of the storm was of short duration, for by
one on the morning of Thursday the wind had moderated
considerably, although it continued to give constant employment to the various crews, by repeatedly veering and coming
upon the vessels suddenly, and from unexpected points.
The circumstances of the following day, with the disaster
that ensued, have been recorded by an eye-witness, who
was on board one of the ships.

A morning more dark than this cannot well be imagined.
The fog even obscured the lights on the several vessels, and
rendered the lanterns scarcely of any use to those on board;
while a cold and unwholesome sleet descended without
intermission. We conceived that we had passed the Isle of
Wight about midnight, but as no lights could be discerned
from the land, our true position could not be accurately
ascertained. The *Harlequin*, which we regarded as our
piloting as well as our protecting vessel, was a little a-head
of the fleet; and as she repeatedly discharged her guns to
reveal her course to us, we found no great difficulty in
keeping in her wake. At two P.M. the convoy hauled her
wind, and fired signals for the whole of the fleet to keep
between her and the land, so as to prevent any of those
petty marauders, in the shape of privateers, from molesting
us at a time when the *Harlequin* was not in a position to
guard the vessels under her charge.

At three o'clock in the afternoon the gale again increased,
but still we were far from considering ourselves in any
immediate danger. Shortly after that hour, however, the
Harlequin mistook our situation, as her captain imagined

we had all weathered Beachy Head, whereas we had not made nearly so much way. So entirely was our convoy deceived by that supposition that she advanced ahead of us, and stood more in for the land, while the whole fleet, as in duty bound, followed her example. This course we kept until the *Harlequin*, with the six foremost ships, ran aground about four o'clock, when the crews of the seven vessels were in the jaws of death almost as soon as danger was apprehended.

Words can scarcely convey an idea of the horrors by which we were now surrounded. The breakers dashed furiously against us, bringing the vessels in dreadful contact with each other, and then with resistless violence passed over the decks, sweeping away everything in their progress. The shrieks of the sufferers, the crashing of the timbers, the fluttering of the rent sails, the howling of the storm, and the thundering roar of the billows that menaced us with instant destruction, must have appalled the stoutest heart. Yet cowardly supineness never for a moment prevented us from doing our duty to each other. All that men could accomplish under such distressing circumstances was effected, and we have the gratifying reflection that by our united efforts many valuable lives were preserved. But the confusion and danger to which we were thus unexpectedly subjected, were rendered all the more terrible by the darkness that enveloped us, and hid all other objects but our own deplorable condition from our sight.

In the horrible dilemma which had thus overtaken us, we were not so absorbed in what was to be done for our own preservation as to neglect giving the requisite information to those ships that were still afloat, that they might by timely warning avoid the cause of our disaster. Signal-guns were therefore fired by the vessels aground, while rockets were exploded from the *Harlequin;* and by these means the other sixteen ships were warned of their danger. Instantly hauling their wind, they all with difficulty weathered Beachy Head in safety, and but for the information thus tendered at an extreme moment, in all human probability each of these vessels would have been a partaker of our distressing fate.

So long as the guns on board the stranded vessels were in a state to be used, recourse was had to the firing of signals of distress, in order to arouse the people on shore to the urgent danger of our situation. The murmuring of voices— for we could see no one by reason of the fog—at length convinced us that the repeated explosions had brought a crowd of persons to the beach, with the humane intention of rendering all possible assistance. The presence of sympathisers so near lent for the moment a gleam of hope to our spirits, but the conviction was soon forced upon our minds that the pitchy darkness of the atmosphere must prevent us from discerning our would-be deliverers, and also interpose an almost impassable obstacle to their rendering us the so much-needed help. The dejection that seized us when our solitary ray of hope became extinguished was almost overpowering, and augmented the horrors produced by the violence of the elements around. Every hand on board our ship was now actively employed, however, although in constant expectation of death, and momentarily witnessing the destruction of fellow-seamen, who had so shortly before been full of life and vigour. The cries of the poor mariners as they were washed from their only ground of safety, their vessels, mingled at intervals with the roaring of the storm, and added poignancy to the misery we endured. The confused sounds from the beach now became more distinct and powerful, evincing that the concourse of people there continued to increase ; but in the impenetrable gloom that enveloped us no possible advantage could be derived from that circumstance. However, we bore our misfortunes like men, and waited in expectation of another day bringing more favourable opportunities for the rescue of the survivors of our crews.

Tediously indeed did the moments pass, from the time of our striking upon the shore till the first faint streaks of daylight appeared over the edge of the horizon. During the night the sounds that came from the beach had told us that every aid within the compass of human means would be rendered as soon as the sunrise permitted the wrecks to be distinguished by the people on shore. But, alas! though the darkness was in some measure dispelled by the dawn, the violence of the storm abated not, and the picture of misery which the day disclosed was even more horrifying than we had prepared ourselves to expect.

The vessels which had been stranded in Seaford Bay proved to be the *Weymouth*, 180 tons, John Llewellyn, master, laden with cork, barilla, and tobacco, and with a crew of eleven men; the *Traveller*, Thomas Bowman, master, with eight of a crew, and laden with shumac and fruit; the *Albion*, John Jermond, master, with a general cargo, and a crew of nine; the *Unice* of New York, William Bowes, master, with a crew of ten, and a valuable cargo of cotton; the *February*, a Prussian ship of 460 tons, in ballast, and with a crew of sixteen men; the *Midbedach*, of 350 tons, also a Prussian ship, with fourteen persons on board, and a costly cargo of merchandise; and the convoy, *Harlequin*, under the command of Lieutenant Anstruther of the Royal Navy.

When daylight enabled us to view the destruction caused by the storm, we found that the *Albion* and two other vessels had almost become total wrecks, while the numerous buoyant articles, that had formed portions of their cargoes, were floating about at the caprice of the waves. Many of the men of these ships, some clinging to fragments of wreckage, others to the masts and rigging, were beating up against the breakers, as they endeavoured to reach the shore.

Several of the poor fellows perished while struggling to get to the beach, although the most strenuous efforts were being put forth by the humane individuals there congregated to save the unfortunate seamen from a watery grave. But others besides the sympathetic and helpful had been attracted to the scene. There were some who, unmoved by the agonising shrieks of the exhausted and dying men, were only intent on plunder and rapine. Nor could the ghastly corpses that the tide sometimes cast among the objects of their covetousness suspend their iniquitous practices for a moment, or arrest them from glutting over the spoils acquired in the most shameless manner from the miseries of their fellow-creatures.

The *Harlequin* was the centre ship on shore, and daylight discovered her to be in a most wretched condition. To lighten the hull, her guns had been thrown overboard, and her masts had gone by the board with appalling crashes, killing two brave fellows as they were at work upon the deck. As it was but too evident the convoy must speedily go to pieces, it became a consideration of the first importance to save the lives of the remainder of her crew. Upon the beach in front of the vessel the onlookers had crowded in vast numbers, as the fact of the *Harlequin* being the armed convoy of the others excited popular interest in her favour. She was also known to have by far the larger number of hands on board than any that were wrecked, and this circumstance lent an additional attraction to the curious as well as to the humane spectator.

When the vessels first grounded the tide was at the ebb, consequently at the return of the flood our position was rendered deplorable and desperate, as the breakers impelled us forward and started our timbers at every shock. At high-tide we were drifted within a few yards of the shore; but the waves lashed the strand with so much violence that we were unable to take advantage of our proximity to the

beach, by swimming thereto.   Indeed, had we jumped overboard with such a purpose, our lives must speedily have
paid a penalty for our temerity.

In the hope of establishing a communication with the
shore, a cask, with a hawser affixed, was let down from the
Harlequin, and after some difficulty it was floated, and at
last borne by the breakers to its destination.   The rope
was instantly secured by the people on the beach, and by
the means of a passage thereby effected all the men of the
Harlequin, including a passenger, were saved from their
perilous position on the wreck.   But a heartrending scene
then ensued ; for it was found that the passenger's wife and
two infant children were still on board.   The poor mother
stood on deck with her little ones, and implored that some
measures might be adopted for the safety of her children ;
and to the honour of British seamen, her pitious appeal was
not made in vain.

Two sailors of the *Harlequin's* crew, who had just been
landed from the vessel, pushed off in a boat, and the progress of the frail craft through the breakers was watched
with breathless interest by all who needed not to attend
more immediately to their own preservation.   With great
difficulty, and at the hazard of their lives, the men at
last reached the side of the wreck, when they called upon
the frantic mother to descend, holding out their arms
meanwhile to receive her.   The poor woman peremptorily
declined to do so, however, until her children had been
secured, and the brave seamen, finding that their purpose
could not otherwise be accomplished, got on board the hull
and brought the children and their mother safely ashore.
The children were first lashed to the bodies of the sailors,
in such a manner as would not impede the movements of
the men, then the woman was lowered into the boat, and
all arrived without injury on land, amidst the cheers of the
spectators.   Shortly after that gallant rescue had been

accomplished, the hull of the convoy broke up into fragments.

The *Weymouth* had been driven higher upon the beach than any of her consorts, in consequence, perhaps, of the water being deeper in that part of the bay, and a projection of the cliff from the shore staying in some measure the formation of the sandbank to the eastward of the cliff, where the *Weymouth* subsequently went in pieces. The fate of this ship, previous to her being wrecked, had been singularly unfortunate. About a month before the disaster she had been captured in the Bristol Channel by a French privateer, when Captain Llewellyn, his wife, and a ship's boy, were put by the enemy into a boat, when seven leagues at sea, and run ashore at the Land's End. But the joy of the Frenchmen over their prize was but of short duration; for a few days after the event, the *Weymouth*, with ten French seamen on board, was recaptured by the *Plover* sloop-of-war, when close under the enemy's fort of St. Maloes, from the guns of which several shots were fired at the intrepid British sloop. The *Weymouth* having then been taken to Scilly, Captain Llewellyn and his apprentice proceeded thither, and a crew having been procured, the vessel was brought to Plymouth, where the captain had remained to settle matters pertaining to the recapture, giving the vessel into the charge of the mate to sail under convoy for the Downs.

When on board his ship, Captain Llewellyn had divided his favours between his apprentice and a pet raccoon; and when the *Weymouth* was aground the boy determined to save the life of the animal, in token of the gratitude he felt for the invariable kindness of his master. The boy was drawn ashore through the breakers by a rope, with the raccoon firmly held in his arms. Another of the crew was in like manner saved through the humane efforts of Mr. Ginn, a government official, who threw a rope upon the deck when all other means of saving life had failed. The

4

end of the line having been secured around the body of a sailor, he was dragged through the waves and up to the summit of the cliff in safety. Previous to Mr. Ginn's successful effort, however, four of the crew had attempted to reach the shore by means of a boat, but all had perished on the way.

To the west of the *Weymouth* lay the *Traveller*, the crew of which were all saved; but the brig and its cargo were entirely lost. The next vessel was the *Albion*. Part of this ship's original cargo had been opportunely landed at Plymouth, but the remainder, with the vessel, was swallowed up, dispersed, or destroyed by the raging waters. All the crew, however, were happily preserved.

The first ship to the east of the *Harlequin* was the *Unice*, and prior to her running ashore she had been in most excellent condition; nearly a thousand pounds having being expended upon her in America, a few months previous to her fatal voyage. Through the exertions of Mr. Close of Newhaven, assisted by some officers of the 81st Regiment, quartered at Seaford Barracks, the lives of the captain and crew of the vessel were saved, together with a large portion of the cargo. The vigilance of these gentlemen was also largely instrumental in detecting and preventing that system of wholesale plunder which hardened men had adopted, in defiance of all laws human or Divine.

The next vessel was the *February*, with a crew of sixteen souls, fifteen of whom unfortunately perished. Having unshipped her cargo at Plymouth, she was in ballast, and is supposed to have dropped her anchor when she struck, which prevented her from being drifted in at the return of the tide. Falling over upon her side, the sea ran completely over her, and no assistance could be rendered from the shore to her despairing crew. Driven to the last extremity, the poor men got on the masts and rigging, and feelingly petitioned for aid that was beyond all human ability to bestow. The sight was heart-breaking, and there were few who witnessed it without betraying by their tears how deeply they were affected. The tremendous buffeting by the waves to which this ship was exposed presently carried away her fore and mizzen masts; the main-mast, therefore, soon became the only point of refuge. But the weight of sixteen men, under the circumstances, was more than the main-mast could bear, and it ultimately gave way. At that instant shrieks of horror filled the dark and turbulent atmosphere, and all the crew were feebly struggling in the water—one only being rescued from the very jaws of death.

The Prussian ship *Midbedach* was also exposed to all the fury of the storm; and eleven, out of a crew of thirteen men, were hurried into eternity. A great part of the wine that was included in this vessel's lading was preserved, but the remainder of her cargo was nearly all lost. The wine-butts floated to a considerable distance when the hull broke up, but the Customs' officers eventually secured these for the owners.

All the shipwrecked men who could, by the most resolute efforts, be rescued from their awful position, were saved by ten on the morning after the calamity, one only excepted. The preservation of this sailor deserves particular notice. The situation of the wrecks was within a short distance of Blatchington; and the commanding officer of the military detachment there stationed, Captain Brown, together with his subordinate officers, and all the available men of the 81st Regiment, took a most humane and active part in the endeavours put forth to save lives and property. While so occupied, a lieutenant of the 81st, Mr. Derenzy, after various successful efforts in rescuing men from death, discovered a poor mariner in the last agony of exhaustion, sometimes beneath and sometimes above the billows, feebly fighting with the breakers, and with his hope of reaching the shore almost on the point of expiring. Soon after the attention of Mr. Derenzy had been attracted towards him, the drowning man sank as if in the cold embrace of dissolution, when the feelings of the officer were wrought to a pitch of torture, and he exclaimed—" I'll save that poor fellow, or perish in the attempt."

Instantly the lieutenant plunged into the foaming surge, and was for some moments wholly lost to the observation of the spectators upon the beach. When he could be discerned, it was seen that he had grasped the clothing of the object of his solicitude with one hand, while with the other he was attempting to make good his return to the land. At this critical moment a heavy fragment of wreckage struck the gallant officer on the temple. The blow was forcible, and deprived him of his senses. He could no longer strive with the waves, but he still held the sailor in his grasp until both sank together. All these incidents of a most exciting scene were painfully witnessed by one of Mr. Derenzy's brother officers, a Mr. Pringle, who without hesitation resolved to make a personal attempt to rescue his loved and valued friend. Accordingly he threw himself into the seething surge, and after the most strenuous efforts reached Mr. Derenzy. But the latter still held the seaman tenaciously, and to guide him shorewards proved to be impossible. After repeated struggles to attain his purpose, Mr. Pringle at last succumbed to the force of the waters, and both of the officers, as well as the poor mariner, lay among the breakers apparently lifeless.

At this momentous juncture a fearful anxiety was betrayed by the men of the 81st, and soon the cry was raised, " Our officers are drowning—let us save them, or die in their company." With a spontaneous consent the soldiers speedily formed with their outstretched arms a line extending from the beach to the spot among the breakers where the bodies lay. Firmly grasping the hands of each other, the soldiers stood among the angry waves while the living line thus constituted was extended for some distance upon the beach by landsmen eager to take a part in the attempted rescue. Amidst sensations of an indescribable character the three objects of tearful solicitude were brought ashore, when restoratives were at once applied to each, and eventually with highly gratifying results. Although all three continued unconscious for some time after their deliverance from the waves, they were at length happily brought back to life, their country, and their friends.

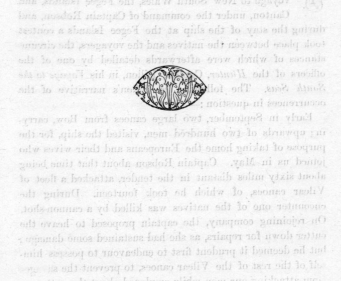

THE HUNTER.

THIS British vessel sailed in 1812 from Bengal, on a voyage to New South Wales, the Fegee Islands, and Canton, under the command of Captain Robson, and during the stay of the ship at the Fegee Islands a contest took place between the natives and the voyagers, the circumstances of which were afterwards detailed by one of the officers of the *Hunter*, Captain Dillon, in his *Voyage to the South Seas*. The following is Dillon's narrative of the occurrences in question :—

Early in September, two large canoes from Bow, carrying upwards of two hundred men, visited the ship, for the purpose of taking home the Europeans and their wives who joined us in May. Captain Robson about that time being about sixty miles distant in the tender, attacked a fleet of Vilear canoes, of which he took fourteen. During the encounter one of the natives was killed by a cannon-shot. On rejoining company, the captain proposed to heave the cutter down for repairs, as she had sustained some damage ; but he deemed it prudent first to endeavour to possess himself of the rest of the Vilear canoes, to prevent the savages from attacking our men while employed about the cutter, as it would be necessary to have that boat ashore at high-water.

On the morning of the 6th September, the Europeans belonging to the ship were all armed with muskets, along with those from Bow, and the party was placed under the command of Mr. Norman, the first-officer of the *Hunter*. We landed at a place called the Black Rock, where the two canoes shortly after joined us ; the Bow chiefs having with them a hundred of their men. The boats and canoes then put off into deep water, so as to prevent their getting aground at the ebbing of the tide.

Upon our landing, the Europeans began to disperse into small parties of two, three, aud four in a group. I begged of Mr. Norman to order the men to keep close together, but no attention was paid to my entreaty. We proceeded over a level plain without interruption till we arrived at the foot of a hill, which we ascended ; and then a few natives shewed themselves, and tried to irritate us by their shouts and gestures. Turning to the right, Mr. Norman went along a path leading to some native huts, while I followed him with seven other Europeans, and the Bow chiefs with one of their men. Here a few savages tried to dispute our passage ; but on one of them being shot dead, the rest retreated. Mr. Norman now caused the huts to be set on fire ; an act of wanton destructiveness that cannot be defended. Shortly after we heard furious yells in the direction of the road by which we had ascended. The character of the sounds led the Bow chiefs to understand that some of their men, as well as Europeans, had been killed by the Vilear natives, who had lain concealed until we had ascended to the table-land, when they attacked our straggling parties, of whom only two individuals escaped.

There were ten musket-men in our party, with the Bow chiefs and a follower. We immediately got out of the thicket on to the table-land, where there were three of the islanders, who called out to us that several of our men were killed, and that we would share the same fate. Before descending to the plain, a young man named John Graham separated from us, and ran into a thicket on the left of the road, where he was speedily pursued by three savages and despatched. As we descended, we discovered that the plain between us and the boats was covered by thousands of infuriated and armed natives, who had prepared to give us a warm reception. When we got to the bottom of the hill, the savages stood on each side of the path, brandishing their weapons, and with their persons and countenances besmeared with the blood of our slaughtered companions.

At this moment a native, who had stealthily followed us down the declivity, threw a lance at Mr. Norman, who, pierced through the body by the weapon, ran a few yards and then fell apparently dead. Turning round sharply, I fired at the native and reloaded my piece as quickly as possible; but when I looked for my companions I found that they had fled in all directions, while the assembled islanders had quitted the path to pursue our flying men. I therefore dashed on as fast as I could, but had not gone above a few yards when I came upon the dead body of William Parker, which was lying across the path. Taking Parker's rifle from the ground where he had fallen, I beat a retreat from the scene of bloodshed.

The natives, now observing me, gave chase; and to make good my escape from their vengeance, I was obliged to throw away Parker's musket, as well as a pistol that I carried in my belt. I reached the foot of a small hill that stood in the plain, but found it impossible to get to the boats on account of the nearness of my pursuers. Observing some of our men upon my right, I called out to them—"Take the hill! take the hill!" We got to the summit, where the following persons mustered with all possible speed:— Charles Savage, Luis, a Chinaman, and Martin Bushart, with Thomas Dafny and William Wilson. The three former resided at Bow, the others were seamen belonging to the ship. Dafny had been wounded in several parts of the body, and the point of a spear had pierced his shoulder, having entered from behind, and come out in front, under the collar-bone. Fortunately, the rock to which we escaped was so steep that few persons could ascend at a time, but the savages shot arrows at us from the base of the acclivity.

I now took command of the party, and stationed each man in the best way possible under the circumstances. I did not allow more than one or two muskets to be fired at a time, and kept the wounded man loading for the others. Several of the natives, approaching too near, were immediately shot by us, which caused the remainder to keep at a respectful distance from the rock ; but the savages had now gathered in the plain beneath us in considerable force, and surrounded our position with vehement yells, as a spectacle was about to be enacted of the most horrid and revolting character. Fires were speedily prepared, and ovens heated for the reception of the bodies of our ill-fated companions who had been slain ; and, while the cannibals sung and danced with joy over their prizes, each corpse was placed in an oven, to be baked as a repast for the victors.

By this time the fury of the savages was somewhat abated, and they began to listen to our offers of agreement. I reminded them that eight of their men were prisoners on board the *Hunter*, and told them that, if we were killed, these men would be put to death, but if we were spared, we would cause them to be released immediately. The head-priest, who is regarded as a deity by the Fegee Islanders, asked if these men were still alive. I replied that they were, and I would send a man to the captain to order them to be released, if he would convey my messenger safely down to the boat. This the priest promised to do, and I prevailed upon Dafny, who was wounded and without arms to defend himself, to venture upon this mission, under the escort of the venerable savage. Dafny was to inform Captain Robson of our horrid position, and that it was my particular request that he should release one half of the prisoners, after showing them a large chest of ironmongery, whales' teeth, etc., which he might promise to give to the other four, with their liberty, the moment we returned to the vessel in safety.

Dafny did as directed, and I did not lose sight of him until he got on the ship's deck. A cessation of arms now took place ; while several chiefs ascended the hill with professions of friendship, and offered security if we would go down among them. To this I would not accede, nor allow any of my men to do so, till Charles Savage, who had resided on the islands for more than five years, and spoke the native dialect fluently, begged permission to go down, as he had no doubt their promises would be kept, and he would be able to procure a peace, and obtain our safe return to the vessel. Overcome by his importunities, I at last consented, but told him that he must leave with me his musket and ammunition. This he did, and proceeded to the spot where Bonaser was seated, surrounded by chiefs, who appeared happy to receive him. Unknown to me, the Chinaman, Luis, had stolen down the opposite side of the hill to place himself under the protection of a chief with whom he was acquainted, and to whom he had rendered important services in former wars. The islanders, finding they could not prevail on me to place myself in their power, set up a yell that rent the air. At that moment Savage was seized by the legs, and with his head placed in a well of fresh water, was held in that state by six men until he was suffocated. At the same instant a powerful native got behind Luis, and with a huge club knocked the upper part of the Chinaman's skull to pieces.

There were now only three of us left upon the hill, and we

were furiously attacked by the cannibals, who pressed closely upon us. Wilson being a bad shot, we kept him loading the fire-arms, while Bushart and I fired them off. Having four muskets, two always remained loaded. Bushart was an excellent marksman. With twenty-eight discharges he shot twenty-seven of the savages; only once missing his aim. I also killed and wounded some of the enemy, who, finding they could not conquer us without great loss to themselves, kept off and vowed vengeance. The human bodies being now prepared, they were taken from the ovens and shared out to the different tribes of cannibals, who devoured their repast with avidity.

Having now no more than seventeen cartridges left, we determined that as soon as darkness set in we would place the muzzles of our muskets to our hearts, with the butts to the ground, and discharge the pieces into our breasts; thus to avoid the danger of falling alive into the hands of these cruel and merciless men. At this moment the boat put off from the ship and got close to the landing-place, where we could see the eight prisoners being brought on purpose to give them their liberty. I could not imagine how the captain could be persuaded to act in this strange manner, as the only hope of our lives being spared was by allowing only a part of the prisoners to land, and by keeping the others on board, to give an incentive to the liberated islanders to intercede with their friends on shore to spare our lives, that we might in return protect their countrymen when we got on board the *Hunter*.

Shortly after the prisoners landed they were conveyed unarmed up the rock to me. The eight natives were preceded by the priest, who informed me that Captain Robson had released them, and sent a chest of cutlery, etc., on shore for the chiefs, with orders for us to deliver our muskets to them, when the priest would see us safely to the boats. These terms I refused. The priest then turned to Bushart and harangued him on the policy of our complying. The thought now entered my head of making the priest a prisoner, and either to kill him or regain our liberty. Accordingly, I tied Savage's musket with my neckcloth to the belt of my cartridge-box, and presenting my own musket to the priest's head, told him I would instantly shoot him if he attempted to run away, or if any of his countrymen offered to molest us. I then directed him to proceed before me to the boat, threatening him with immediate death in case he did not comply with my orders. Thinking it prudent to obey, the priest led the way for us down the hill, and as we passed along through the multitude of natives, he exhorted them not to molest us, for if they did so he would be shot, and they would consequently incur the wrath of the gods, who would be angry at their disobedience of the divine commands, and would cause the sea to rise and swallow up the islands and all the inhabitants. The warning of their spiritual adviser caused all the cannibals to be seated forthwith upon the grass.

The priest proceeded towards the boats, with the muzzles of Bushart's and Wilson's muskets at his ears, while the muzzle of mine was placed between his shoulders. On nearing the water he made a sudden stop. I ordered him to go on, but this he refused to do, declaring he would go no farther, and I might shoot him if I pleased. Threatening to take him at his word if he persisted in his obstinacy, I asked him why he would not go to the water's edge. He replied, " You want to take me on board and put me to the torture." There being no time to lose, I told him to stand still, for I would shoot him if he attempted to move before I got into the boat. We then walked backwards to the waterside, and up to our breasts in the water, where we embarked ; but we had no sooner got on board our boat than the islanders came down to the beach, and with their bows and slings saluted us with showers of arrows and stones.

Being now out of danger, however, we returned thanks to Divine Providence for our escape, and proceeded towards the ship, which we reached just as the sun was setting. I expostulated with Captain Robson on his extraordinary conduct in causing so many human beings to be unnecessarily sacrificed. He made some absurd apologies, and inquired if we were the only persons who had escaped. I replied that such was the case, but if the natives could have made proper use of the muskets which fell into their hands on that occasion, we must all have been killed.

THE PATRICK HENRY.

AN American vessel, the *Patrick Henry*, sailed from New York for Curaçoa in July 1813, and when within a week's journey of her destination was attacked by a crew of desperadoes, hailing from the piratical shores of the West Indies. The merchantman was commanded by Captain Tuttle, a worthy representative of the old school of master-mariners, and the crew consisted of a set of as daring seamen as ever trod the forecastle of a ship. Both the captain and his men had fought in the War of Independence, so that they were not tyros in the art of warfare; but the resources of the commander, at a critical moment, were not limited to the ordinary tactics or means of defence usually relied upon for the safety of a vessel and her crew during an encounter with an enemy upon the high seas. The *Patrick Henry* carried only one passenger on this adventurous voyage; and the services of the gentleman in question were called into requisition to repel the onslaught of the pirates, and contribute not a little to the discomfiture of these marauders. The following account of the incidents is from the pen of this naval volunteer of a past generation :—

I was sitting alone in the cabin when the captain came down and told me there was a vessel just appearing on the horizon to windward, and asked me to go and see what she was, for he could not make her out at all. I went on deck, mounted into the maintop, and began my scrutiny.

"Well, what is she?" asked the captain from the deck.

"I can hardly make her out, but I think she is a schooner."

"What's her course?"

"South-west by south, I think; about the same as ourselves." I remained in the top for a few minutes, and continued looking at the stranger. "She seems fonder of the sea than I am," I continued, "for she might have her top-sails and topgallants, and studding-sails to boot, all set, instead of slipping along under her lower-sails."

The captain made no answer, but was looking hard at her with his naked eye. I now perceived through my glass a white speck above her fore-sail, flapping against the mast. "Well," I said, "she must have heard me, for there goes her foretop-sail."

The captain now went to the companion for his glass, and after looking attentively at her for a short time, "What's that?" he asked. "Is that her square-sail she's setting? I can't very well see from the deck."

I looked again. "Yes, 'tis her square-sail; as I'm alive, she's changed her course, and is bearing down upon us."

But by this time the captain had mounted the rigging, and was standing beside me; he was eyeing the distant vessel keenly. After having apparently satisfied himself, he asked me to go with him to the cabin, as he wished to talk with me alone. We descended to the deck, and I followed him to the cabin. He motioned me to take a seat, and after carefully shutting the door—

"I rather expect," said he, "that fellow's a pirate."

"Pirate?" I asked in alarm.

"Yes, I say pirate, and I'll tell you why. In the first place, you see, he'd no business to be sneaking along in that do-little sort of a way, as when we first saw him; who ever, that had any honest business to do, would allow such a fine breeze to go by without shewing more canvas than a powder-monkey's old breeches to catch it? Next, you see, what the mischief has he to do with us, that, as soon as he clapped eyes on us, he must alter his course, and be so anxious to get out his square-sail? Again, he looks just like one of those imps of mischief, with his low black hull and tall raking masts. No use talking; the only thing is, what shall we do? The *Patrick Henry* ain't a Baltimore clipper, and that 'ere blackguard will walk up to us like nothing. If we let them aboard, it's most likely we'll all walk the plank, so we'd better try to keep 'em out. We've only got an old rusty carronade and two six-pounders, and I don't believe there's a ball on board, we came off in such a hurry. There's two muskets and an old regulation rifle down in my state-room, but they ain't been fired I don't know when, and I'd as lief stand afore 'em as behind 'em. But our ship's as handsome a looking craft as you'll see; and couldn't we look wicked-like now, and try to frighten that cut-throat-looking rascal?"

I confess I was at first startled at the captain's opinion of the strange sail; but his cool and collected manner impressed me with confidence in his management, and I told him he knew best what we should do, and I would second him as well as I could. He walked up and down the cabin twice; then rubbing his hands together, as if pleased with his own idea—

"I have it," he cried; "I'll just go on deck to put things in order, and in the meantime you'd better amuse yourself looking out your pistols, if you have any; for if he won't be content with a look at us we'll have to fight."

I hurriedly took my fowling-piece and pistols from their

cases, for I fortunately had both; and though I somehow refused to allow myself to believe there would be any occasion for their use, yet I loaded them all with ball, and in each of the pistols put a brace; this done, I went on deck, where I found the captain surrounded by his crew, telling them his suspicions and plan of action.

"Maybe," said he, "we'll have to fight; if them scoundrels have a mind to try us, they'll send a boat on board, and I want to know if you'll help me to keep 'em off. You see it's most likely they'll make you walk the plank, whether you fight or not, if they get on board; and I calculate, if you do just as I tell you, we'll frighten 'em."

There was a hearty "Ay, ay, sir!" to this short and pithy harangue.

"Thankee, thankee, boys," said the captain. "Now, we'll not shew another stitch of canvas, but seem to take no more notice of that fellow than if we didn't see him; and if he does try to come aboard, then we'll shew 'em what we can do."

The crew were soon busy, in obedience to his orders, cutting up a spare foretopgallant-mast in logs of about four feet long. These were immediately painted black, with a round spot in the centre of one end, so as to bear a tolerable resemblance to pieces of cannon, and with the two old six-pounders, were placed, one at each port, on our deck, five on a side; but the ports were to be kept closed until the captain gave the order to open them, when they were to be raised as quickly as possible, and the logs thrust out about a foot. A platform was then made on the top of the long-boat, which was fixed between the fore and main-masts, and the carronade, or fourteen-pounder, was hoisted up. These things being arranged, the captain went below, and the crew mustered in knots, to wonder and talk of what was to be done.

In the meantime we had been standing on our course,

5

and had not shifted or hoisted a single sail, but were as if perfectly regardless of the schooner. Not so with her, however, for besides a large square-sail and squaretop-sail on the fore-mast, she had run out small foretop-mast stud- aing-sails, and onward she came right before a pretty smart breeze, yawing from side to side, at one moment sinking stern foremost into the trough of the sea, as an enormous wave rolled out from under her, and at the next forced headlong onwards by its successor, while a broad white sheet of foam spread out around her, giving beautiful relief to the jet-black colour of her hull, testifying how rapidly she was going through the water. I could not help thinking of the captain's expression, for she certainly did "walk up to us like nothing," and as there appeared not much time to lose, I went down to the cabin to assume my weapons. The captain was there arranging some papers, and a bottle was before him, into which he had put a letter.

"Maybe," said he, "something 'll happen to me; for if them 'ere bloodthirsty wretches won't be cheated I shall be the first to suffer; and natural enough too, for all the mis- chief they'll suffer will be by my orders, just because I didn't like to be overhauled like an old tarpaulin by every rascal that chooses to say, 'Heave-to,' on the high seas. But never mind; only, should you escape, just drop the bottle and letter overboard, if you think you can't deliver it yourself."

I had never seriously considered the probability that I might also be killed in an approaching *mêlée*, for I thought that the captain intended to throw open his ports and shew his sham guns, and that the schooner would take fright. But when he began to talk about death in such a serious strain, I began to feel very uncomfortable, and not being naturally a warrior, I wished myself anywhere else than on board the *Patrick Henry*. There I was, however, without a chance of escape; and I suggested to the captain that it would be as well for me to put a letter into the bottle also, in case of any accident to both of us, which was agreed to; and we arranged that if either survived, and had the opportunity, the letter of the unfortunate should be safely forwarded to its destination. After this little piece of preparation, the captain took me by the hand and said:—

"'Tis well. Are you willing to share with me the post of danger? Do not suppose I am unaccustomed to the perils of a sea-fight. No; I've supported the glory of my country in many a gallant action, and have witnessed the death of those honoured and esteemed as the sons of liberty. You are a passenger, and should be under my protection, yet I ask you to share my danger. I wish some one to stand by me on the platform, and help me to manage the swivel. Hands are scarce, and I don't know where else to place you."

The hardy fellow's eyes glistened as he made the proposal, to which I instantly agreed. We went on deck, and the men were still hanging about waiting for orders. These were soon given. The cooper and the carpenter were ordered to bring up all hatchets and other offensive and defensive weapons, and, with the muskets and rifle, these were distributed among the crew, who were told to use them in repelling any attempt to board.

The schooner had now come down within half-a-mile of us, when she suddenly took down her square-sail, and hauled her wind, to have a look at us. I dare say she did not know what to make of our seeming indifference. Presently a cloud of smoke burst from her side, and a ball came skipping over the water, and passed astern of us.

"I thought so," said the captain. "Now, lads, show her our stripes."

A ball of bunting flew up to the end of our mizzen-peak, rested an instant, and fluttered out into the American ensign. The smoke drifted away from the schooner, and she ran up at her gaff the ensign of the Columbian Republic.

"That's just the way with them blackguards," said the captain; "they're always making a fool of some republic."

Scarcely were the words out of his mouth when another column of smoke burst from the schooner, and another ball came skipping along towards us, but catching a swell, it plunged in, and we saw no more of it.

"That fellow, now, I take it, is a good shot, so we'll not wait for another. Clue up the main-sail, boys; haul aft the main-braces; clue up the fore-sail; luff her, man, luff her a little more—steady," burst from our captain's mouth. The orders were obeyed with the quickness of a well-disciplined crew, and our ship was hove-to.

"Now, my lads, take your stations, four to each port, on the weather side, but do nothing till I tell ye."

The men took their stations as directed by each log on the weather side, and I followed the captain to the platform where our carronade was mounted. It was loaded to the muzzle with bits of iron, musket-balls, lumps of lead, and various other missiles, for the captain had conjectured truly —there were no balls on board. The schooner hove-to, and a boat was lowered, and crowded with men. It approached rapidly, pulled by eight rowers. The muzzle of our carronade was depressed as much as possible, and made to bear on the water about fifty yards from the ship. The captain stood with his speaking-trumpet in one hand, and a handspike, with which he shifted the position of the gun as required, in the other. The schooner's boat approached, and was pulling rapidly to get alongside.

"Now, sir, keep steady, and obey my orders coolly," said the captain in an under-tone. "Boy, fetch the iron that's heating in the galley—run!"

The boy ran, and returned with the iron-rod heated at one end, which was handed to me.

"When I tell you to fire—fire, as you value your life and those on board."

The captain now put his speaking-trumpet to his mouth and hailed the boat, which was within a hundred yards of us. "Stop—no nearer, or I'll blow you all out of the water. Keep off, keep off, or, I say, I'll——"

At that instant the man at the bows of the boat, who appeared to take the command, gave an order, and a volley from several muskets was fired at us. I heard the balls hit about me, and turned to look for the captain to receive my order to fire. He was on one knee behind the cannon, and holding it by the breech.

"Why, captain! what's the matter? Are you hit?"

He rallied. "Nothing—they're coming!" He gave another hoist to the gun, cast his eye hurriedly along its barrel—"*Fire*, and be quick!"

I needed not a second bidding, for the boat was close alongside. The smoke burst from the touch-hole with a hiss, and for an instant I thought the gun had missed fire, but in the next it exploded with a tremendous report, that deafened me.

"Throw open your ports, boys, and shew them your teeth," roared the captain through his trumpet, and his voice sounded hideously unnatural.

In an instant every port was up, and our guns protruded their muzzles. I had fancied that I heard a crash, followed by wild screams, immediately upon the discharge of the cannon; but the report had deafened me, and the smoke, which was driven back in my face, had so shrouded me that I could not see. The unearthly shout of the captain had also for the moment driven the idea from my mind, and I now grasped my gun to repel boarders. But my hearing had not deceived me, for as the smoke was borne away to leeward, the whole scene of destruction burst upon my sight. The cannon had been most truly pointed, and its contents had shivered the hapless boat, killing or wounding almost every person in her.

The longest lifetime will hardly efface that scene from my mind. The stern of the boat had been carried completely away, and it was sinking by the weight of the human beings that clung to it. As it gradually disappeared the miserable wretches struggled forward to the bows, and with horrid screams and imprecations battled for a moment for what little support it might yield. The dead and the dying were floating and splashing around them, while a deep crimson tinge shewed how fatal had been that discharge. Ropes were thrown over, and everything done to save those who were not destroyed by the cannon-shot, but only three out of the boat's crew of twenty-four were saved; the greater number went down with the boat to which they clung.

The whole scene of devastation did not last ten minutes, and all was again quiet. The bodies of those who had been shot did not sink, but were driven by the wind and sea against the side of the ship. From some the blood was gently oozing, and floating around them; others, stiff in the convulsion in which they had died, were grinning or frowning with horrible expression. One body, strong and muscular, with neat white trousers, and a leathern girdle in which were stuck two pistols, floated by, but the face was gone; some merciless ball had so disfigured him that all trace of human expression was destroyed. He was the pirate captain.

But where was the schooner? She lay-to for a few minutes after the destruction of her boat; and whether alarmed at our appearance, or horrified at the loss of so many of her men, I know not, but she slipped her fore-sail and stood away as close to the wind as possible. We saw no more of her.

The excitement of the scenes we had just passed through prevented our missing the captain; but so soon as the schooner bore away, all naturally expected his voice to give some order for getting again under weigh. But no order came. Where was he? The musket discharge from the boat, with the unearthly voice that conveyed the orders for the ports to be thrown open, flashed across my mind. I ran to the platform. The captain was there, lying on his face beside the gun that he had pointed with such deadly effect. He still grasped the speaking-trumpet in his hand, and I shuddered as I beheld the mouthpiece covered with blood.

"The captain's killed!" I cried, and stooped to raise him.

"I believe I am," said he; "take me to the cabin."

A dozen ready hands were stretched to receive him, and he was taken below and carefully laid on a sofa.

"Ay," he said, "I heard the crash; my ear knows too well the crash of shot against a plank to be mistaken, and my eye has pointed too many guns to miss its mark easily now. But tell me, is any one else hurt?"

"No, thank God," I said; "and I hope you are not so badly hit."

"Bad enough. But cut open my waistcoat—'tis here."

A mouthful of blood stopped his utterance, but he pointed to his right side. I wiped his mouth, and we cut off his waistcoat as gently as possible. There was no blood, but on removing his shirt we discovered, about three inches on the right of the pit of the stomach, a discoloured spot about the size of half-a-crown, darkening towards its centre, where there was a small wound. A musket-ball had struck him, and from there being no outward bleeding, I feared the worst. We dressed the wound as well as circumstances would permit; but externally it was trifling—the fatal wound was within. The unfortunate sufferer motioned for all to leave him but me, and calling me to his side—

"I feel," he said, "that I am dying. The letter—promise me that you will get it forwarded; 'tis to my poor widow.

I've tempted this death often and escaped, and 'tis hard to be struck by a villain's hand. But God's will be done!"

I promised that I would personally deliver the letter, for I intended returning to New York from Curaçoa.

"Thank you truly," said the dying man. "You will then see my Helen and my child, and can tell them that their unfortunate husband and father died thinking of them. This ship and cargo are mine, and will belong to my family."

A sudden flow of blood prevented his saying more. I tried to relieve him by change of posture, but in vain; he muttered some incoherent sentences, by which his mind seemed to dwell upon former scenes of battle. He rallied for a moment, and with a blessing for his family, and the name of Helen on his lips, he ceased to breathe.

The body of our unfortunate captain was next day committed to the waves, amidst the tears of us all, and our voyage was prosecuted to an end without further interruption.

THE COMMERCE.

ON the 24th of June 1815, the American brig *Commerce*, James Riley commander, sailed from New Orleans for the Western Coast of Africa, touching on the way at Gibraltar. The vessel was nearly new, and was well fitted in every respect, her carrying capacity being about two hundred and twenty tons. George Williams and Aaron Savage were respectively her first and second mates, and the brig's crew consisted of six seamen, a black cook, and a cabin-boy. Arriving at Gibraltar, some wines and spirits were shipped, in addition to the cargo of flour and tobacco with which the *Commerce* had left New Orleans. An old man, Antonio Michel, was likewise taken on board, when the vessel went on her way for the Cape de Verd Isles on the 23rd of August.

After having been five days at sea, the captain discovered that he had passed the Canary Islands without observing them. This was to be accounted for by the thick weather that prevailed, and the fog still continued to increase. On the night of the 28th of August the brig was suddenly found to be in the midst of breakers, and she struck upon a rock without further warning; every man upon deck being started from his position by the violence of the shock. As she bilged immediately, it was determined to take to the boats in the hope that land might be at no great distance from the brig, and the efforts of the crew were now directed to getting up provisions and water from the hold. In the morning, however, land was found to be so near that Riley thought a line of communication between the brig and the shore might be formed by means of a rope. Accordingly, a hawser was carried through the breakers by Riley himself and one of his seamen, at the hazard of their lives. Having fixed one end of the rope securely on the beach, the whole of the crew were speedily landed, together with some wine and provisions, and several barrels of water. Two of the boats were also got ashore, one receiving an injury in its passage to the beach.

Setting themselves actively to work, the crew soon constructed a tent by means of their oars and two sails. They next endeavoured to repair the boats, so as to fit them for going out to sea, in the event of the abandonment of the vessel proving absolutely necessary. While the men were employed, a man was observed approaching, and Captain Riley thought the aspect of the comer to be more terrific than anything he had yet seen in a human being. The skin of the man was dusky, but brighter than a negro's; his mouth was unusually large, and his eyes were of a fiery red; his parted lips disclosed a set of sharp teeth of a pearly whiteness; while a ragged and scanty piece of woollen cloth was his only covering, save his matted locks and long black beard. Two old women and several children, together with a young woman of eighteen or twenty years, speedily joined the head of the family, who had acted as their pioneer. They brought an English hammer, which had probably belonged to some vessel previously wrecked upon the coast, and also carried an axe and some long knives, the latter being in sheaths suspended from their necks. Having assembled round the

crew of the *Commerce*, these Arabs commenced an indis-
criminate plundering of the effects which had been landed
from the ship. Trunks, chests, and boxes were broken
open and emptied of their contents; the clothing being
carried by the spoilers to the neighbouring sand-hills, and
spread out to dry. Beds were also emptied and the feathers
scattered before the wind, to the amusement of the younger
denizens of the desert.

As they departed with their plunder, the Arabs made
signs that they would return in the morning, and the crew
prepared to pass the night under the shelter of their tent,
after eating a hearty meal which they had cooked with the
aid of a fire that one of the children had kindled on the
beach. In the morning the old Arab again appeared,
accompanied by his wives and two young men, and
apparently with the object of getting possession of the tent.
Pointing to the wreck, he menaced Riley and his party with
a spear. This act of hostility would probably have been
resented by the Americans, had not the sight of a drove
of camels and their drivers approaching, made them glad to
put off in the long-boat towards the wreck, which was still
above water. After loading the camels with the tent and
provisions, the Arabs stove-in the heads of the casks and
emptied the contents on the sand. They then gathered
together and made a bonfire of everything that remained,
including the navigating instruments, books, and charts of
the vessel. The further misfortunes and sufferings of the
mariners are given in

CAPTAIN RILEY'S NARRATIVE.

We now made preparations to leave the brig, by getting
a few bottles of wine and some slices of salt pork. No
water could be procured. Our oars lost, we split a plank
for oars, and attempted to shove off; but a surf, striking
the boat, filled her. The sight of our deplorable situation

seemed to excite pity in the breasts of the savages who had driven us from the shore. They came down to the water's edge, bowed themselves to the ground, beckoned us to come on shore, and made repeated signs of peace and friendship. Finding we would not come on shore, one of them ran and fetched a goat-skin of water. The old man came into the water with it, up to his armpits, and beckoned me to come and drink. Being thirsty, and finding we could not get water any other way, I went to the beach, where the old man met me, and gave me the skin of water, which I carried off to the wreck. This done, he wished to go on board, while I waited on the beach till his return. Seeing no possibility of escaping but with their assistance, I went on shore, where the old man and his companions expressed every demonstration of goodwill and peace. I let the old man pass to the wreck, while I remained on the beach. When my men hauled him on board, I endeavoured to make them understand that they must keep him till I was released; but the noise of the surf prevented their hearing me.

After he had satisfied his curiosity by looking attentively at everything he could see, and inquiring for baftas, for firearms, and for money, he came on shore. When he was near the beach, and I about to meet him, I was seized by two of the stoutest Arabs, and at that very instant the women and children presented their knives to my breast. To strive against them were instant death. I was obliged to remain quiet. The countenances of all around me assumed the most horrid and malignant expressions. They gnashed their teeth at me, and struck their daggers within an inch of my head and body. The young men held me fast, while the old one, seizing a sharp scimitar, laid hold of my hair as if to cut off my head. I concluded my last moments were come. But the old man, after drawing the scimitar lightly across the collar of my shirt, released me.

When the old man had quitted his hold, and I hailed my

people, their hopes began to revive, and one of them named Porter came on the hawser to know what they should do. I told him all the money they had on board must be instantly brought on shore. He was in the water at some distance, and on account of the noise occasioned by the surf, could not hear what I added—namely, not to part with the money until I should be released. He went on board, and all hands put their money, to the amount of about one thousand dollars, into a bucket and slung it on a hawser. Porter shoved it along before him near the beach, and was about to bring it to the place where I sat. With considerable difficulty, however, I prevented him, as the surf made such a roaring that he could not hear me, though he was only a few yards distant; but he at last understood my signs, and stayed in the water until one of the young men went and received it from him. The old man had taken his seat alongside of me, and held his scimitar pointed at my breast.

The bucket of dollars was brought and poured into the old man's blanket, when he bade me rise and go with them; he and the young men urging me along with their daggers, and the women and children with their knives. In this manner they made me go over the sand-drifts to the distance of three or four hundred yards, where they seated themselves with me on the ground. The old man proceeded to count and divide the money. He made three heaps, counting into each heap by tens, and so dividing it exactly, gave to the two young men one-third, to his two wives one-third, and kept the other to himself. All secured the dollars by tying these in pieces of our clothing. During this process they had let go my arms, though they still kept around me. I thought my fate was now decided, if I could not by some means escape. I knew they could outrun me, and would undoubtedly plunge their weapons to my heart if I failed in the attempt. However I resolved to risk it, and made a slight movement with that view, at a moment when I thought all eyes were turned away; but, seeing my manœuvre, one of the young men made a lounge at me with his scimitar. I eluded the force of the blow by falling backwards as the weapon pierced my waistcoat. He was about to repeat it, when the old man bade him desist. The money being now distributed and tied up, they made me rise, as they were all about to leave the beach. There appeared no possibility of escape, when the thought was suggested to me to tempt their avarice. I then made them understand that there was more money in the possession of the crew. This seemed to please them, and they instantly turned towards the beach, sending the money off by one of the young men and a boy. When they approached to within one hundred yards of the shore they made me seat myself on the sand between two of them, who held me by the arms, bidding me order the money to be fetched. I knew there was none on the wreck or in the boat; but I imagined if we could get Antonio Michel on shore I should be able to make my escape. I hailed accordingly, and made signs to my people for one to come towards the beach, but as they saw that my situation was critical, none of them were inclined to venture, and I waited more than an hour, was often threatened with death, and made to halloo with all my might, until I became so hoarse as scarcely to make myself heard around me. The pity of Aaron Savage at last overcame his fears. He ventured on the hawser, and reaching the beach in safety, was about to come up to me, when I endeavoured to make him understand by signs that he must stay in the water, and keep clear of the natives, if he valued his life; but not being able to hear me, my guards, who supposed I was giving him orders to fetch the money, obliged me to get up and approach him a little, until I made him understand what I wanted. He then returned to the wreck, and I was taken to my former station.

Antonio came ashore. The natives instantly flocked round, expecting more money; but finding he had none, the adults beat him, and the children cut him with their knives. He begged for his life upon his knees, but they did not regard his entreaties. In hopes of saving him from the fury of these wretches, I told him to let them know by signs that there was money buried where the tent had stood. A new spy-glass, a saw, and other articles had been buried there, together with a bag of four hundred dollars. They went to the spot and commenced digging.

I was seated on the sand between the old man, with his spear pointing to my heart, and the stoutest young man, with his scimitar pointing to my head. Both weapons were within six inches of me, and my guards within a foot on each side. I considered that as soon as anything was found by the men who were digging, they would inform those who guarded me; and as I was pretty certain that both of them would look round as soon as the discovery of any treasure was announced, I carefully drew my legs under me, in order to be ready for a start. The place where they were digging was partly behind us; and on their making a noise, both my guards turned their heads towards them, when I instantly sprang out from beneath the weapons, and flew to the beach. I was running for my life, and soon reached the water's edge. Knowing I was pursued and nearly overtaken, I plunged into the sea head-foremost, and swam under water as long as I could hold my breath; then rising to the surface, I looked round on my pursuers. The old man was within ten feet of me, and up to the chin in water. He was about to dart his spear through my body, when a surf rolled over me, saved my life, and dashed him and his comrade on the beach. I was at some distance westward of the wreck, but swimming as fast as possible towards her, while surf after surf broke in towering heights over me, I was enabled, by almost superhuman exertions, to reach the wreck, when I was taken into the boat by the mates and crew. I was so far exhausted that I could not immediately witness what passed on shore, but was informed that my pursuers stood motionless at the edge of the water until I was safe in the boat, when they ran towards poor Antonio, and plunging a spear into his body, laid him dead at their feet. Then they picked up what things remained, and made off together. I saw them dragging Antonio's lifeless trunk across the sand-hills, and felt an inexpressible pang that to me alone was his massacre imputable. But on my recovery, when I reflected that there were no other means whereby under Providence the lives of ten men who had been committed to my charge could have been preserved, I concluded I had not done wrong; nor have I since had occasion to reproach myself for being the innocent cause of his destruction.

Hostilities had now commenced, and we could not doubt but the merciless ruffians would soon return in force and massacre us all as they had done Antonio. The wind blowing strong, and the surf breaking twenty or thirty feet high, the hope of getting to sea in our crazy long-boat was indeed but faint. She had been thumping alongside the wreck and on a sand-bank all day, taking in as much water as two men constantly employed with buckets could throw out. The deck and outside of the wreck were fast going to pieces, and the other parts could not hold together. The low tide, together with the sand-bar that had been formed by the washing of the sea from the bow of the wreck to the beach, had very much lessened the danger of communicating with the shore during the day, but the tide was now returning to sweep everything from the wreck, aided by the wind, which blew a gale on shore every night. Either to remain on the wreck, or to go on shore, was almost certain death. The boat could no longer be kept afloat alongside; and, being without provisions and water, if we put to sea we must soon perish. We had neither oars nor rudder to the boat, nor compass nor quadrant to direct our course, but as it was our only chance, I resolved to get if possible to sea; expecting, nevertheless, that we would be swallowed up by the first surf, and launched into eternity.

In the first place, a man was sent on shore to get two broken oars that were still lying there, while I made my way into the hold in search of fresh water. I dived in at the hatchway, which was covered with water, and after coming up under the deck on the larboard side, found, as I expected, just room to breathe, and to work among the floating casks, planks, and wreck of the hold. After much labour I found a water-cask partly full and the bung tight. With much trouble a small keg was filled, and a good drink given to all hands. The man now returned with the oars, and he also went of his own accord and got the bag of dollars. We got the small boat's sails into the boat, with a spar that would do for a mast, and the brig's foretop-mast staysails, the keg of water, a few pieces of salt pork, a live pig weighing about twenty pounds, and a few damaged figs. Everything being now ready, I endeavoured to encourage the crew; representing to them that it was better to be swallowed up altogether than to suffer ourselves to be massacred by the savages.

As we surveyed the dangers that surrounded us, wave followed wave, breaking with a dreadful crash, and there appeared no possibility of getting safely beyond the breakers without a particular interference of Providence in our favour. Every one trembled with apprehension, and each imagined that the moment we ventured past the vessel's stern would be his last. I then said, "Let us pull off our hats, my companions in distress." It was done in an instant, when, lifting up my eyes towards heaven, I exclaimed: "Great Creator and Preserver of the Universe, who now seest our distresses, we pray Thee to

6

spare our lives, and permit us to pass through this over-whelming surf into the open sea, but if we are doomed to perish, Thy will be done; we commit our souls to the mercy of Thee our God, who gavest them; and O, universal Father! protect and preserve our widows and children."

The winds, as if by Divine command, at this very moment ceased to blow. We hauled the boat out. The dreadful surges that were nearly bursting upon us suddenly subsided, making a path for our boat about twenty wards wide, through which we rowed her out as smoothly as if she had been on a river in a calm, whilst on each side of us, and not more than ten yards distant, the surf continued to break twenty feet high, and with unabated fury. We had to row nearly a mile in this manner. All being fully convinced that we were saved by the immediate interposition of Divine Providence, joined in returning thanks to the Supreme Being for this mercy. As soon as we reached the open sea, and had gained some distance from the wreck, the surf returned, combing behind us with the same force as on each side of the boat. We next fitted the mast, and set the small boat's mainsail.

The wind veering to the eastward, we were enabled to fetch past the point of the cape, though the boat had neither keel nor rudder. It was sunset when we got out, and night coming on, the wind as usual increased to a gale before morning, so that we expected to be swallowed up every moment. After a consultation, it was resolved to keep to sea instead of returning again to the cruel shore. After two days of stormy weather, on the 31st it became more moderate, but the weather was very thick and hazy. Our pig being nearly dead for the want of water, we killed it, taking care, however, to save its blood, which we divided and drank, our thirst having become almost insupportable. We also divided the pig's liver, intestines, etc., among us, and ate some of these to satisfy in some degree our extreme thirst. Thus this day passed away; no vessel was yet seen to relieve us.

The night came on very dark and lowering; the sky seemed big with an impending tempest. The wind blew hard from the N.E., and before midnight the sea combed into the boat in such quantities as several times to fill her more than half-full. All hands were employed in baling out the water, each believing that every approaching surge would bury him for ever in a watery grave. Sharp flashes of lightning shot across the gloom, rendering the scene doubly horrible.

Day came on amidst these accumulated horrors; it was the 1st of September. The wind continued to blow hard all this day and the succeeding night with great violence. Worn down by fatigue, hunger, and thirst, scorched by the burning rays of the sun, with our water fast diminishing, as well as our strength, every hope of succour by meeting with a vessel entirely failed us; so that in the afternoon of the 2nd of September we put about and made towards the coast. On the morning of the 7th we discovered land, and continued to approach it, driving along to the southward by a swift current until sunset. The surf was breaking high among the rocks near the shore, which we were very near, and seeing a small spot with the appearance of a sandy beach, we made towards it. In our track numerous fragments of rock showed their craggy heads, over which the surf foamed as it retired with a dreadful roaring. Landing, we got out of the boat with the little remains of our water and provisions, and night coming on, we prepared a place in the sand on which to lie. After wetting our mouths with water, and eating a few slices of pork, we lay down to rest.

On the morning of September the 8th, as soon as it was light, being much refreshed by our undisturbed sleep, we agreed to leave all that was cumbrous or heavy, and try to make our way to the eastward, in the hope of finding a place to dig for water while we had strength. Our burning thirst was now rendered more grievous than ever by our having eaten a few mussels, extremely salt, that were found on the rocks. Having agreed to keep together, and render each other assistance, we divided amongst us the little water we had, every one receiving his share in a bottle, in order to preserve it as long as possible; then taking a small piece or two of pork, which we slung on our backs in a spare shirt or piece of canvas, and leaving all our clothes but those we had on, we bent our way towards the east. Before starting I buried the bag of dollars, and induced every man to throw away all he had, as money had been the cause of our former ill-treatment, by tempting the natives to practise treacherous and cruel means to extort it from us. We now proceeded, as well as we were able, close to the water's side.

The land was either nearly perpendicular, or jutted over our heads to the height of five or six hundred feet, and we were forced to climb over masses of sharp and craggy rocks from two to three hundred feet high; then to descend from rock to rock until we reached the water's edge. After waiting for a surf to retire, we rushed one by one past a steep point, up to our necks in the water, to the rocks on the other side, by clinging to which we kept ourselves from being washed away by the next surf, until with each other's assistance we clambered up beyond the reach of the greedy billows. But surmounting one obstacle seemed only to open to our view another still more dangerous. At one place we were obliged to climb along a narrow ledge of rocks between forty and fifty feet high, and not more than eight inches broad; while the least slip must have plunged us into the frightful abyss below. Our shoes were nearly all worn off; our feet were lacerated and bleeding; the rays of the sun beat upon our emaciated bodies; while not a breath of air cooled our almost boiling blood. In crawling through one of the holes between the rocks, I had broken my bottle and spilled the little water it contained. Thus passed this day with us, and when night came on it brought with it new distresses. We had advanced along the coast not more than about four miles this day, and without finding any change for the better in our situation, whilst our strength was diminishing, and no circumstance occurred to revive our hopes.

We spent the two succeeding days in clambering among the rocks under the high cliffs, all the while suffering from hunger. After unremitting exertions, we found a place by which we ascended to the plain above, where no object was seen as far as the eye could reach—not a tree, shrub, or spear of grass that might give the smallest relief to expiring nature. We travelled along the edge of the cliff. A little after sunset I was encouraging the men to proceed, when one exclaimed, "I think I see a light." It was the light of a fire.

Joy thrilled through my veins, and hope again revived me. We determined to wait till morning before presenting ourselves to the Arabs. All agreed to go forward and meet the natives on the morning of September the 10th. As soon as they discovered us they ran towards us in the most frantic manner with drawn scimitars, and stripped us amid the most savage yells. A strife now ensued among our captors with respect to dividing the plunder and prisoners. They cut each other with their weapons in the most horrid manner, so that the blood ran in streams. After watering the camels and loading them, the Arabs departed for the interior. We were forced to walk and drive the camels, while the sand was so soft and yielding that we sunk up to our knees every step. Thus we mounted the sand-hills. The blazing heat of the sun's rays darting on our naked bodies, the sharp rocks and stones cutting our feet and legs to the bone, in addition to our excessive weakness, which dysentery had increased, rendered our passage through this chasm so severe that we were almost deprived of life. I was obliged to stop, until, by the application of a stick to my sore back, I was forced up to the level ground where the camels lay down to rest.

The Arabs had been much amused by our difficulty in ascending the height, and kept up a laugh while they were whipping us forward. The women and children were on foot as well as themselves, and went up without the smallest inconvenience; though it was extremely hard for the camels to mount, and before the animals got to the top they were covered with sweat and froth. Having now selected five camels for the purpose, they put us on behind the humps, to which we were obliged to cling by grasping the long hair with both hands. The backbone of the one I was on was only covered with skin, and was as sharp as the edge of an oar's blade. I was slipping down to his tail every moment, but was forced, however, to keep on, while the camel, rendered restive at the sight of his strange rider, was all the time running about among the drove, and making a most woeful bellowing. As they have neither bridles, halters, nor anything wherewith to guide them, all I had to do was to stick on as well as I could.

The Arabs, both men and women, were very anxious to know where we had been thrown on shore, and being satisfied by me on that point, as soon as they had given the women directions how to steer, each man mounted his camel, seating themselves on the small round saddle, and crossing their legs on the animals' shoulders. They then set off to the westward at a speedy trot, leaving us under the care of the women, some of whom were on foot, and urged the camels forward as fast as they could run. The motions of the camel, not unlike that of a small vessel in a heavy sea, were so violent as soon to excoriate my naked body. The inside of my legs and thighs were dreadfully chafed, so that the blood dripped from my heels, while the intense heat of the sun had scorched and blistered us so that we were covered with sores, and without anything to administer relief. Thus bleeding and smarting under the most excruciating pain, we continued to advance in a south-eastern direction, on a surface of sand, gravel, and rock, covered with small sharp stones.

The night came on, with no indication of our stopping. A cold wind now began to blow, chilling our blood, which ceased to trickle down our lacerated legs. But although the wind saved our blood, it acted on our blistered skins, and increased our pain beyond description. We begged to be permitted to get off, but the women paid no attention to our entreaties, and were intent only on getting forward. We designedly slipped off the camels when going at a full trot, risking our necks by the fall, and tried to excite their compassion to get a drink of water for us; but they paid no attention to our prayers, and kept the camels running faster than before.

This was the first time I had attempted to walk barefooted since I was a school-boy. We were obliged to keep up with the camels by running over the stones, which were nearly as sharp as gun-flint, and cut our feet to the bone at every step. Now my fortitude and philosophy failed me. I searched for a stone, intending to knock out my brains with it; but searched in vain. This paroxysm, however, passed off in a minute or two, when reason returned; and I recollected that my life was in the hand of the Power that gave it, and that "the Judge of all the earth would do right." Then running with all my remaining strength, I soon came up with the camels, regardless of my feet and pain, and felt perfectly resigned to the will of Providence and the fate that awaited me.

At daylight, September the 13th, we were called on to proceed. The females struck their tents and packed them on camels, together with all their stuffs. They made us walk and keep up with the camels, though we were so stiff and sore that we could scarcely refrain from crying out at every step. In the course of the morning I saw George Williams. He was mounted, and had been riding with the drove about three hours. I hobbled along towards him. His camel stopped, and I was enabled to take him by the hand. He was still entirely naked. His skin had been burned off, and his whole body was so inflamed and swelled, as well as his face, that I only knew him by his voice, which was very feeble. He told me that he had been obliged to sleep naked in the open air every night; that his life was fast wasting away amidst the most dreadful torments; that he could not live one day more in such misery; that his mistress had taken pity on him, and anointed his body that morning with butter or grease. "But," said he mournfully, "I cannot live. Should you ever get clear of this dreadful place, and be restored to your country, tell my dear wife that my last breath was spent in prayers for her happiness." He could say no more; tears choked his utterance. His master arrived at this time and drove on his camel, and I could only say to him, "God bless you," as I took a last look at him, and forgot for a moment my own misery while contemplating his extreme distress.

Sometimes riding, sometimes walking, we continued to wander over the desert; suffering intensely from the heat of the sun by day and the cold winds by night. Receiving no nourishment during this period, except a little camel's milk daily, hunger had preyed upon my companions to such a degree as to cause them to bite off the flesh from their arms. I was forced to tie the arms of one of my men behind him; while two of them, having caught one of the boys out of sight of the tents, were about to dash the young Arab's brains out with a stone for the purpose of eating his flesh, when luckily I came up and rescued the child from their voracity. They were so frantic with hunger as to insist upon having one meal of his flesh, when they would die willingly. At length, on the 21st, about the middle of the day, two strangers arrived, riding two camels laden with goods. Their names were Sidi Hamet and Seid, from the confines of Morocco.

Hamet was fortunately on his way to Morocco ; and, after much debate and altercation with the owners, he succeeded in purchasing five of us, with a view to carrying us to Swearah, or Mogadore, where I assured him we would be redeemed the moment we arrived. This stipulation was confirmed to the satisfaction of Hamet, and after having exacted from me the most solemn protestations that I spoke the truth, he assured me, if it proved otherwise, my own life and the perpetual slavery of my companions would be the forfeit. Sidi Hamet's means did not allow him to purchase any more of the crew, and they were left behind, scattered in different parts of the desert. We had no reason to regret our change of masters. Hamet was comparatively a humane man. He bought an old camel, nearly dead with age, which he killed, and allowed us a bountiful repast on its blood and entrails. He made shoes for us of its skin, and gave to each a piece of an old blanket to protect us from the sun. Thus clad and refreshed, we started on our tour.

In a few days we arrived at a part of the desert which was very sandy. We sunk nearly up to the knees at each step in the sand, which was scorching hot. The camels were stopped, and all of us mounted, when we saw before us a vast number of immense sand-hills, stretching as far as the eye could reach. We soon arrived at these hills, and were struck with horror at the sight: huge mountains of loose sand, piled up like drifted snow, towered two hundred feet above our heads on every side, and seemed to threaten destruction to our whole party. The loose sand, blown by the trade winds, cut our flesh meanwhile like hailstones.

After a painful march across the desert we came in sight
of the ocean, about the middle of October, and travelled
along the coast. On the 17th, the black tops of high mountains appeared in the distant horizon to the eastward. We
soon came to cultivated land. On October the 22nd we
rode by turns, crossing deep hollows until the afternoon,
when we were forced to have recourse to the sea-beach to
get past one of these deep places, the sides of which were
so steep as to render a passage down impracticable. When
we gained the beach, we found ourselves on a narrow strip
of land which was then dry, the tide being out; this extended in length eight or ten miles ; but from the water's
edge to the perpendicular cliffs on our right, not more than
ten yards. These cliffs appeared to be one hundred and
fifty feet in height. When we came to the sea I went in
and let a surf wash over me, that I might once more feel its
refreshing effects ; but my master, fearing that I would be
carried away by the receding waves, told me not to go near
them again. We proceeded along this narrow beach, and
had passed over half its length when we observed four men,
each armed with a musket and scimitar, spring from
beneath the jutting rocks to intercept our march. Our
masters were at this time on their camels, but they instantly
leaped off, at the same time unsheathing their guns. The
foe was but a few paces from us, and stood in a line across
the beach. Sidi Hamet, holding his gun ready to fire
demanded if it were peace? One of them answered, "It is
peace," and extended his hand to receive that of Sidi
Hamet, who gave him his right hand, suspecting no
treachery, but the fellow grasped it fast, and would have
shot him in a moment, but at this critical juncture two of
Hassan's men came running towards us, each having a
double-barrelled gun in his hand, ready to fire. The robbers
saw them as they turned the point, and the fellow who had
seized Sidi Hamet's hand instantly let go, turning the

affair off with a loud laugh, and saying he only did it to frighten him. His excuse was deemed sufficient, merely because our men did not feel themselves sufficiently strong to resent the insult, and we proceeded; but these fellows, who were very stout and active, hovered around us slaves, endeavouring to separate us from our masters, as it appeared, in the hope of seizing us as their own. Sidi Hamet observing this, ordered me with my men to keep close to the camels' heels, while he and his company kept between us and the banditti. When they found our masters too vigilant for them, the robbers took French-leave of us, and ran along the beach with incredible swiftness.

Soon after this event our masters, who were brothers, drove off some camels, which they were obliged to restore. Their disappointment produced a terrific quarrel about the division of their slaves. They clenched each other like lions, and, with fury in their looks, each tried to throw the other to the ground. Seid was the largest and stoutest man. They writhed until both fell, but Sidi Hamet was undermost, until by superior activity or skill he disengaged himself from his brother's grasp, and both sprang upon their feet. Instantly they snatched their muskets, and each retiring a few paces, with great rapidity and indignation tore the cloth covers from their guns, which they presented at each other. Sidi Hamet, having had a moment's reflection whilst priming and cocking his piece, discharged both his pistols in the air, and presented his naked breast to Seid, who declined firing, but wreaked his vengeance on Aaron Savage and my cabin-boy; the latter he seized by the breast and dashed to the ground with all his strength. The force of the blow beat the breath from the boy's body, and he lay stretched out apparently dead. He was resuscitated with difficulty. After suffering great hardships, we arrived at the Widnoon, or River Noon, in the south part of Suse. In three days after we entered the village of Stuca. Fortunately

Mr. Wiltshire, the English consul resident at Mogadore, agreed to ransom us, and we proceeded towards that place. We continued our journey without any material interruption until we arrived in the vicinity of Mogadore, or Swearah. Here our deliverer, who had received news of our coming, dismounted from his horse, and was prepared to behold some of the most miserable objects his imagination could paint. I heard the exclamation, in Spanish, "Ali estan"—"there they are." At this sound we looked up and beheld our deliverer, who had at that instant turned his eyes upon us. He started back one step with surprise. His blood seemed to fly from his visage for a moment, but recovering himself a little, he rushed forward, and clasping me to his breast, he ejaculated—"Welcome to my arms, my dear sir; this is truly a happy moment." He next took each of my companions by the hand, and welcomed them to their liberty, while tears trickled down his cheeks, and the sudden rush of generous and sympathetic feelings nearly choked his utterance. Then raising his eyes, he said, "I thank Thee, great Author of my being, for Thy mercy to these my brothers." He could add no more; his whole frame was so agitated that his strength failed him, and he sunk to the ground. We, on our part, could only look up towards heaven in silent adoration, while our hearts swelled with indescribable sensations of gratitude and love to God, who had conducted us through so many scenes of danger and suffering; had controlled the passions and disposed the hearts of the barbarous Arabs in our favour, and had finally brought us to the arms of a friend. After a pause, when Mr. Wiltshire had in some measure recovered, he said : "Come, my friends, let us go to the city; my house is already prepared for your reception." We then rode off slowly towards Mogadore.

On our arrival Mr. Wiltshire conducted us to his house, and spared neither pains nor expense in procuring every comfort, and in administering with his own hand, night and day, such refreshments as our late sufferings and debility required. Of the miserable condition to which I had been reduced, one fact will witness. At the instance of Mr. Wiltshire I was weighed, and fell short of ninety pounds, though my usual weight for the previous ten years had been over two hundred pounds. Unerring Wisdom and Goodness has since restored me to the comforts of civilised life, to the bosom of my family, and to the blessings of my native land.

THE GALLEY OF THE DART.

IN the year 1816, His Majesty's war-sloop *Dart* was stationed in the British Channel for the purpose of rendering it at least difficult for the smugglers of the South Coast to prosecute their nefarious traffic with impunity. On the evening of the 1st of March the vessel lay safely moored at Dartmouth, under the command, for the time being, of the first-lieutenant, as the captain was ashore. The latter officer having been informed of the movements of one of the smuggling craft of which he had been in search, immediately communicated the intelligence to his deputy on board, with instructions that steps should be taken to arrest the contraband ship before it reached the land. In obedience to the commander's orders, an expedition was organised, and set out under the charge of the first-lieutenant, who has left a thrilling account of his adventures on the momentous occasion. The following is that officer's story :—

We had just put in from a short cruise, the work of the day was finished, and preparations had been made by most of the officers and men for spending a day or two on shore. All was fun and frolic on board at the expectation of this

pleasure, when I received a letter from the captain inform-
ing me that a smuggling vessel was expected on the coast,
and directing me to send the second-lieutenant with the
galley, armed, to look out between Torbay and Dartmouth
during the night. Now, my brother officer had that night
resolved to go on shore to see his sweetheart; and not
being in love myself, I volunteered to take his place.
Before going off, I put on a suit of "Flushing" over my
jacket and trousers. The galley was soon hauled alongside,
and the arms, bittacle, and other necessary articles being
deposited in her, six seamen, one marine, and myself, took
our places;—the painter was cast off, and with muffled oars
we commenced paddling her out of the harbour. We were
soon at a distance from the *Dart*, which lay like a sea-mew
on the water: her rigging gradually disappeared; the
lights of the near and overhanging houses shone for a
minute or two between her masts and yards; and nought
remained in view astern save the lofty black land and the
glittering lights of the elevated town; for the bark had
vanished from our sight, never to be again beheld by the
greater part of my crew.

We entered the harbour of Torbay. On arriving off
Brixham (the place where I thought it likely the smuggler
would attempt), we kept a bright look-out, occasionally
lying-to on our oars, in order to catch the sound of the
flapping canvas, or of the rippling water under the bows of
the expected vessel; we were exposed to the cold night,
and successive heavy showers. We then pulled further
out, but having neither seen nor heard anything to excite
suspicion, we determined on shaping our course home-
wards, and in the event of reaching Dartmouth Range
before daylight, to remain there on the look-out during
the remainder of the night. As we pulled towards Berry
Head, a heavy ground-swell seemed to indicate an
approaching gale. We had some difficulty in rounding the

pitch of the " Berry," for a heavy sea was running off it;
and we shipped several seas over the stern-head before we
accomplished our purpose. On clearing it, the sea ran
clearer and the breeze seemed to have died away. Our
situation was melancholy enough, for nought was to be
heard save the roar of the breakers around us. A solitary
star occasionally gleamed through the heavy clouds that
sailed past it. The galley rose slowly over the mountain
swell, under her muffled oars. Following the lay of the
coast, we pulled to the westward; with, on our larboard
side, nothing but a dirty horizon, and on the other side
breakers and an iron-bound shore; and even these were
occasionally lost sight of as the boat slowly sunk in the deep
hollow of the swell. At half-past one we reached the
entrance of the sound that separates the "Mewstone" from
the main; and not having seen anything peculiarly dangerous
in the passage before, I steered directly through it, ordering
the bowman to keep a good look-out, and of course very
careful myself. In this manner we half-threaded the
passage; and the "Ay, ay, sir!" of the bowman, to my oft-
repeated order of "Keep a good look-out forward," was still
ringing in my ears, when, to my great surprise, the boat
struck on something forward, the bowman crying out,
" There's a rock under the bow, sir!" "Back off all!"
" Jump out, bowman, and shove the boat astern!" were the
orders instantly given. Neither, however, could be obeyed;
for the descending swell immediately left the boat suspended
by the gripe; and she being of that class appropriately
called " *Deaths!* " instantly fell on her broadside. The next
sea rushed over the starboard-quarter, and with the last
words of the order—" Throw the ballast-bags overboard! "
on my lips, she sank under me; while for a second or two
the men forwards appeared high and dry out of the water.
It was but for a second or two! she shipped off the rock,
sank, and not a splinter of her was ever again seen.

On first feeling the boat sink under me, I knew our case was desperate, and that it was "every man for himself, and God for us all." I could swim much better than most people, and had great confidence in the water; but benumbed as I was with the cold, at such a distance from the land—on such a coast, and with such a sea on shore—it appeared that little short of a miracle could save me; and all thoughts of assisting others were entirely out of the question. My first object was to avoid the grasp of my drowning crew (more particularly that of the unfortunate marine, whom but a few seconds before I had seen comfortably nestled, apparently fast asleep, behind me); therefore, while the poor fellow sprang and clung instinctively to that part of the boat that was still above water, with an idea of finding footing on the rock, I seized the strokeman's oar that lay on the water near me, and giving myself what little impetus my sinking footing would admit of, I struck out of the starboard-quarter of the boat in the opposite direction. After a few hasty strokes, I looked behind me to see if the poor marine was near, when a scene presented itself that may have been the lot of many to behold but few have lived to describe. The "Death" was gone! But as I rode on the crest of the wave, the sparkling of the sea beneath me, and the wild shrieks that rose from the watery hollow, too plainly pointed out the fatal spot where the poor fellows were sinking in each others' embrace. For a few seconds a sea rose, and hid the place from my view; and on again getting a glimpse of it, the sparkling of the water was scarcely discernible, and a faint murmur only crept along the surface of the waves. Another sea followed; as it rose between me and heaven, I saw on its black outline a hand clutching at the clouds above it—a faint gurgle followed, the sea rolled sullenly by—and all was dark and silent around me!

I had just beheld within a few yards of me the dying

7

struggle of—as I then thought—my whole crew, and everything seemed to announce that my own life was prolonged for only a few short minutes; for allowing I succeeded in reaching the shore, the surf threatened my destruction on the rocks. And should I weather this danger, the precipitous coast only promised a more lingering death at the cliff's foot. But—thanks to the Almighty!—my presence of mind never deserted me; a ray of hope flashed across my mind in spite of the apparent hopelessness of my situation. I as calmly weighed all the chances against my reaching the shore, and prepared for the attempt, as if I had been a looker-on, instead of an actor in the dreadful scene.

In addition to the suit of "Flushing" over my jacket and trousers, I was enveloped in a large boat-cloak, which it became my first object to get rid of. Accordingly, with the help of the oar (that supported me while doing so), I stripped off my two jackets and waistcoat; and my two pair of trousers would have followed also, had I not dreaded lest the heavy "Flushing" should be entangled round my ancles in the first place; and in the second, considered that both them and my shoes would preserve me from being cut by the rocks, should I succeed in reaching them. Thus lightened, and with the oar held fore-and-aft-wise under my left arm, I struck out boldly for the shore; and being God only knows how long in the water—for to me it appeared an age—I got into the wash of the breakers; and after receiving some heavy blows, and experiencing the good effects of my "Flushing fenders," I secured a footing, and scrambled up above the break of the waves.

As I lay on the rock, panting, breathless, and nearly insensible, the words—"Save me, save me, I am sinking!" appeared to rise with the spray that flew over me. At first, stupified with exertion and fatigue as I was, I fancied that the wild shriek that had accompanied the sinking boat still rung in my ears; till the repeated cry, with the addition of my own name, aroused me from my state of insensibility, and on glancing towards the surf, I saw a man struggling hard to gain the shore. Never shall I forget the sensation of that moment; I could not lift up a finger to save him. At this time the oar that had saved my life fortunately floated into the exhausted man's hands; and after a hard struggle he appeared to gain a footing—he lost it! Again he grasped the rock! The next moment saw him floating at some distance in the foam! Once more he approached and clung to the shore. My anxiety was dreadful—till, rising slowly from the water, and scrambling towards me, the poor fellow's embrace informed me that I was not the only survivor; while his faltering exclamation, "They are all drowned, sir!" too plainly assured me that we alone were saved. After a time we managed to gain the use of our legs; and then, what with stamping upon the rock and flapping our arms across our chests, we contrived to knock a little warmth into ourselves; and that point gained, we commenced our attempt to scale the face of the cliff that hung lowering over our heads. By mutual assistance, and with some difficulty, we mounted about twenty or thirty feet; and I had just begun to solace myself with the idea that the undertaking was not so difficult as I had supposed it, when, on reaching out my arms to catch a fresh hold of the rock before me, I found my eyes had deceived me as to its distance, and falling forward, I with great difficulty saved myself from pitching headlong into a chasm that yawned beneath me, and through which the sea dashed violently. In fact, the high land had deceived us. We were only on a rock!

I was almost struck with consternation at this discovery. There was no alternative but to remain where I was till chance sent a boat to my relief, or death took that office on itself. My heart sunk within me. For a few minutes I gazed eagerly around me from the peak of the rock, in hopes of seeing some possible way of extricating myself, when, observing nothing but a circle of foam, I descended to the nearest ledge in the deepest despondency, and casting myself alongside of my companion, sat in silent despair. My shirt clung with icy coldness to my body, and notwithstanding we huddled as closely as possible, my shivering frame told me that it was rapidly losing, through my late exertion, the little strength I had gained; I felt assured, that if I remained where I was, daylight would find me a corpse. What, then, was to be done? To remain was certain death. Death appeared equally certain should I try to leave the rock; still, however, by the latter course there was a slight chance in my favour, and drowning I preferred to dying by inches where I was.

I therefore resolved to gain the main, or sink in the attempt; but on asking my fellow-sufferer whether he would accompany me, he seemed thunderstruck at the proposal, so earnestly pointed out the danger of the attempt, and his own weakness, and clinging to me, so pathetically entreated me that I should remain where I was, that we might at least have the consolation of dying together, that I not only ceased from urging him, but appeared to give up the idea of leaving the rock myself. This, however, was only done to elude his grasp; for a few minutes after, under the pretence of looking for a more sheltered place, I left him, and descending the rock, reached the edge of the channel that separated me from the main.

There a scene presented itself that plainly pointed out the danger of the undertaking. The distance across, indeed, was not very great; but the whole channel was one sheet of foam, along the edges of which appeared the long black tangle that adhered to the rocks, except when a heavy black sea, rolling through the passage, drove the one before it, and flowed over the other; an apparently perpendicular cliff hung over the whole. It was an awful sight! For a moment my heart failed me. There was, however, no alternative; for my own fate, and the fate of the poor man above me, depended on my reaching the opposite side; so watching a "smooth," and committing my spirit to the Almighty, I sprang forward, and found myself nearly in the middle of the channel. A few strokes brought me to the cliff's foot; but neither holding nor footing could I gain, except what the tangle afforded. Again and again did I seize the pendant slippery weeds, and as often did the drawback of the sea, and my own weight, drag me with a giant's force from my hold, and rolling down the face of the rock, I sank several feet under water.

Bruised, battered, and nearly exhausted, with the sea whizzing in my ears and rattling in my throat, I thought my last moments had arrived. Once more I rose to the surface, and digging my nails into the rock, I seized the sea-weed with my teeth, and clung in the agonies of death. Another tremendous sea rose, and as it violently rushed over me, I lost my hold, and rose on its surface up the face of the rock. It reached its greatest height; and in the act of descending, I caught a projecting point above the weeds, and at the same instant my left leg was thrown over another. The sea again left me, and gasping for life, I hung over the abyss once more; successive seas followed, but only lashed the rocks beneath me, as if enraged at having lost their prey. I once more breathed freely; hope revived; the dread of being forced away caused me to make an almost superhuman effort. I gained a footing; and climbing upwards, in a short time even the spray fell short of me. God be praised! I was safe.

Having ascended about thirty or forty feet (for then only did I consider myself above the reach of the waves), I stopped to take rest. There I remained a short time, and between the roar of the breakers occasionally heard distinctly the shrill shrieks of the poor isolated wretch beneath

me, and the frantic, oft-repeated exclamation of "Mr. ——,
for the love of God, don't leave me!" I endeavoured to
console him by telling him that, if I succeeded in getting up
the cliff, I would procure immediate help; but as the cries
continued as loud and frantic as before, I presumed I was
neither seen nor heard, and again commenced my ascent.
Panting, and almost breathless—sometimes with tolerable
ease, and at others clinging to the perpendicular face of the
cliff, and hanging over the pitch-black ocean—I continued
ascending, till not only the cries of the man were lost, but
even the roar of the sea was only faintly heard, and at
length reached the summit of the cliff. At that critical
moment, exhausted nature sunk under the fatigue of the
night. On suddenly seeing the heavens all around me, I
appeared for an instant air-borne—my legs sunk under me.
I fell rapidly, head-foremost, I know not where. I believe
I shrieked. My senses left me.

How long I lay insensible I know not. On opening my
eyes, I was agreeably surprised to find myself in the centre
of a furze bush, and felt much inclined to sleep. Fortunately, I recollected that this would probably prove fatal
to me; I aroused from my lethargy, but felt as if in the
night-mare, for my body would not move for some time, and
it seemed as if an iceberg lay on my bosom. The ground
beneath me had a rapid descent from the sea (which had
occasioned my heavy fall, and led me to believe I was falling
down the cliff), and with some struggling, I worked myself
out of the furze bush, and rolled down for some distance.
This broke the spell, and turning my head inshore, I kept
tumbling about till the blood began to circulate, and I was
conscious of that acute pain which none but those who have
been frost-bitten can form any idea of. At length I felt the
prickles of the furze bush, with which I was covered over
like a porcupine, and can with truth say, that that was the
happiest moment of my life.

Resolving to travel inland, I came on the track of cart wheels, which brought me to a respectable house; and after narrowly escaping being shot for a robber, was admitted, and made as comfortable as circumstances permitted. My wet clothes were shifted, and a capital supper placed before me. I made known who I was, and the circumstances of the disaster, and the need my fellow-sufferer stood in of assistance. Men were placed along the shore with lights, to keep up his spirits, and tell him that help would be forthcoming in the morning. Those on the cliffs showed their lights the whole night; but as I afterwards heard, were not seen by the seaman. At daylight, however, a boat pulled to the westward, the very one which we had spoken with in Torbay during the night; the crew having landed, had not gone far before they saw something like a bundle lying on the rocks. It was my unfortunate shipmate. As they could not reach him, he was towed off by a rope, and after three days' care and nursing recovered.

I have already said that not a splinter of the boat was ever picked up that I know of; some of the gear was, however, for a day or two after, the crew of a Torbay boat were rather surprised at seeing a spar floating *on end* in the water near them. On sending their punt to pick it up, they found that it was a boat's mast, with a corpse hanging to the end of it, by one hand firmly clenched round the tie. The body was buried in the churchyard of Brixham.

THE MEDUSA.

THIS French frigate, under the command of Captain Chaumareys, sailed from Aix for the coast of Africa on the 17th of June 1816, for the purpose of taking possession of colonies on behalf of the Government. She was accompanied by three smaller vessels, and the voyage of the *Medusa* was marked by circumstances of extreme peril, rendered all the more calamitous through the callous selfishness of a portion of the crew. When off Cape Finisterre one of the frigate's seamen fell into the ocean, and he was left to perish through the carelessness and apathy of his shipmates and officers. This was but the first of a series of fatal disasters attributable to the same dastardly cause.

On the tenth day of the voyage an error of thirty leagues appeared in the reckoning, and three days after that discovery the ship entered the tropics, where, with an imbecile disregard of danger and every precaution to guard against accident, the ceremony identified with "crossing the line" was performed by the crew, while the officers abetted the men in their revelry and inattention to the navigation of a vessel that was now running headlong to destruction. Leaving the command of the ship to a man who had passed

the ten preceding years as a prisoner of war in England,
the captain presided over the scene of disgraceful merri-
ment in which his men indulged. A few persons on board
remonstrated against such an inexperienced person as Mons.
Richfort taking charge of the frigate at such a time. All
remonstrances, however, were in vain. They continued
their course and occasionally heaved the lead, but without
slackening a single sail, although it was ascertained that
they were now on the banks of Arguise, and in dangerous
waters. There were indeed various indications of the
shallowness of their course, but Richfort persisted in his
opinion that he was sailing in a hundred fathoms of sea,
until his flagrant error was demonstrated by the ship
grounding in sixteen feet of water.

At the moment of the disaster the *Medusa* had on board
six boats, and after a few bungling and futile attempts had
been made to get her afloat, all hope of saving her was
abandoned, a raft was constructed, and the boats launched.
A dreadful scene was now enacted. Without discipline or
order the men rushed over the sides of the ship, each eager
only to save his own life. Those who were the earliest to
reach the boats stubbornly refused to admit the after-comers,
although there was still ample room therein. This selfishness bore terrible fruit, for some of the seamen immediately
surmised that a plot had been formed to abandon them to
their fate, and determined to use their arms against those
who it was suspected had betrayed them. Instead of
endeavouring to allay the fears and anger of his men,
Captain Chaumareys quietly stole out of a port-hole into his
own boat, and left a large number of his crew to shift for
themselves.

The construction of the raft had been conducted without
an intelligent appreciation of its requirements. In length
about sixty-five feet, and in breadth about twenty-five, the
middle of this floating platform was the only part that

could be considered comparatively secure; but the space was so small that fourteen persons could only lie thereon with difficulty. One hundred and fifty, however, sought safety from the wreck upon the frail structure, and those who were compelled to stand were in continual danger of slipping into the ocean, from between the yawning planks, while the waves washed the raft from all sides, and frequently immersed the unfortunate occupants up to their waists. The senior midshipman of the *Medusa*, M. Coudin, was suffering from a severe bruise on one of his legs, and was incapable of moving; but notwithstanding his disabled condition, to this young officer was assigned the command of the raft, while his superiors, in the most cowardly fashion, went into safer positions in the boats. It is true that a promise was extorted from the captain that the poor middy would be relieved and allowed to go into one of the boats, but the promised concession was never granted. Of the hundred and fifty persons thus crowded together under Coudin's charge, one was a soldier's wife, twenty-nine were sailors, and the remainder were soldiers. The total number of souls on board the frigate, when she set out upon her expedition, was four hundred, and included the newly-appointed governor, M. Schmaltz, and other functionaries of the French settlement of Senegal.

The governor, who had planned the raft, had intended that a good supply of provisions should be shipped thereon, for the subsistence of those in the boat as well as the persons upon the raft, and that the latter means of safety was to be taken in tow by each of the six smaller craft. In terms of this arrangement the boats at length put off from the wreck, but these had not rowed more than three leagues when the tow-line, attaching the raft to the captain's boat, suddenly broke, and the mishap, or treacherous act it may have been, became a signal to all the other boats to cut their cables and abandon the raft and its occupants to the mercy of the waves. One after another the boats went out of sight, and left the remainder of the *Medusa's* living freight either to a scene of desperate revelry on the wreck, or to be tossed about at the caprice of the ocean upon a few planks hastily bound together.

The first night spent by the sufferers upon the wreck was a stormy one, but the hope of revenge kept many of the men from brooding over the terrible nature of their situation. All the provisions that had been collected were found to consist of some saturated biscuits, only sufficient for one meal, and a few casks of wine. A pocket-compass was by chance discovered, but the instrument fell through the raft into the sea, and there was nothing left to indicate their position on the trackless waters. As no one had partaken of food since the morning of the disaster, some wine and biscuit had been distributed. During the succeeding twelve days that these miserable beings spent upon the deep, no other food was eaten by them, except such as is most revolting to human nature. As soon as daybreak enabled the men to see each other, twelve of their number were found crushed and dead between the planks, while several more were missing. The whole mortality of the first night, however, could not be accurately ascertained, by reason of some of the soldiers taking the billets of their deceased companions, thereby to receive a double allowance of wine.

During the second night many were washed off the raft, while others were smothered by the pressure caused by so much crowding towards the centre of the structure. In the near prospect of dissolution the soldiers drank to excess, and in their drunken madness rebelled against all attempts to secure anything like discipline amongst the cast-a-ways. One soldier, who pretended to rest himself upon the side, was discovered in the act of cutting the ropes that bound the timbers together, and the traitor was at once thrown into the sea. Another had to be dealt with in a like manner for similar treachery. These dastardly actions were found to result from a preconcerted rebellion on the part of several of the men, rather than from the fiendish disposition of individual malcontents, but at last the discontent was suppressed, and the rebellious soldiers abjectly sought for mercy upon their knees. The quiet that ensued was but of short duration, however, for at midnight the rebellion was renewed with increased fierceness. Those without weapons used their teeth with cruel energy upon the upholders of order. One of the latter was wantonly bitten in the leg, even when a number of the infuriated madmen were beating the sufferer's head with their carbines, previous to throwing the insensible body overboard. After a night of savage butchery, morning dawned, when the raft was seen to be the bearer of sixty-five dead bodies, and it was found that two casks of wine, and all the fresh water, had been thrown into the sea during the progress of the awful conflict. The fortitude even of the strongest now began to succumb under their trials, and several of the survivors were afflicted with severe mental derangement.

The day following that outbreak of treacherous cruelty was marked by comparative quietude. It had become necessary to limit each man's daily allowance of wine. The mast, which had carried their signals of distress and a sail, had been wantonly cut down during the encounter, but the spar was re-erected, and again the woeful bunting floated in the wind. After endeavouring in vain to catch some fish, the survivors were now compelled by the cravings of famine to feed upon the dead bodies of some who had fallen victims in the night. As the darkness set in for the third time since the *Medusa's* disaster, the most plaintive cries proceeded from the poor wretches upon the raft, and before another morning broke upon the sufferers, ten more of their number had been relieved of their misery by death.

The fourth day brought fine weather, but did not otherwise mitigate the horrors of the situation, excepting that some flying-fish alighted upon the raft, and, being instantly secured, afforded for a solitary meal a change in the diet of the survivors. The fourth night was marked by another perfidious attempt to destroy the raft. The majority of the rebels being thrown overboard during the fight that followed the discovery of the plot, only thirty were found alive next morning; but these were all either wounded or sick almost to death, and with the skin of their legs corroded by the action of the salt water. Only one cask of wine was now left, and two soldiers detected in the act of robbing from the scanty store were instantly pitched into the waves as a punishment for their selfishness. Despair now seized the remainder of the men. Death having taken a boy from the sorrowful community, only twenty-seven souls were left to eke out their miserable existence as best they could. A council was held by the stronger of the survivors, who determined to rid themselves of the encumbrance occasioned by the weaker occupants of the raft consuming a share of the common store. Accordingly, twelve poor wretches, too feeble to offer an availing resistance to the inhuman resolution of the others, were immediately thrown into the ocean, along with the greater number of firearms and other weapons aboard the raft.

The fifteen surviving, but famishing individuals now left had little hope of existence for more than a few days after they had carried out their murderous intentions towards their companions, and their misery was increased rather than abated after the inhuman deed. Their scanty aliment was of the most nauseous and loathsome kind, and almost appeared to intensify instead of appeasing their hunger. Even a butterfly, which had alighted upon the sail, and was held by some of the miserable beings to be a harbinger of relief, was regarded as a desirable mouthful by some greedy eyes. Several sea-birds also hovered over the raft, but it was impossible to catch any, and the presence of the fowls only lent augmented pain to the starving men. The most trifling article of food now became a source of contention. A small quantity of toilet-spirit, a lemon, a little garlic, and the daily distribution of wine, all in their turn gave occasion for quarrelling. Individual suffering and wretchedness had blunted the better instincts of humanity, destroyed every vestige of social action, and smothered all solicitude for the common good.

In the most excruciating tortures the survivors passed the next three days, when they constructed a smaller raft, with a view to make for some strange but perhaps friendly coast. The second raft was, however, found to be insufficiently buoyant for the purpose, and with much regret the idea of navigating their way to land was abandoned by the miserable men, and all gave up hope of ever being rescued from a fate which had already overtaken one hundred and thirty-five of their comrades. But the French brig *Argus* had been despatched for the relief of the sufferers, and that vessel, while in search of the *Medusa's* wreck, fortunately sighted the signals of distress that floated over the despairing cast-a-ways, and all were received on board. The perils of the rescued men were nevertheless not at an end; for a fire breaking out at night in the brig, they were again in danger of perishing.

Of those who had embarked on the raft, one hundred and fifty persons, fifteen only, as we have seen, were taken on board the brig, and six of these died from the effects of their wounds and exposure shortly after their arrival at St. Louis. The remaining nine, although so altered in appearance as to have become objects of pity to all but the most obdurate and inhuman of their species, were subjected to the neglect of their shipmates who had previously got there in safety by means of the *Medusa's* boats. Of the six boats that were cut adrift from the raft after having left the wreck, the two in which the governor and the captain had embarked arrived at Senegal, while the four other craft made the shore at different points and landed their passengers, many of whom suffered greatly before getting ashore. But the vicissitudes experienced in the boats were comparatively light when compared with the misfortunes encountered after landing by those who had left the *Medusa* in her pinnace. Madlle. Picard, one of the sufferers in question, having left a record of the events, the following is a portion of her story :—

Shortly after landing, or about seven in the morning, a party was formed to penetrate into the interior, for the purpose of finding some fresh water. Some accordingly was found at a little distance from the sea by digging among the sand. Every one instantly flocked round the little wells, which furnished enough to quench our thirst. This water was found to be delicious, although it had a sulphureous taste ; its colour was that of whey. As all our clothes were wet, and in tatters, and as we had nothing to change them, some generous officers offered theirs. My stepmother, my cousin, and my sister, were thus dressed ; for myself, I preferred keeping my own. We remained nearly an hour beside our beneficent fountain, then took the route for Senegal ; that is, a southerly direction, for we did not know exactly where that country lay. It was agreed that the females and children should walk before the caravan, as the general body was called, that they might not be left behind. The sailors voluntarily carried the youngest on their shoulders, and every one took the route along the coast. Notwithstanding it was nearly seven o'clock, the sand was quite burning, and we suffered severely, walking without shoes, having lost them while landing. As soon as we arrived on the shore, we went to walk on the wet sand to cool us a little. Thus we travelled during the night, without encountering anything.

Early on the morning of the 9th we saw an antelope on a little hill; it instantly disappeared, before any of the party had time to shoot it. The desert seemed to our view one immense plain of sand, on which not a blade of verdure was seen. However, we still found water by digging in the sand. In the forenoon two officers of marine complained that our family incommoded the progress of the general body. It is true the females and the children could not walk so quickly as the men. We walked as fast as it was possible for us; nevertheless, we often fell behind, which obliged them to halt till we came up. These officers, joined with other individuals, considered among themselves whether they would wait for us, or abandon us in the desert. I will be bold to say, however, that but few were of the latter opinion. My father being informed of what was plotting against us, stepped up to the chiefs of the conspiracy, and reproached them in the bitterest terms for their selfishness and cruelty. The dispute waxed warm. Those who were desirous of leaving us drew their swords, and my father put his hand upon a poniard, with which he had provided himself on quitting the frigate. At this scene we threw ourselves between them, conjuring him rather to remain in the desert with his family than seek the assistance of those who were perhaps less humane than the Moors themselves. Several people took our part, particularly M. Bégnère, captain of infantry, who allayed the dispute by saying to his soldiers: "My friends, you are Frenchmen, and I have the honour to be your commander; let us never abandon an unfortunate family in the desert, so long as we are able to be of use to them." This brief but energetic speech caused those to blush who wished to quit us. All then joined with the old captain, saying they would not leave us, on condition that we would walk a little quicker. M. Bégnère and his soldiers replied, they did not wish to impose conditions on those to whom they were desirous of doing a favour; and the unfortunate family of Picard were again on the road with the whole caravan.

About noon, hunger was felt so powerfully among us, that it was agreed upon to go to the small hills of sand which were near the coast, to see if any herbs could be found fit for eating: nothing, however, was procured but poisonous plants, among which were various kinds of euphorbium. Convolvuli of a bright green carpeted the downs; but on tasting their leaves we found them as bitter as gall. The party rested in this place, whilst several officers went farther into the interior. They returned in about an hour, loaded with wild purslain, which they distributed to each of us. Every one instantly devoured his bunch of herbage, without leaving the smallest branch; but as our hunger was far from being satisfied with this small allowance, the soldiers and sailors betook themselves to look for more. They soon brought a sufficient quantity, which was equally distributed, and devoured upon the spot, so delicious had hunger made that food to us. For myself, I declare I never ate anything with so much appetite in all my life. Water was also found in this place, but it was of a nauseous taste. After this truly frugal repast we continued our route. The heat was insupportable in the last degree. The sands on which we trod were burning; nevertheless, several of us walked on these scorching coals without shoes; and the females had nothing but their hair for a cap. When we reached the sea-shore, we all ran and lay down among the surf. After remaining there some time, we took our route along the wet beach. On our journey we met with several large crabs, which were of considerable service to us. Every now and then we endeavoured to slake our thirst by sucking their crooked claws. About nine at night we halted between two pretty high sand-hills. After a short talk concerning our misfortunes, all seemed desirous of passing the night in this place, notwithstanding we heard on every side

8

the roaring of leopards. Our situation had been thus perilous during the night; nevertheless, at break of day, we had the satisfaction of finding none missing.

Early on the following morning we resumed our march, bearing towards the east, in the hope that we might find water. Although disappointed in this, we were gratified in observing that the country was less arid, and that it produced a species of vegetation. Some of the party went on before to make observations, and on their return they told us they had seen two Arab tents upon a slightly rising ground. We instantly directed our steps thither. We had to pass great downs of sand, very slippery, and arrived in a large plain, streaked here and there with verdure; but the turf was so hard and piercing that we could scarcely walk over it without wounding our feet. Our presence in these frightful solitudes put to flight three or four Moorish shepherds, who herded a small flock of sheep and goats in an oasis. At last we arrived at the tents after which we were searching, and found in them three Mooresses and two little children, who did not seem in the least frightened by our visit. A negro servant, belonging to one of the officers, interpreted between us and the women, who, when they had heard of our misfortunes, offered us millet and water for payment. We bought a little of that grain at the rate of three francs a handful; the water was got for three francs a glass—it was very good, and none grudged the money it cost. As a glass of water with a handful of millet was but a poor dinner for famished people, my father bought two kids, for which twenty piastres were charged. We immediately killed them, and the Moorish women boiled them for us in a large kettle.

Having again set out, we met several Moors, or Arabs, who, after saluting us in a friendly manner, conducted us to their encampment. We found a Moor in the camp who had previously known my father in Senegal, and who spoke a little French. We were all struck with astonishment at the unexpected meeting. My father recollected having employed long ago a young goldsmith at Senegal, and discovering the Moor Amet to be the same person, shook him by the hand. After that good fellow had been made acquainted with our shipwreck, and to what extremities our unfortunate family had been reduced, he could not refrain from tears. Amet was not satisfied with deploring our hard fate; he was desirous of proving that he was generous and humane, and instantly distributed among us a large quantity of milk-and-water, free of any charge. He also raised for our family a large tent of the skins of camels, cattle, and sheep; because his religion would not allow him to lodge under the same roof with Christians.

The Moors having furnished us with asses on hire, we proceeded on our journey towards Senegal, and regaining the shore, we were gratified at seeing a ship out at sea, but sufficiently near for those on board to take notice of the signals of distress that we immediately displayed from the beach. In answer to our appeal the vessel approached the land, when the Moors who accompanied our party went into the sea and swam to it. In about half-an-hour we saw these friendly assistants returning, pushing before them three small barrels. Arrived on shore, one of them gave a letter to the leader of our party from the commander of the ship, which was the *Argus*, a vessel sent to seek after the raft, and to give us provisions. This letter announced a small barrel of biscuits, a tierce of wine, a half-tierce of brandy, and a cheese. Oh, fortunate circumstance! We were very desirous of testifying our gratitude to the generous commander of the brig, but he instantly set out and left us. We staved the barrels which held our stock of provisions, and made a distribution. Each of us had a biscuit, about a glass of wine, a half-glass of brandy, and a small morsel of cheese. Each drank his allowance of wine at one gulp;

the brandy was not even despised by the ladies. I, however, preferred quantity to quality, and exchanged my ration of brandy for one of wine. To describe our joy whilst taking this repast is impossible. Exposed to the fierce rays of a vertical sun, exhausted by a long train of suffering, deprived for a long time of the use of any kind of spirituous liquors, when our portions of water, wine, and brandy mingled in our stomachs, we became like insane people. Life, which had lately been a great burden, now became precious to us. Foreheads, lowering and sulky, began to unwrinkle; enemies became most brotherly; the avaricious endeavoured to forget their selfishness and cupidity; the children smiled for the first time since our shipwreck: in a word, every one seemed to revive from a state of melancholy and dejection.

About six in the evening my father, finding himself extremely fatigued, wished to rest himself. We allowed the caravan to move on, whilst my stepmother and myself remained near him, and the rest of the family followed with their asses. We all three soon fell asleep. When we awoke, we were astonished at not seeing our companions. The sun was sinking in the west. We saw several Moors approaching us, mounted on camels; and my father reproached himself for having slept so long. Their appearance gave us great uneasiness, and we wished much to escape from them, but my stepmother and myself fell quite exhausted. The Moors, with long beards, having come quite close to us, one of them alighted, and addressed us in the following words:—" Be comforted, ladies; under the costume of an Arab you see an Englishman who is desirous of serving you. Having heard at Senegal that Frenchmen were thrown ashore on these deserts, I thought my presence might be of some service to them, as I was acquainted with several of the princes of this arid country." These noble words from the mouth of a man we had at first taken to be

a Moor, instantly calmed our fears. Recovering from our
fright, we rose and expressed to the philanthropic Englishman the gratitude we felt. Mr. Carnet, the name of the
generous Briton, told us that our caravan, which he had
met, waited for us at about the distance of two leagues.
He then gave us some biscuit, which we ate; and we then
set off together to join our companions. Mr. Carnet wished
us to mount his camels, but my stepmother and myself,
being unable to persuade ourselves we could sit securely on
their hairy haunches, continued to walk on the moist sand;
whilst my father, Mr. Carnet, and the Moors who accompanied him, proceeded on the camels. We soon reached a
little river, of which we wished to drink, but found it as
bitter as the sea. Mr. Carnet desired us to have patience,
and we should find water at the place where our caravan
waited. We forded that river knee-deep. At last, having
walked about an hour, we rejoined our companions, who
had found several wells of fresh water. It was resolved to
pass the night in this place, which seemed less arid than
any we saw near us. The soldiers being requested to go
and seek wood to light a fire, for the purpose of frightening
the ferocious beasts which we heard roaring around us,
refused; but Mr. Carnet assured us that the Moors who
were with him knew well how to keep all such intruders
from our camp.

After a rest of a few hours we all continued our march,
with the exception of Mr. Carnet, who left the party for
the purpose of procuring the means of satisfying our hunger.
At noon the sun's heat became so violent that even the
Moors themselves endured it with difficulty. We then
determined on finding some shade behind the high mounds
of sand which appeared in the interior; but how were we
to reach them? The sands could not be hotter. We had
been obliged to leave our asses on the shore, for they would
neither advance nor recede. The greater part of us had

neither shoes nor hats; notwithstanding, we were obliged to go forward almost a long league to find a little shade. Whether from want of air, or the heat of the ground on which we seated ourselves, we were nearly suffocated. I thought my last moments were come. Already my eyes saw nothing but a dark cloud, when a person of the name of Borner, who was to have been a smith at Senegal, gave me a boot containing some muddy water, which he had had the precaution to keep. I seized the elastic vase, and hastened to swallow the liquid in large draughts. One of my companions, equally tormented with thirst, envious of the pleasure I seemed to feel, and which I felt effectually, drew the foot from the boot, and seized it in his turn; but it availed him nothing. The water which remained was so disgusting that he could not drink it, and spilt it on the ground. Captain Bégnère, who was present, judging, by the water that fell, how loathsome that must have been which I had drunk, offered me some crumbs of biscuit, which he had kept most carefully in his pocket. I chewed that mixture of bread, dust, and tobacco; but I could not swallow it, and gave it all masticated to one of my younger brothers, who had fallen from inanition.

We were on the point of quitting this furnace when we saw our English friend approaching, who brought us provisions. At this sight I felt my strength revive, and ceased to desire death, which I had before called on to release me from my sufferings. Several Moors accompanied Mr. Carnet, and every one was loaded. On their arrival we had water, with rice and dried fish in abundance. Every one drank his allowance of water; but had not ability to eat, although the rice was excellent. We were all anxious to return to the sea, that we might bathe ourselves, and the caravan put itself on the road to the breakers of Sahara. After an hour's march of great suffering we regained the shore, as well as our asses, which were lying in the water.

We rushed among the waves, and, after a bath of half-an-hour, reposed ourselves upon the beach.

We had yet another long and fatiguing journey before us before we reached the Senegal river, where we expected to find boats waiting to convey us to the town of St. Louis. During the day we quickened our march; and for the first time since our shipwreck, a smiling picture presented itself to our view. The trees, always green, with which that noble river is shaded, the humming-birds, the red-birds, the paroquets, the pomerops, and others, which flitted among their long yielding branches, caused in us emotions difficult to express. We could not satiate our eyes with gazing on the beauties of this place, verdure being so enchanting to the sight, especially after having travelled through the desert. Before reaching the river, we had to descend a little hill covered with thorny bushes. It was four o'clock in the afternoon before the boats of the government arrived, and we all embarked. Biscuit and wine were found in each of them, and all were refreshed. After sailing for an hour down the stream we came in sight of St. Louis, a town miserable in appearance, but delightful to our vision after so much suffering. At six in the evening we arrived at the fort, where the late English governor and others, including our generous friend Mr. Carnet, were met to receive us. My father presented us to the governor, who had alighted: he appeared to be sensibly affected with our misfortunes, the females and children chiefly exciting his commiseration; and the native inhabitants and Europeans tenderly shook the hands of the unfortunate people; the negro slaves seemed even to deplore our disastrous fate. Everything was done to relieve our necessities, and render us comfortable after our dangers and fatigues.

Having followed the fortunes of some of the *Medusa's* crew and passengers, as narrated by Madlle. Picard, we have now to notice the vicissitudes of the unfortunate men who were left by their countrymen to apparent destruction upon the wreck.

On the departure of the boats and raft from the frigate, it was found that there remained seventeen sufferers, some of whom had clung to the ship as their only hope of safety, while others had been too intoxicated to engage in the scramble for places on the raft or in the boats. Finding themselves abandoned to their fate, several of the men endeavoured to secure as much of the provisions stowed in the vessel as were available, in order to sustain their lives until rescued from their dangerous position by a passing ship, or by the efforts of their friends. Accordingly some wine and brandy, biscuit and bacon, were collected, and these stimulants and articles of food served as rations to the survivors for a number of days. But at length the store of provisions which had been gathered together became exhausted, without any further effort being made to reach the larger quantities of food that were in the hold. After forty-two days had been spent in an agony of fear and suspense, twelve of the more active of the men gave up all hope of being relieved, and in a fit of desperation constructed a raft, upon which they embarked with a small stock of food, leaving five of their companions upon the wreck. Some time afterwards the shattered timbers of this raft were driven ashore by the waves, and the certainty of the men's destruction was thus placed unhappily beyond a doubt. One seaman, who had refused to go with the raft, even trusted his safety to the fragile keeping of a hen-coop, and in this way sought to reach land; but when at the distance of a cable's length from the *Medusa*, the hen-coop capsized, and the desperate voyager was drowned. There now remained only four souls upon the ill-starred ship, and they severally determined to stay thereon until death or succour came to put a period to their misery. To one of these poor wretches relief soon came, for, worn out with hunger and fatigue, he sank under his sufferings and died. The three who now remained upon the wreck shunned each other's society, and passed the tedious hours in different parts of the ship. So suspicious did they become in their feelings towards each other, that no one ever met his fellow sufferer without rushing at him with a drawn knife.

Having secured his own safety in the most cowardly and despicable manner, the governor, M. Schmaltz, bethought himself that it would be at least a wise, if not a profitable, proceeding to save the specie and stores which he knew to be stowed upon the *Medusa's* wreck. Accordingly, he caused a schooner to be fitted and despatched from Senegal for that purpose, seven days after the survivors from the raft had been landed. After two ineffectual attempts had been made to reach the wreck, and the schooner had again returned from a fruitless mission, she was a third time despatched, and reached the *Medusa* fifty-two days after the disaster; when the captain and crew of the schooner beheld, with the utmost astonishment, three spectral occupants of the unfortunate frigate, who welcomed those who had thus unexpectedly come to their relief. After the emaciated survivors had been put aboard the schooner, and received proper attention and care, everything of value that could be removed from the wreck was also taken in charge, in terms of the governor's orders; then the schooner returned to Senegal, where many hearts beat with exultation at the thought that some of their personal effects would be restored to them. In this hope, however, the poor survivors were disappointed; for upon some of the frigate's officers and men going on board the schooner, on her arrival at St. Louis, and inquiring as to what had been saved, they were told that all the salvage was now the property of those who had secured it, and that it would be publicly sold in the market-place of the town for the benefit of the salvors. This threat was carried out to the letter, and the clothes, appointments, and stores of the ship-wrecked Frenchmen were sold by their piratical country-men, while the unhappy owners of the merchandise looked on the fair which their misfortunes had occasioned with feelings of disappointment and smothered rage. For the honour of humanity, however, a brighter scene closes this sorrowful drama. Though plundered by some of their own nationality, and cruelly neglected by the officials of their own government, who ought to have befriended them, the wretched survivors of the *Medusa's* crew and passengers were kept from utter starvation by a few Englishmen—men whom all Frenchmen then regarded as their natural enemies.

THE ALCESTE.

ON the 21st of January 1817, the British frigate *Alceste*, commanded by Captain Murray Maxwell, sailed from Whampoa for England. The ambassador to China, Lord Amherst, and his suite were on board, after having fulfilled a special mission to the Emperor of the Celestial Empire at Pekin. When twenty-eight days at sea, the frigate made Gaspar Island, and then stood on for the Straits of Banca. Between Banca and Pulo Leat every precaution was taken to guard against accident while passing through that dangerous channel, but although the lead was continuously going, the vessel struck with terrific force upon a sunken reef, and there remained fixed. As it was found impossible to get the frigate off the rock without a fatal risk being incurred, the best bower-anchor was let go to keep her fast, while the pumps were abandoned, as these were found wholly inadequate to cope with the great inrush of water through the large holes that had evidently been made in the hull. One of the sufferers by the disaster has given a graphic account of the stirring adventures through which Captain Maxwell and his men successfully passed, and the narrative presents a pleasing contrast to that regarding the cowardice and selfishness of the *Medusa's* commander, and the fearful results to be attributed to the panic and lack of discipline among the crew of the French frigate. In detailing the events that followed the striking of the *Alceste* upon the reef, the writer says :—

Notwithstanding the perilous situation of the ship's company, every one was cool and collected. The boats were hoisted out, and Lieutenant Hoppner, with a barge and cutter, proceeded with Lord Amherst and suite to the nearest part of the island, which appeared to be about three miles distant. In the meantime every exertion was made to save what provisions and useful articles could be obtained from between decks by means of diving. A raft was also constructed, on which were placed the heavier stores and baggage. By the return of the boats which had carried Lord Amherst on shore, we learnt the great difficulty of effecting a landing, as the mangrove trees grew out to a considerable distance in the water; and it was not till ranging along shore for three miles that a small opening appeared, through which, by scrambling from rock to rock, we at last obtained a footing on *terra firma.* Here, by cutting away a quantity of the smaller jungle at the foot of a hill, a space was soon cleared, where, under the shade of the loftier trees, we bivouacked for that day and night. Parties were now despatched for water, but none could be found on the island; and the crew began to suffer terribly from thirst. A consultation was now held, and it was determined to send Lord Amherst and suite in the two boats to Java; from which place he was to send a vessel immediately to rescue those who remained on the island. Those who went in the boats amounted to forty-seven, and had with them a very slender stock of provisions: consisting of a side of mutton, a ham, a tongue, about twenty pounds of coarse biscuit, and some few more of fine ; seven gallons of water, the same of beer, as many of spruce, and thirty bottles of wine. After pulling outwards a little way to clear all the rocks, they made sail to the southward, attended by the best wishes of every man on the island, and were soon out of sight.

The number left behind was two hundred : men and boys, and one woman. After appointing a party to dig a well in a spot which was judged the most likely to yield water, the first measure of Captain Maxwell was to remove our bivouac to the top of the hill, where we could breathe a cooler and purer air—a place in all respects not only better adapted to the preservation of our health, but to our defence in case of attack. A path was cut upwards, and a party employed in clearing away and setting fire to the underwood on the summit. This last operation tended much to free us from the ants, snakes, scorpions, centipedes, and other reptiles which generally abound in such a climate. Others were employed in removing our small stock of provisions, which were deposited, under a strict guard, in a sort of natural magazine, formed by the tumbling together of some huge masses of rock on the highest part of this eminence. On board the wreck a party was stationed endeavouring to secure what they could of provisions and arms, and to save any public stores that might be found. For this purpose there was a communication between the shore and the ship whenever the tide permitted. During the previous two days every one had experienced much misery from thirst. A small cask of water, which was the only one that could be obtained from the ship, was scarcely equal to a pint for each person in the course of that period ; and perhaps no question was ever so anxiously repeated as,—" What hope from the well ?" About eleven at night the diggers had got as far down as twenty feet, when they came to a clayey or marley soil ; that immediately above being a red earth, which seemed rather moist, and had nothing saline to the taste. At a little past midnight a bottle of muddy water was brought to the captain as a specimen, and the moment that it was understood to be fresh, the rush to the well was such as to impede the workmen; it therefore became necessary to place sentries to enable the sinkers to complete their task, and permit the water to settle a little. Fortunately, about this time a heavy shower of rain fell, and by spreading sheets and table-cloths, and wringing these when saturated, some relief was afforded. Bathing in the sea was also resorted to by many, in order to drink by absorption, and it was fancied this also afforded relief.

During Thursday the 20th, our well afforded a pint of water for each man. It had a sweetish taste, something like the juice of the cocoa-nut; but nobody found fault therewith. On the contrary, it diffused that happiness which they only can feel who have suffered the horrible sensation of thirst under a vertical sun, while subjected to a harassing and fatiguing duty. This day was employed in getting up everything from the foot of the hill. Boats passed to and from the ship, but unfortunately almost every thing of real value to us, in our present case, was under water. We hoped, however, that as no bad weather was likely to arise, we might be enabled, by scuttling the ship at low-water, or by burning her upper works, to acquire many useful articles.

On Friday the 21st, the party stationed at the ship was soon after daylight surrounded by a number of Malay proas, apparently well armed, and full of men. Without a single sword or musket for defence, our men had just time to throw themselves into the boat alongside, and make for the shore, chased by the pirates. Finding two of our other boats' crews push out to the assistance of their comrades, the Malays returned and took possession of the ship. Soon afterwards it was reported from the look-out rock that the savages, armed with spears, were landing at a point about two miles off. Under all the depressing circumstances of hunger, thirst, and fatigue, and menaced by a cruel foe, it was gratifying to find that the British spirit was still staunch and unsubdued. The order was given for every man to arm himself as best he could, and it was obeyed with the utmost promptitude and alacrity. Rude pike-staves were formed by cutting down young trees; while small swords, dirks, knives, chisels, and even large spike-nails sharpened, were firmly affixed to the ends of these poles; and those who could find nothing better hardened the end of the wood in the fire, and bringing it to a sharp point, formed a tolerable weapon. There were, perhaps, a dozen cutlasses; the marines had about thirty muskets and bayonets, but could muster no more than seventy-five ball cartridges among the whole party. We had fortunately preserved some loose powder, drawn from the upper-deck guns after the ship had struck, and the marines, by hammer-ing their buttons into a round shape, and by rolling up pieces of broken bottles in cartridges, did their best to supply themselves with a sort of langrage, which would have some effect at close quarters. Strict orders were given to the men not to throw away a single shot until sure of their aim. Under the direction of the captain, Mr. Cheffy, the carpenter, and his crew were busied in forming a sort of abattis by felling trees, and enclosing in a circle the ground we occupied. By interweaving loose branches with the stakes thus driven in, a breastwork was constructed which afforded us some cover, while calculated to impede the pro-gress of any army unsupplied with artillery. That part of the island on which we had landed was a narrow ridge, not above a musket-shot across, bounded on one side by the sea, and on the other by a creek extending upwards of a mile inland, and nearly communicating with the sea at its head. Our hill was the outer point of this tongue, and its shape might be very well represented by an inverted punch-bowl —the circle on which the bowl stands would then represent the fortification, and the inner space our citadel. It appeared from the report of scouts, a short time after the first account, that the Malays had not actually landed, but had taken possession of some rocks near this point, on which they deposited a quantity of plunder brought from the ship ; and during the day they continued these predatory trips to the vessel.

In the evening all hands were mustered under arms, and a motley group they presented. It was satisfactory, however, to observe that, rude as were our implements of defence, there seemed to be no want of spirit to use them if occasion offered. The officers and men were therefore marshalled regularly into different divisions and companies, their various posts assigned, and other arrangements made. An officer and party were ordered to take charge of the boats for the night ; and these were hauled closer into the landing-place. An alarm which occurred during the night showed the benefit of these regulations; for on a sentry challenging a noise among the bushes, every one was at his post in an instant, and without the least confusion.

On Saturday morning the 22nd, some of the Malay boats approached the place where ours were moored ; and with the view of ascertaining whether the savages had any inclination to communicate with us upon friendly terms, the gig, with an officer and four hands, pulled gently towards them, while the bow of a tree was waved (a symbol of peace everywhere), showing the usual demonstrations of friendship, and of a desire on our part to speak to them ; but all was vain, for they were merely reconnoitring our position, and immediately pulled back to the rock.

The second-lieutenant, Mr. Hay, was now ordered to proceed to the ship with the barge, cutter, and gig, armed in the best way we could, and regain possession of the *Alceste*, either by fair means or by force, for the pirates did not appear at this time to have more than eighty men. Those on the rocks seeing our boats approach, threw all their plunder into their vessels and made off. Two of their largest proas were now at work on the ship ; but on observing their comrades abandon the rock, and the advance of the boats, they also made sail away, after having set fire to the ship, which they did so effectually, that in a few minutes the flames burst from every port, and she was enveloped in a cloud of smoke. The boats were consequently unable to board her, and returned to the shore.

Here was a period to every hope of accommodation with these people, if indeed any reasonable hope could ever have been entertained on that head. The Malays, and more especially those wandering and piratical tribes who roam about the coasts of Borneo, Billiton, and the wilder parts of Sumatra, are a race of savages perhaps the most merciless and inhuman to be found in any part of the world. The Battas are literally cannibals. In setting fire to the ship they gave a decided proof of their disposition towards us. But, although with no good intention, they merely did what we intended to do ; for by burning her upper works and decks, everything buoyant could float from below, and be more easily secured.

The ship continued burning the whole of the night, and the flames, which could be seen through the opening of the trees, shed a melancholy glare around, and excited in us the most mournful ideas. This night all hands were suddenly under arms again, from a marine firing his musket at what he very properly considered a suspicious character, who appeared advancing upon him, and refused to answer after being repeatedly hailed. It turned out afterwards that the branch of a tree, half-cut through the day before, had given way under one of a race of large baboons, which we found about that time disputing with us the possession of the island. At the well, where there generally was kept a good fire at night, on account of the mosquitoes, the sentries had

9

more than once been alarmed by these gentlemen showing their black faces from behind the trees. They became so troublesome to some ducks we had saved from the wreck that on several occasions, when the monkeys got among them, the water-fowl instinctively sought the society of man for protection.

On the following morning the boats were sent to the smoking wreck, where it was found that some flour, a few cases of wine, and a cask of beer had floated up from the hold. This last was announced just at the conclusion of Divine service, which was held in the mess-tent, and a pint of beer was ordered to be served out to each man, a command that called forth three cheers. This seems to be the only manner in which a British seaman can give vent to the warmer feelings of his heart. It is his mode of thanksgiving for benefits received; and it equally serves him to honour his friend, to defy his enemy, or to proclaim his victory. This day we continued improving our fence, and clearing away a glacis immediately around it, that we might have fairplay with these barbarians should they approach. They had retired between a little islet, called Pulo Chalacca, or Misfortune's Isle, about two miles from us, and seemed waiting for reinforcements; for some of their party had made sail towards Billiton.

At daylight on Wednesday the 26th, two of the pirate proas, each with a canoe astern, were discovered close in with the cove where our boats were moored. Lieutenant Hay, a straightforward fellow, who had the guard that night at the boats, immediately dashed at the Malays with the barge, cutter, and gig. On perceiving this, the pirates cut adrift their canoes, and made all sail, chased by our boats. They rather distanced the cutter and gig, but the barge gained upon them. On closing, the Malays evinced every sign of defiance, by placing themselves in the most threatening attitudes, and firing their swivels at the barge.

This discharge was returned by Mr. Hay with the only musket he had, and as they came nearer, the Malays threw their javelins and darts, several of which fell into the barge, but without wounding any of our men. Soon after the pirates were grappled by our fellows, when three of them having been shot, and a fourth knocked down with the butt-end of a musket, five more jumped overboard and drowned themselves, and two were taken prisoners, one of whom was severely wounded. The close style of fighting is termed by seamen "handling an enemy."

The Malays had taken some measures to sink their proa, for she went down almost immediately. Nothing could exceed the desperate ferocity of these people. One who had been shot through the body, but who was not quite dead, on his being removed into the barge with a view of saving him, as his own vessel was sinking, furiously grasped a cutlass which came within his reach, and it was not without a struggle wrenched from his hand. He died in a few minutes. The consort of this proa, firing a parting shot, bore up round the north part of the island, and escaped. Their canoes, which we found very useful to us, were also brought on shore, with several articles of plunder from the ship. These appeared to be the two identical proas that set fire to her. During the time our boats were in chase, Mr. Fisher, anxious to secure one of the canoes which was drifting past with the current, swam out towards it. When within a short distance of his object, an enormous shark was seen hovering near him, crossing and recrossing, as they are sometimes observed to do before making a seizure. To have called out might probably have unnerved him (for he was yet unconscious of his situation), and it was resolved to let him proceed without remark to the canoe, which was the nearest point of security. Happily he succeeded in getting into it; whilst the shark, by his too long delay, lost a very wholesome breakfast. One of the prisoners was rather elderly, the other young, and when brought on shore both seemed to have no hope of being permitted to live, but sullenly awaited their fate. On the wounds of the younger being dressed, however, the hands of the other untied, and food offered to each, with other marks of kindness, they became more cheerful, and appeared especially gratified at seeing one of their dead companions, who had been brought on shore, decently buried.

In the forenoon, immediately after this encounter, fourteen proas and smaller boats appeared standing across from the Banca side; and soon after these anchored behind Pulo Chalacca. Several of their people landed, carrying bundles, which they left in the wood and returned for more. We had some hope, from the direction in which they first appeared, as well as from their anchoring on this spot, which was the rendezvous fixed at the departure of Lord Amherst, that they might have been sent from Batavia to our relief. The morning of Thursday the 27th, however, perfectly relieved us from any further discussion on the subject, for the rajah and his suite proceeded to plunder the wreck, which by this time they had espied. It is probable they were not certain of our real situation on the first evening, but supposed, from seeing the uniforms, colours, and other military appearances, that some settlement, as at Minto, in the island of Banca, had been there established. This supposition may also account for their civility in the first instance; for from the moment their happy-like spirit was excited by the wreck, and they saw our real condition, there were no more offerings of fish or of cocoa-nut milk.

To have sent the boat openly to attack them was judged impolitic, as it would only have driven them off for a time, and put them on their guard against surprise by night, should it have been thought necessary to do so. They could deprive us of little; for the copper bolts and iron-work, about which they were now most interested, were not to us of material importance. We had the day before moved the boats into another cove, more out of sight from the overspreading branches of the trees, and safer in case of attack : being commanded by two strong little forts, one having a rude drawbridge, erected on the rocks immediately above it, and wattled in, where an officer and picket were nightly placed. A new serpentine path was cut down to this inlet, communicating with our main position aloft.

On Friday the 28th, the Malays were still employed on the wreck. A boat approached us in the forenoon ; but on the gig going out to meet it, they refused to correspond, and returned to their party. No relief having appeared from Batavia, and the period having elapsed at which, as we now thought, we had reason to expect it, measures were taken, by repairing the launch and constructing a fine raft, to give us additional powers of transporting ourselves from our present abode before our stock of provisions was entirely exhausted. On Saturday the 1st of March, the Malays acquired a great accession of strength by the arrival of fourteen other proas from the northward, probably of the old party, and the new-comers joined the others in breaking up the remains of the wreck.

At daylight on Sunday the 2nd, a still greater force joined the despoilers during the night, when the pirates, leaving a number at work on the wreck, advanced with twenty of their heaviest vessels towards our landing-place, fired one of their patereroes, beat their gongs, and otherwise making a hideous noise, anchored in a line about a cable's length from our cove. We were instantly under arms, while the party covering the boats was strengthened, and scouts sent out to watch their motions, as some of their boats had gone up the creek, at the back of our position, and to beat about, lest any of the enemy should be lying in ambush from the land. About this time the old Malay prisoner, who was under charge of sentries at the well, and who had been incautiously trusted by them to cut some wood for the fire, hearing the howling of his tribe, left his wounded comrade to shift for himself, ran off into the woods and escaped, carrying with him his hatchet. After waiting a short time in this state of preparation, and finding that they made no attempt to land, an officer was sent a little outside the cove, in order to discover their further intentions and course of action. After some deliberation, one of their boats, with several men armed with creeses, or crooked daggers, approached. Here, as usual, little could be made out, except a display of their marauding spirit, by taking a fancy to the shirt and trousers of one of the young gentlemen in the canoe; but on his refusing to give them up, they used no force.

In the afternoon some of the rajah's people, whom we at first considered our friends, made their appearance, as if seeking a parley. On communicating with them, they gave us to understand by signs, and as many words as could be made out, that all the Malays except their party were extremely hostile to us; that it was the determination of the others to attack us that night; and they urged also that some of their people should ascend the hill in order to protect us. Their former conduct and present connections displayed so evidently the treachery of this offer that it is needless to say it was rejected, and we gave them to understand that we could trust to ourselves. They immediately returned to their gang, who now assumed a most menacing attitude. In the evening, when the officers and men were assembled as usual under arms, in order to inspect them and settle the watches for the night, the captain spoke to us with much animation, and almost as follows:—

"My lads, you must all have observed this day, as well as myself, the great increase of the enemy's force (for enemies we must now consider them), and the threatening posture they have assumed. I have, on various grounds, strong reason to believe they will attack us this night. I do not wish to conceal our real state, because I do not think there is a man here who is afraid to face any sort of danger. We are now strongly fenced in, and our position is in all respects so good, that, armed as we are, we ought to make a formidable defence against even regular troops. What then would be thought of us if we allowed ourselves to be surprised by a set of naked savages, with their spears and creeses? It is true that they have swivels in their boats, but they cannot act here. I have not observed that they have any matchlocks or muskets; but if they have, so have we. I do not wish to deceive you as to the means of resistance in our power. When we were first thrown together on shore we were almost defenceless; only seventy-five ball cartridges could be mustered—we have now sixteen hundred. They cannot, I believe, send up more than five hundred men; but with two hundred such as now stand around me, I do not fear a thousand—nay, fifteen hundred of them. I have the fullest confidence we shall beat them. The pike-men standing firm, we can give them such a volley of musketry as they will be little prepared for; and when we find they are thrown into confusion, we will sally out among them, chase them into the water, and ten to one but we secure their vessels. Let every man, therefore, be on the alert, with his arms in his hands; and should these barbarians this night attempt our hill, I trust we shall convince them that they are dealing with Britons."

Perhaps three heartier cheers were never given than at the conclusion of this short but well-timed address. The woods echoed again; whilst the picket at the cove, and those stationed at the wells, the instant the hurrahs caught their ear, instinctively joined their sympathetic cheers to the general chorus. There was something like unity and concord in the sound which rung in the ears of the savages, and no doubt our cheers had a dispiriting effect upon the enemy, for about eight P.M. they were observed making signals with lights to some of their tribe behind the islet. If ever mariners had a strong inducement to fight, it was on the present occasion, for everything combined to animate us. The feeling excited by a savage, cruel, and inhospitable aggression on the part of the Malays—an aggression adding calamity to misfortune—roused every mind to a spirit of just revenge; and the appeal which the captain had made to us on the score of national character was not likely to let that feeling cool. That the enemy might come seemed to be the anxious wish of every heart. After a slender but cheerful repast the men lay down as usual on their arms, whilst the captain remained with those on guard to superintend his arrangements. An alarm during the night showed the effect of preparation on the people's minds; for all like lightning were at their posts, and returned growling and disappointed because the alarm was a false one.

Daylight, on Monday the 3d, discovered the pirates exactly in the same position in front of us; ten more vessels having joined them during the night, making their number now at least six hundred men. The plot began to thicken, and our situation became hourly more critical. Their force rapidly accumulating, and our stock of provisions daily shortening, rendered some desperate measure immediately necessary. That which seemed most feasible was by a sudden night attack, with our four boats well armed, to carry by boarding some of their vessels, and by manning these, to repeat our attack with increased force. The possession of some of their proas, in addition to our own boats, might, it was thought, enable us to shove off for Java in defiance of them. Any attempt to move on a raft, with their vessels armed with swivels playing round it, was evidently impossible. Awful as our situation now was, and every hour becoming more so, with starvation staring us in the face on one hand, and without a hope of mercy from the savages on the other, there were no symptoms of depression or gloomy despair. Every mind seemed buoyant, and if any estimate of the feeling which prevailed could be collected from the manner and expression of all, there appeared to be formed in every breast a calm determination to dash at the pirates and be successful, or to fall as became men in the attempt to be free.

About noon on this day, while various schemes and proposals were projected as to the mode of executing the measures in view, Mr. Johnstone, who had mounted the look-out tree, one of the loftiest on the summit of our hill, descried a sail at a great distance to the southward, which he thought larger than a Malay vessel. The buzz of conversation was in a moment hushed, and every eye fixed anxiously on the tree for the next report—a signalman and telescope being instantly sent up. The ship was now lost sight of from a dark squall overspreading that part of the horizon, but in about twenty minutes she emerged from the cloud, and was announced to be a square-rigged vessel. "Are you quite sure of that?" was eagerly inquired. "Quite certain," was the reply; "it is either a ship or a brig, standing towards the island under all sail." The joy this happy information infused, and the gratitude of every heart at the prospect of deliverance, may be more easily conceived than described. It occasioned a sudden transition from one train of thought to another, as if we were all waking from a disagreeable dream. We immediately displayed our colours on the highest branch of the tree to attract attention, lest she should only be a passing stranger.

The pirates soon discovered the proximity of the ship, and the circumstance occasioned an evident stir among them. As the tide was ebbing fast, it was thought possible, by an unexpected rush to the edge of the reef, to get some of the enemy under fire, and secure them as prisoners. They seemed, however, to have suspected our purpose, for the moment the seamen and marines appeared from under the mangroves, the nearest proa let fly her swivel among a party of the officers, who had been previously wading out-wards; and the whole of the proas instantly got under weigh, and made sail, fired at by our people, but unfor-tunately without effect, for, in addition to the dexterous management of their boats, the wind enabled the pirates to weather the rocks. Two only in tacking struck upon a reef to windward of us, but got off again. It was pleasing to see the anxiety of the marines to keep their powder dry, by buckling their cartouch boxes on their breasts, and swivelling their muskets above that level, as they loaded and fired, while the seamen with their pikes, like water-dogs, pushed out to support them. It was fortunate, however, that this attack took place when it did, and that it had the effect of driving the enemy away; for had they stood their ground, we were as much in their power as ever, as the vessel was obliged to anchor to the leeward of the island, twelve miles distant. The vessel sent to our relief proved to be the *Ternate*, one of the East India Company's cruisers, which had been despatched to our aid by Lord Amherst on the day of his fortunate arrival at Batavia. Mr. Ellis and his com-panions, on their arrival in the *Ternate* at Fort Maxwell, were received with heartfelt acclamation by the whole gar-rison under arms. This fortification and its inhabitants had altogether a very singular and romantic look. Some of the wigwams, or dens, as they were called, were neatly formed of branches, and thatched with the palm leaves scattered about at the feet of the lofty and majestic trees which pleasantly shaded our circle. The rude tents of others, and the ragged appearance of the men, with pikes and cutlasses in their hands, gave by fire-light a wild and picturesque effect to the camp far beyond any the imagina-tion can portray. The ship's company were now embarked as soon as practicable, and safely reached Batavia.

The ship *Cæsar* was chartered to take the ambassador, Lord Amherst, and suite, together with the crew, to England. After touching at the Cape of Good Hope, we reached St. Helena on the 27th of June. The Emperor Napoleon was there in exile. The party had an interview with him, and being received with great courtesy, all were highly gratified with their reception. Lord Amherst presented to the Emperor the several gentlemen, beginning with Captain Maxwell, to whom the distinguished prisoner bowed with great dignity, and said that his name was not unknown to him; observing that the captain had commanded on an occasion where one of his frigates, *La Pomone*, was taken in the Mediterranean. "Your government must not blame you for the loss of the *Alceste*," said the Emperor, "for you have taken one of my frigates." To each of the party he had also something to say, and we retired highly gratified with our visit. On the arrival of Captain Maxwell in England, he was honourably acquitted of the loss of the *Alceste*, and his conduct highly applauded. In the court Lord Amherst, being examined, stated "that he had selected Captain Maxwell, on the occasion of the embassy, from motives of personal friendship, as well as from the high opinion he entertained of his professional character; which opinion had been much increased by the events of this voyage." Captain Murray Maxwell afterwards received the honour of knighthood.

THE CABALVA.

ON the 14th of April 1818, this vessel sailed from Gravesend for China, in company with the East Indiaman *Lady Melville*. She was in charge of an experienced pilot, and started with a fair wind, but under a hazy sky. At eleven A.M. on the 17th, while going at the rate of seven miles an hour, the *Cabalva* touched the ground with several shocks, which alarmed the pilot, and he ordered the helm to be put about. Having got afloat, it was soon afterwards found that a leak had been sprung, and there were nine inches of water in the well. The officers having consulted together as to getting into port for repairs, or proceeding on the voyage, they unfortunately decided to adopt the latter alternative, and a number of the seamen were obliged to keep the pumps at work without intermission day and night. The ship proceeded on her way with a fair wind until off the Cape of Good Hope, where the *Scalesby Castle* was spoken, and the information tendered that when the *Cabalva* passed the Owen-light vessel the latter had drifted some miles towards the shore. This explained the cause of the accident to the *Cabalva*, and exonerated her captain, officers, and pilot from all blame on that account. A few days after a gale came away, and during its continuance the ships parted company, but after doubling the Cape the *Cabalva* was favoured with better weather, and all on board expected to arrive without further mishap at Bombay, where the captain intended to dock his vessel for repairs, as the gale had increased the leak considerably. That expectation was not realised, however, for the ship became a total wreck ere many days had passed. The following account of the perils and preservation of the crew is from the pen of one who suffered by the calamity :—

Tuesday, July the 7th. At four in the morning the watch was relieved as usual, and I was called on deck to keep the morning watch, under the second officer. Having received orders to keep a good look-out, I stationed two men on the fore-yard, and one on each cat's-head, and mustered the forecastle watch. It was now the darkest part of the night, but the stars were shining, the sky was clear, the wind moderate, and we were going under easy sail at the rate of seven-and-a-half miles an hour. I had been walking the waist nearly half-an-hour when the men aloft repeatedly sung out—" Breakers on the larboard bow ! hard a-port ! hard a-port ! it is too late ! it is all over ! hard a-port ! "

Instantly aware that there was no time to lose, I ran aft to the wheel, after repeating the words to the officer of the watch. The helm flew a-port, the ship rounded-to, and then stopped at once with a shock that affected her whole frame ; shaking the masts, and spinning the wheel round till the helm was hard a-starboard again. Everybody ran up from below. The last shock had thrown most of them out of their hammocks and cots, and the upper-deck was crowded with people, the greater number of whom were half-naked. The voices of the captain and officers were now and then heard amid a horrid crashing and parting of beams, ribs, masts, and yards, and the overwhelming roar of the surf.

" Clear away the boats ! " was the cry ; but few set to work, for the surf was knocking the ship about so dreadfully that we could scarcely keep our feet.   " Cut away the main-mast ; cut away the fore-mast ; stand clear the masts." An awful silence ensued for a few minutes ; and then by repeated blows they tumbled, masts, yards, and sails, with a tremendous crash.

The break of day was hailed with three cheers.   Then some of the officers and sailors were employed in clearing away the large cutter, which was at length effected ; and as soon as she was afloat, a number of active young men jumped into her, pushing back some weak and helpless wretches, and leaving them to shift for themselves.   Captain Dalrymple was asked to go in her, but refused.   I crawled on the forecastle, and took a good hold round the best bower-anchor stock.   The ship was now washed quite in two, the poop and forecastle being the only parts out of the water, and over these the surf was continually breaking. I saw the captain, and most of those who had been left, swimming to leeward of the wreck, between timbers, ribs, yards, and spars, half-afloat and half-drowning.   The large cutter, with about thirty people aboard, danced over the surf with wonderful lightness till she touched the rocks, when a tremendous surf broke over her, and washed every person out, dashing them against the rocks.

The number of people to leeward of the wreck was fast diminishing ; some were drowned, and others reached the rocks singly, or on rafts and pieces of wreck.   I only saw twenty or thirty, and these were nearly overcome by fatigue. Amongst them were Captain Dalrymple, the fifth mate, and two midshipmen.   In contrast with that I heard three or four sailors making merry in the captain's cabin over some bottles of wine and brandy.   In the meantime the long-boat, which was large enough to hold all who were left, got clear of the wreck.   The captain, the fifth mate, and about

twenty men, with myself, sought refuge in her, but she was
soon stove to pieces, close to the wreck, and then every one
tried to save himself as well as he could. Several were
drowned in the attempt.

Shortly after I got on a large raft made of booms, which
was now breaking adrift from the wreck. The captain with
much difficulty reached this raft, and two midshipmen, with
about twenty sailors, managed also to got thereon. The
spars unfortunately turned broadside to the surf, which
rolled them about so furiously that few of us could keep
our hold. Several had their limbs broken. After being
lashed by successive surfs, the raft was thrown upon a rock.
The captain and several sailors were washed away, and the
rest reached the rock quite exhausted and dreadfully bruised.
We there found many of our shipmates sitting in a state of
inactivity, instead of trying to better their situation. The
reef was covered with pieces of wreck, and bales of cloth,
casks, chests, etc., were strewed about in abundance. The
people were in a state of unruly confusion, though the
officers endeavoured to maintain some sort of order. Meanwhile the water was rising fast, and it was evident that the
rock would soon be submerged. Perceiving that nothing
was to be done where we were, I walked off towards some
sand-banks, without well knowing for what purpose. Five
or six sailors followed me. We walked on very slowly
over hard rocks, barefooted, and up to our middle in water,
and were fortunate enough on our passage to meet with a
young shark, which was killed after half-an-hour's chase,
and promised to make a good meal for ten or twenty
persons. We dragged it along, and arrived about noon on
a little sand-bank, where part of our people were already
assembled. They were all provided with a fair allowance
of cherry brandy or wine, the effects of which most of them
had begun to feel. Some were asleep, some quarrelling and
fighting, some skylarking, some catching birds; but I could

prevail on none of them to return to the wreck and endeavour to save some provisions and water before the ship went totally to pieces. They answered me in such fine terms, and made such long harangues, that I gave over the task, convinced that there was not a sober man amongst them! Tired, and bruised all over, I lay down on the sand, and slept comfortably for some time. When I awoke I found almost all the ship's company collected around me; they had brought from the wreck some pork, wine, and fresh water, which, with the shark and two or three lobsters, afforded a meal for upwards of a hundred people. The tide flowing in the afternoon completely inundated the rock, and the wind drove everything light and floatable over to the sand-bank. We busily employed ourselves in picking up whatever useful articles we could find. A fire was now lighted by striking a razor against a piece of glass, with the assistance of some rags and some gunpowder which had been thrown on the rock quite dry. In the evening we built a tent out of a part of the wreck, and covered it with pieces of cloth. But this did not accommodate above forty of our number.

Wednesday, July the 8th. An early breakfast was served this morning, consisting of a small slice of pork and a dram of beer to each person. We then set out in different parties. Some volunteered to wade to the wreck, partly to get provisions and water, but principally to secure the large cutter; while another party went to the adjoining sand-bank, where a variety of casks, cases, and pieces of wreckage were cast up. Some remained to erect a flagstaff, to enlarge the tent, and to spread a sufficient quantity of cloth out to the sun to dry against night. We set out for the wreck, and after having waded for two hours up to our middles in water, fell in with the large cutter, with the people who had been left behind. The boat contained some provisions, and from the wreck we also got some, which we carried back with us, when we were received with great joy by our companions on account of our success. By the result of this excursion our hopes and spirits began to revive. Our stock of provisions consisted of five sheep, six pigs, twenty-four fowls, fifty pieces of pork and beef, a keg of flour, three casks of beer, four dozen of wine, one dozen of cherry brandy, and five pine-cheeses, but neither biscuits nor water. The party who had gone to the sand-bank returned with twenty pieces of pork, but nothing more. An officer's watch was set at eight P.M., partly to watch the motion of the water, to look out for ships, and keep the fire in, but chiefly to guard the provisions.

Thursday, July the 9th. At daybreak all went again to work, except the sick, the lazy, and the drunken. The carpenter and his mates began to repair the large cutter, the sailmaker to make sails, and the boatswain to make ropes by twisting three pieces of muslin together. The chief mate with one party set out for the sand-banks, and I took another to the wreck. All that we met with were some sail-ropes and two or three dozen of wine. We found to our great joy the captain's cutter, which we took back with us to the tents for the carpenter to repair. We found that in the course of the day the following articles had been collected—four butts of fresh water, four casks of beer, three dozen of wine, fifty pieces of pork and beef, a drowned pig, and some sails and ropes.

Friday, July the 10th. The carpenter and sailmakers continued their work in fitting out the large cutter. We determined the latitude and longitude of our situation, and found that this shoal was the "Cargados Garrayos Reef," and we calculated that the Isle of France was the nearest inhabited land, bearing S.W. by S., and distant two hundred and fifty miles. Parties set out in different directions to collect provisions, while some tried their luck in fishing, and others employed themselves in repairing the tents and

10

preparing the victuals. The chief mate and myself, with some of the sailors, set out for a neighbouring sand-bank to see what we could pick up, and there we built a raft of some spars we found on the beach. We then loaded the raft with about thirty pieces of pork and about three dozen of wine, which we brought home with us.

Saturday, July the 11th. This day we spent in similar occupations. The number of tents had increased to sixteen, and the people divided themselves into messes, every mess having a tent of its own. Two allowances of provisions were served each day, one at seven A.M., the other at six P.M., each ration consisting of about two ounces of meat and a coffee-cup of beer. About five P.M. the parties returned after very unsuccessful excursions. While we were at dinner, we heard three cheers outside the tent, and ran out to see what was the matter; when we found that one of the sailors, while digging a hole in the sand, had found fresh water, to the surprise and joy of us all. The fluid was of a milky colour, and rather brackish, but a great blessing, notwithstanding its indifferent quality.

Sunday, July the 12th. No work was done to-day, and in the afternoon the people assembled around the cutter, when Mr. Ayres, the purser, delivered a religious address.

Monday, July the 13th. The boat being nearly ready for sea, it was now determined that she should be launched the next morning, and sail for the Mauritius. I was appointed to command her, and Mr. Ayres and eight seamen were to accompany me. The day passed in the necessary preparations for the voyage. Our provisions for the boat consisted of four pieces of pork, twenty cakes of flour and water, a pine-cheese, eight gallons of porter, sixteen gallons of water, six bottles of wine, and three of cherry brandy. We had three masts with lug-sails, eight oars, two buckets for baling out any water that might get into the boat, two or three muskets, and some gunpowder. A quadrant, two watches, and a long seal, were the only instruments to navigate her, as neither compass nor chart could be found.

Tuesday, July the 14th. The morning of our departure having arrived, the boat's crew had a more substantial meal than usual, and at five o'clock we set off, amidst the repeated cheers and prayers of the *Cabalva's* officers and men. The weather being very squally and wet, we could not get an observation at noon, and were often obliged to take in the fore-sail, and heave-to under a close-reefed mizzen. At sunset we were enabled to make a tolerably accurate estimate of our course, which we judged to be S.W. by S. A long night followed, in which we sought for sleep in vain, as the sea was constantly washing over the boat, and kept us employed in baling out the water.

Wednesday, July the 15th. The sun rising clear this morning, our course appeared to be S.W. by S., and the rate of sailing about five knots an hour. At noon we got a pretty accurate observation : lat. 18° 30′. We continued our course under a close-reefed fore-sail and mizzen, keeping the boat's head to the wind, as near as we were allowed by the sea, which often rose to such a prodigious height as to require the whole attention of the man at the helm ; for the least inattention would have caused the shipping of heavy seas, and probably the swamping of the boat. Indeed, during the continuance of the squalls, the helm was obliged to be put down every four or five minutes to turn her head to the billows, which would have sunk her at once if they had struck her on the side. The waves came over us continually, so that three hands were employed constantly day and night in baling.

The sun not setting clear, and the night being squally and rainy, we could only guess our course by the wind to be S.W. by S. till it cleared up for a while about two in the morning, when I perceived, by the bearing of the Southern Cross, that we had broken off to S.W. by W., and I was afraid of getting to leeward of the Mauritius. The discovery of our real course was a sore disappointment, for we began to despair of regaining our ground, and were on the point of giving up all hope of reaching Port Louis, and bearing away for Bourbon.

Thursday, July the 16th. The breaking of day filled us with new hope and vigour, although the weather continued squally, and the sky cloudy and hazy. But it is impossible to describe our sensations when, on the larboard-bow, we saw land, which we knew to be Round Island, close to the Mauritius. We found ourselves abreast of Port Louis at noon, although twelve or fourteen miles to leeward. The wind drawing round to the south, right in our teeth, we could gain no way by working to windward. We therefore took in the sails, got the oars out, and pulled hard for two hours; but the sea running high, we did little good, and set the three lugs with all reefs out. Night coming on, our situation became alarming, for we feared that we would be blown off the island, and be obliged to make for Bourbon. Happily for us, after sunset we got a slant wind, which enabled us to work in-shore, but not knowing the entrance of the harbour, and the night becoming hazy, we made a rope fast to one of the ballast-bags, and came to an anchor in nine feet water, close to the land, at two in the morning.

Friday, July the 17th. At daybreak we weighed anchor, and pulled four miles along shore, when we descried the harbour, and got safely in about eight o'clock. When we got to the landing-place a crowd of people gathered around us. Our appearance was truly ludicrous. Only one of us had a hat; the rest wore muslin turbans, or ladies' fancy caps; three had jackets; the rest wore mantles of different coloured cloth, with holes for the naked arms; two or three had trousers, but there were neither shirts, stockings, nor shoes among the party! Our faces and arms had been so exposed to the scorching rays of the sun that we had more the appearance of savages than of Europeans. The people who crowded around us were very kind. They brought us bread, coffee, grog, and fruit; and many of them invited us to their houses.

The purser went ashore to state our case to the company's agent, while I got the boat secured. I then went with one of the inhabitants, a kind-hearted Frenchman, who urged me to go and breakfast with him. After breakfast I went in search of Mr. Ayres, and was happy to find that our wishes were most readily met by the company's agent and the commanding naval officer. The *Magicienne* frigate was ready in an hour after our arrival to go to the relief of the *Cabalva's* crew. Mr. Ayres, two of the boat's crew, and myself, went on board the frigate, while the rest remained at Port Louis. His Majesty's brig the *Challenger* was appointed to accompany us. We met with a very hearty reception on board the *Magicienne* from Captain Purves and his officers. The account which we gave of our misfortunes and sufferings surprised and interested them greatly. The officers were never tired of hearing our adventures repeated; and in return they supplied all our wants, and made us as comfortable as possible.

On Sunday the 20th July, the men that were on the look-out at the mast-head sung out, " Breakers on the larboard-bow ! Hard a-port !" These most portentous words remained impressed on my mind from the first morning of our disaster, and I thought we were again on the rocks; but we happily escaped all danger this time, and worked into leeward of the sand. To our great joy we soon after descried the flagstaff of our shipmates. The chief officer, with eight hands in the captain's cutter, met us at the entrance of the bay, and was heartily congratulated on board the frigate, when he gave us an account of what had occurred to our shipmates since our departure. The chief officer's statement was nearly as follows :—

"After you left us on the sand-bank, we were not able to save anything from the wreck, but we became more expert and successful in fishing. The captain's cutter was repaired, that we might make discoveries northward, and select a spot for our encampment more elevated above the sea; for we had almost given up the large cutter and her crew as lost. We were assembled at prayers to-day, when the boatswain, looking towards the sea, interrupted the service with the words, 'A sail! a sail!' and ran capering about like a mad fellow. The whole congregation immediately ran to the beach, when they cheered for some time; then some fell on their knees to thank God for the deliverance."

The frigate brought up for the night in twelve fathoms water. On Monday morning we weighed again, and the same evening got safely to an anchor within a mile of the sand-bank. Several of the *Cabalva's* officers came off in one of the frigate's boats, which had been sent for them, and we mutually rejoiced at meeting after a short but trying separation. On the following morning the captain of the frigate went ashore, taking with him some bags of biscuits, which proved a great treat to the poor fellows. All the *Cabalva's* crew were embarked in the course of the day. Most of the sailors had concealed some valuables about their persons; but as the men were strictly overhauled as they came on board the *Magicienne*, all were deprived of their plunder. Cloth, muslin, and linen were afterwards served out to them, however, according to their behaviour. On the 28th of July we safely reached Port Louis, and thus our misfortunes terminated in a manner surpassing our most sanguine expectations. May we be ever thankful to the gracious Providence which so wonderfully protected us, from the morning of the wreck till our arrival at the Isle of France

THE HARPOONER.

THIS transport ship having been chartered by the Government, in the year 1818, to carry a large number of soldiers to Canada, she set sail from England with not fewer than three hundred and eighty-five souls on board. These included relief-detachments for several regiments then in the Dominion, with the wives and children of many of the men. Altogether the number of passengers was slightly in excess of the carrying capacity of the vessel, but the voyage was a prosperous one until the dangerous navigation at the mouth of the St. Lawrence, on the American coast, had been reached. From one cause or another—in all probability by reason of not keeping a good look-out during the hazy weather that then prevailed—about nine o'clock on the evening of the 10th of November, the ship struck against a rock called St. Shotts, near Newfoundland. The shock was not very severe, but the atmosphere being dark, and their true position at the time unknown, considerable consternation was engendered among those who crowded the lower-deck of the unfortunate vessel, and the alarm was increased when, a few minutes after the first shock, a second concussion was felt and the hold began to fill from a leak caused by the force of the blows. The wind was now high, with a heavy sea, and the *Harpooner* was encircled by a cluster of formidable rocks that loomed in the darkness, and threatened destruction from all the points of the compass.

Falling over on her larboard beam-end, the ship was driven by the rage of the elements over and among the rocks, and for the purpose of righting her the masts were cut away, some of the seamen falling overboard during the operation. Terror had now seized all on board, and their fear was intensified by fire being communicated to some spirits in the captain's cabin, through the carelessness of some one who had carried a lighted candle too closely to the inflammable liquid. It was with considerable difficulty that a general conflagration on board was prevented. Carried along at the mercy of the waves, the vessel drifted over towards the high cliffs that jutted from the mainland, while the heavy seas rushed over the deck and removed all the fittings thereon that offered any opposition to their destructive violence. The suddenness with which the water poured in upon the occupants of the lower parts of the vessel prevented many from seeking to save themselves by going on deck. The berths and stanchions were carried away, and being washed against the hapless crowd of men, women, and children, rendered many of them senseless, while others were killed by the force with which they were driven against the floating casks and baggage, which had formed the cargo of the vessel and the effects of the passengers and crew. All who could get upon deck found themselves face to face with death. From the crowding and confusion that there prevailed, the orders of the commander to the crew, as well as those of the military officers to their subordinates, were almost wholly unavailing, while the hull continued to strike upon the rocks with such fury as to threaten each moment to dash it into fragments, and to give up all the

remainder of the now frantic people on board to the anger of
the waves. The shrieking mass of men and women, with
their little ones, now pressed towards the larboard side, and
in the terrible crush that prevailed several received severe
injuries. From the moment of the first disaster but little
hope appeared that any would be saved, and now even the
most resolute were unnerved by the influence of the most
abject despair.

About eleven at night, a heavy sea struck the vessel and
washed overboard all the boats from the deck. From that
hour until four o'clock in the morning, the miserable people
on the wreck prayed anxiously for the light of day to break
upon the scene of their misery and hopelessness. Meanwhile the stern-boat had been lowered upon the water, and
into it the first mate and four seamen went, at the risk of
their lives, and pushed off to the shore, which they at length
reached with much difficulty, and effected a landing upon
the mainland, at a point behind a huge cliff, and nearest to
the rock upon which the *Harpooner* had been driven. The
progress of their shipmates was watched with painful interest on the wreck by the crew, who as soon as the others
had got ashore threw a log-line in that direction, so that if
possible a means of communication might be established
between the ship and their friends who had fortunately got
to land. But the darkness, together with the tremendous
surf that beat upon the coast, rendered fruitless repeated
efforts to effect this result in the manner described.

While his men were thus eagerly employed in seeking to
convey a line ashore, it occurred to the master of the vessel
that the purpose for which the crew were striving, amidst
the most awful suspense, terror, and pain, might be effected
through the sagacity and strength of a favourite dog. The
captain determined to follow the plan that had been suggested to his mind, and the animal was speedily brought aft,
when a line was secured around the dog's body, and the

faithful creature thrown in the sea. It would be difficult to describe adequately the sensations of those who witnessed the efforts of the animal as he battled with the breakers, while ever and anon a receding wave dashed him backwards into the sea. Sufficient, that after great exertions, during which the life of the dog and the rising hopes of those for whose safety the animal had been made to go on his errand of mercy, were repeatedly jeoparded, the canine messenger at length reached the rock upon which the seamen stood, and landed in view of the anxious crowd who had watched his passage to the shore.

Having secured the end of the line which the dog had carried from the wreck, the seamen on the rock next hauled ashore a stronger rope that had been attached to the other end by their shipmates. The hawser was then securely fastened to a part of the cliff and to the wreck, and about six in the morning the first person was landed from the *Harpooner* by this means. By an improvement in the adjustment of the rope, and placing each individual in a sling devised for the purpose, many of the sufferers were afterwards extricated with increased facility from their perilous position, although it was with the greatest difficulty that the unfortunate persons could maintain their hold of the line that supported them in their dangerous passage to the land. As the sea washed over them while being hauled ashore, some were found in a state of insensibility on their removal from the sling. When coming ashore, Lieutenant Wilson, a young military officer, lost his life. Being unable to retain his hold of the rope while struck more than once by heavy seas, he fell backwards out of the sling into the waves, and after swimming for a considerable time amongst the floating wreckage, he received a blow upon the head from a heavy spar, and consequently perished. Many lives were also lost through the more daring of the crew and passengers having trusted to secure their safety by swimming ashore ; but some were dashed in pieces upon the rocks by the force of the surf, while others met their death through repeated contact with the broken timbers that were thrown against their bodies by the angry breakers.

After having been the means of saving many valuable lives, unhappily the hawser was at length cut in two, through the constant friction to which it had been subjected while being swung across a sharp rock. As there were no means of replacing the severed line of communication, the spectacle on board the wreck became, if possible, even more deplorable than it had yet assumed since the hour of the calamity. This might largely be attributable to the falsification of those hopes of ultimate rescue which had for some hours infused vigour into the efforts of the workers at the hawser and sling. Shortly after the breaking of the hawser the sea beat upon the wreck with augmented violence, and numbers of those who had been nervously awaiting the moment when they might take their place in the sling and be hauled ashore, were washed overboard. At length the hull broke up along its entire length, and all who had been left on the deck were precipitated into the seething waters. With a feeling of unutterable horror, the party on shore saw the first indication of the breaking-up of the ship at the stern, and the frantic appeals for help that were made by the persons on the rent and riven deck. The cry was raised from those on the rock to their friends on board, "Go forward;" but the advice came too late, for midship and forecastle in turn speedily gave way, and in a few moments the greater number of the men, women, and children thereon had bidden adieu to mortal suffering.

The last person to leave the wreck voluntarily was Lieutenant Mylrea, of the 4th Veteran Battalion. He was upwards of seventy years of age, and one of the oldest subalterns in the British service. When he had seen every other person either safely ashore or beyond the power of assistance, he threw himself on a rock, from which he was rescued some time afterwards. One of those who were spared only to find themselves bereft of all they held dear on earth, was the daughter of Surgeon Armstrong, who lost both of her parents, with her brother and two sisters. The total number of those who perished was two hundred and eight.

The survivors, numbering one hundred and seventy-seven, were landed upon a rock, about one hundred feet above the level of the sea, and at the flow of the tide their place of refuge was totally surrounded by water. During the whole of the night after the wreck the rescued were compelled to remain on the summit of the cliff. Many of the sufferers were without shoes; some were but scantily clothed; and all were exposed, without shelter or nourishment of any kind, to the wind and rain that beat upon their bleak and barren resting-place. A fire had been kindled from pieces of the wreck, and this afforded the only means of comfort to the hungry and sorrowing persons who huddled around the dull and steaming embers.

As daylight appeared the party took advantage of the time of low-water to effect a passage to the land opposite the rock on which they had bivouacked. Nor was their removal to the mainland proper accomplished without difficulty and personal risk. Some were let down the face of the cliff by a rope; while others were seated upon a ladder, and in that manner slipped to the bottom. When all had crossed over the shallow creek, their course was directed towards the humble dwelling of a fisherman, distant about a mile-and-a-half from the scene of their peril, where they remained until the following day. The owner of the miserable shed had not the means wherewith to supply relief to so many necessitous persons. Consequently, a party was organised for the purpose of going farther afield in search of food for themselves, and in order to obtain assistance for their weaker partners in misfortune. After travelling about fourteen miles through a marshy and uninhabited country they reached Trepassy, where the circumstances of the wreck were reported to several of the settlers, who immediately took measures for alleviating the sufferings of the travellers and bringing forward as many as possible of those who had remained at the shed of the fisherman, or had already started on the journey to Trepassy, footsore and weary with their privations.

On the evening of the 13th the greater number of the survivors arrived at the town named. During the journey many had been assisted by the inhabitants, who carried the weak and feeble upon their backs. As the shipwrecked people reached Trepassy they were billeted by the order of a magistrate upon the townsfolk, according to the social position of the latter, and every care was taken to mitigate the distress of the remainder of the *Harpooner's* passengers and crew. At St. Shotts a poor woman, the wife of a sergeant in the Veteran Battalion, had been delivered of a child upon the rock, shortly after her rescue from the wreck. A private soldier, whose leg had been broken, and a woman who had been severely bruised by the disaster, could not be removed from the neighbourhood of the wreck for some time afterwards. All these sufferers received attention, until so far recovered as to be able to bear the fatigue of a journey to Trepassy, and eventually boats were provided by the hospitable settlers for the conveyance of their unfortunate guests to St. John's, where the survivors from the wreck in due course safely arrived.

THE ABEONA.

EARLY in November 1820 this transport-ship was chartered by the Government for the conveyance of emigrants from the Clyde to the British settlements at the Cape of Good Hope, and the destruction of the *Abeona* by fire, when her outward voyage had been about half-completed, created a considerable sensation in the public mind at the time. Having taken on board fourteen passengers at London she proceeded to the Clyde, where the emigrants embarked, to the number of one hundred and twenty-six. The captain, officers, and crew numbered twenty-one persons, and with a fair wind the ship entered the Atlantic from the mouth of the river. Nothing of importance occurred on the passage until the outbreak of the conflagration, which destroyed the vessel and deprived one hundred and twelve of the passengers and crew of their lives, together with all the possessions of many of the emigrants. The following narrative of the burning of the transport was given by Mr. Fisher, the surgeon on board :—

It is with the most painful feelings that I undertake the melancholy duty of giving an account of the destruction, by fire, of the *Abeona* transport when on her way with emigrants to the Cape. About a quarter-past twelve on the afternoon of the 25th of November, Mr. Duff, first mate, was serving out the rum in the lazarette or store-room, when, as it is supposed, the flame of the candle accidentally communicated with the spirits, or other combustible stores. The catastrophe that ensued was alike sudden and awful in the extreme. So soon as the existence of the fire had been made known to the passengers and crew by the volumes of smoke which issued from below, as well as by the alarm that was at once raised by the mate, every exertion was made by the seamen and emigrants in handing the water along, and I joined the men and encouraged them when so employed, until the flames came up in such quantity and fury from the hatchways that all chances of saving the vessel were seen to be hopeless. Our only alternative now was to get the boats out, and to this our attention was directed. Happily for us, we speedily lowered the two gigs which were on the quarters together with the skiff, which was stowed on the booms in the long-boat, which latter craft was now the only one remaining on board that could be used by the crew and passengers as a means of leaving the doomed vessel.

With the intention of launching the long-boat, it was started from the boom to the gangway, and we had her almost clear of the bulwarks. The tackle-falls were taken to the windlass, and the men continued heaving round, assisted by the captain and myself, until we found our position so dangerous that we abandoned the lowering of the boat and sought our safety in the gigs and skiff that were afloat. The captain's boat happened to be under the larboard-bow at the time, and he entered it. I immediately followed him, and we were only a minute or two in the boat when the main and mizzen masts fell overboard on our side of the ship. The fore-mast was now in a blaze, and from this time until the hull of the *Abeona* sunk beneath the waves the horror of the scene momentarily increased.

In a frenzy of fear some of the emigrants leaped overboard and were drowned, as it was impossible to save them. In their efforts to escape from the fury of the flames, others got out upon the bowsprit, and were either knocked off into the sea or killed by the fall of the fore-mast, which went directly forward. We rescued from the ship, as well as from the water, as many as we prudently thought the boats could carry, considering the immense distance that intervened between us and the nearest land, and the innumerable difficulties with which we had to contend. Even those in the boats who beheld their dearest relatives perishing before their eyes, felt constrained to acknowledge that the attempt to save more than we did would only have involved the whole of the occupants of the boats in one common and calamitous fate. This fact and the number of women and children who were saved, are convincing proofs of our impartial behaviour on the melancholy occasion.

The spectacle now presented was one of the most awful and distressing ever beheld by mortal eye. Without being able to render them any succour, we saw some of our fellow-creatures throwing themselves from the bulwarks of the burning ship into the deep, while others were hanging by ropes and eagerly clinging to life, which we all so dearly value, although inevitable destruction stared them in the face whichever way they turned. Unable longer to withstand this saddening manifestation of human misery, we rowed to a distance from the ship, picking up on the way some hammocks, spars, and a cask that were floating by. Before leaving the deck I had a pig given to me by the cook, and I threw the animal overboard; it was taken out of the water by the men in one of the boats, who had previously taken the precaution to secure other two pigs as a provision against starvation on the inhospitable ocean.

Having got a mile or two from the unfortunate *Abeona* the crowded boats lay-to, and we consulted as to the course we would follow under the painful circumstances of our situation. Altogether, we found that our stock of provisions on board the boats amounted to about ten pounds of biscuit, a few bacon hams, and the three pigs which had been secured. Some water we collected by wringing our drenched clothes. That was our slender store of food to sustain the lives of fifty persons, until we either reached land or were rescued by a passing vessel. It was proposed that we should make for the coast of South America. Sanguine indeed must that mind have been which could hope, thus provided, to prosecute successfully a voyage of nearly six hundred miles. But it pleased God, in His omnipotent mercy, that we should be left living witnesses to tell the terrible fate of those who perished. We resolved to remain within sight of the dreadful conflagration, in the hope that it might be seen from some passing ship in the night, and prove the means of our succour from a death by drowning or starvation.

When the fire broke out the weather was moderately calm, and it continued so during the night, with occasional puffs of wind and heavy squalls of rain. The flames abated but little of their energy until between three and four in the morning, when they suddenly ceased to illuminate the water, and the dark cloud of smoke which had hung for fifteen hours over the wreck was slowly driven by a light breeze from the spot where the burning remnants of the hull had sunk into the ocean.

At daylight on the 26th we descried a vessel about two miles distant, with all sail set before the wind, and coming towards us. Our sensations at the time may be more easily imagined than described. As the stranger approached we hailed her and rowed alongside, when we asked to be taken on board. We had then been in the boats during seventeen long and painful hours. Our request was granted with the utmost alacrity.

11

The ship that saved us was a Portuguese merchantman, called the *Condessa da Ponte*, Captain Joaquim Almeida, bound to Lisbon from Bahia, and with the solitary exception of a vessel which had passed us about five days before the burning of the *Abeona*, was the first passing sail we had seen for twenty days previous to our rescue. The flames of our ship had not been observed from the *Condessa da Ponte* during the night, consequently I could not but regard the arrival of a humane commander upon the scene of the calamity as a merciful interposition of Providence on our behalf.

The consideration and kindness experienced by all the survivors from the burning wreck redound very much to the honour of the Portuguese nation, so worthily represented on this occasion by Captain Almeida and his crew. The captain cruised about the spot where we thought the *Abeona* had been from six in the morning until noon, in the hope that some of the poor sufferers might be seen floating about on spars, and saved from a watery grave. In that expectation, however, we were disappointed, for not even a vestige of anything belonging to the burned ship or her unfortunate passengers was discovered. On the 21st of December we arrived at Lisbon, where we received the kindest treatment at the hands of Mr. Jeffrey, the British Consul-General, and the gentlemen connected with the British Factory in that city. The most considerate friendship was also shown to us by the Reverend J. H. Siely and his amiable wife.

Of the crew of the *Abeona*, consisting of twenty-one men and boys, there were seven lost and fourteen saved. Among those who perished, Mr. Duff, the chief mate, was deeply deplored by all who had witnessed his noble self-sacrifice at the final moment. With a generous regard for the passengers who were face to face with death, Duff resolutely refused to save his own life by going on board the small boat : declaring that he would abide the fate of those who were forced to remain with the burning ship. Of one hundred and twenty-six emigrants, who were for the most part from Glasgow and the immediate neighbourhood, only twenty-six were saved. Of the passengers, fourteen in number, who had gone with the ship from London, five were lost.

Various instances of the force of parental affection, and of the most devoted attachment, were exhibited in this dreadful calamity. Of these I shall only mention one or two. Mr. and Mrs. Barrie, from Provan Mill, near Glasgow, appeared to be insensible to their own immediate danger, so wholly engrossed were they in their efforts to save their helpless offspring. Having thrown their eight youngest children into one of the boats, Mrs. Barrie was desired to take her place therein, but she refused to do so until she had found her eldest daughter. Unfortunately, before she could return with the girl, the boat was obliged to be put off from the ship, and both parents were lost, together with their daughter and a son. The fate of Barrie and his wife caused eight children to be orphans. The youngest is only fifteen months, and the infant is cherished by one of his sisters with all the tenderness of a mother. A man named Macfarlane, who had been married but a few days before the sailing of the *Abeona* from the Clyde, plunged overboard with his wife lashed to his back, and endeavoured to swim towards the boats. Finding his strength failing him, however, he turned about and made for the ship. Unable to catch hold of anything to which they might cling for support, the unfortunate young couple sunk together.

THE BLENDENHALL.

THE privations to which shipwrecked persons have been reduced when thrown upon the bleak and sterile coast, or the uninhabited island, have furnished materials for many interesting tales since the first publication of Defoe's *History of Robinson Crusoe*. But all the efforts of the romancer have failed to produce narratives of a more thrilling character than those which have owed their origin to occurrences in actual seafaring life. Although the wreck of the vessel, the name of which forms the title of this chapter, presents nothing unusually sensational, yet the incidents are so much akin to some that have embellished the pages of fiction, as to have rendered the story a popular one, and conduced to its repeated narration in various records of Adventure. An account of the events appeared in *Chambers's Edinburgh Journal*, and it is here slightly condensed :—

In the year 1821 the *Blendenhall*, free trader, bound from England for Bombay, partly laden with broadcloths, was prosecuting her voyage with every prospect of a successful issue. While thus pursuing her way through the Atlantic she was unfortunately driven from her course by adverse winds and currents more to the southward and westward than was required, and it became desirable to reach the island of Tristan d'Acunha, in order to ascertain and rectify the reckoning. This island, which is called after the Portuguese admiral who first discovered it, is one of a group of three, the others being the Inaccessible and Nightingale Islands, situated many hundreds of miles from any land, and in a south-westerly direction from the Cape of Good Hope. The shores are rugged and precipitous in the extreme, and form, perhaps, the most dangerous coast upon which any vessel could be driven.

It was while steering to reach this group of islands that, one morning, a passenger on board the *Blendenhall*, who chanced to be upon deck earlier than usual, observed great quantities of seaweed floating alongside. This excited some alarm, and a man was sent aloft to keep a good look-out. The weather was then extremely hazy, though moderate; the weeds continued; all were on the alert; they shortened sail, and the boatswain piped for breakfast. In less than ten minutes " Breakers ahead!" startled every soul, and in a moment all were on deck. " Breakers starboard! breakers larboard! breakers all around!" was the ominous cry a moment afterwards, and all was confusion. The words were scarcely uttered when, and before the helm was up, the ill-fated ship struck, and, after a few tremendous shocks against the sunken reef, she parted about midship. Ropes and stays were cut away—all rushed forward, as if instinctively, and had barely reached the forecastle when the stern and quarter broke asunder with a violent crash, and sank to rise no more. Two of the seamen miserably perished; the rest, including officers, passengers, and crew, held on about the head and bows—the struggle was for life!

At this moment the Inaccessible Island, which till then had been veiled in clouds and thick mist, appeared frowning above the haze. The wreck was more than two miles from

the frightful shore. The base of the island was still buried
in impenetrable gloom.   In this perilous extremity one was
for cutting away the anchor, which had been got up to the
cat-head in time of need ; another was for cutting down the
fore-mast (the foretop-mast being already by the board).
The fog totally disappeared, and the black rocky island
stood in all its rugged deformity before their eyes.
Suddenly the sun broke out in full splendour, as if to expose
more clearly to the view of the sufferers their dreadful
predicament.   Despair was in every bosom—death, arrayed
in all its terrors, seemed to hover over the wreck.   But
exertion was required, and everything that human energy
could devise was effected.

The wreck, on which all eagerly clung, was drifted by the
tide and wind between ledges of sunken rocks and thundering breakers until, after the lapse of six hours, it entered
the only spot on the island where a landing was possibly
practicable, for all the other parts of the coast consisted of
perpendicular cliffs of granite, rising from amidst deafening
surf to the height of twenty, forty, and sixty feet.   As the
shore was neared, a raft was prepared, and on this a few
paddled for the cove.   At last the wreck drove right in ;
ropes were instantly thrown out, and the crew and passengers (except two who had been crushed in the wreck),
including three ladies and a female attendant, were snatched
from the watery grave which a few short hours before had
appeared inevitable, and safely landed on the beach.

Evening had now set in, and every effort was made to
secure whatever could be saved.   Bales of cloth, cases of
wine, a few boxes of cheese, some hams, the carcase of a
milch cow that had been washed on shore, buckets, tubs,
butts, a seaman's chest (containing a tinder-box and needles
and thread), with a number of elegant mahogany turned
bedposts, and part of an investment for the India market,
were got on shore.   The rain poured down in torrents—all

hands were busily at work to procure a shelter from the weather; and with the bedposts and broadcloths, and part of the fore-sail, as many tents were soon pitched as there were individuals on the island.

Drenched with the sea and with the rain, hungry, cold, and comfortless, thousands of miles from their native land, almost beyond expectation of human succour, hope nearly annihilated, the shipwrecked voyagers retired to their tents. In the morning the wreck had gone to pieces; and planks and spars, and whatever had floated in, were eagerly dragged on shore. No sooner was the unfortunate ship broken up than, deeming themselves free from the bonds of authority, many began to secure whatever came to land; and the captain, officers, passengers, and crew were now reduced to the same level, and obliged to take their turn to fetch water and explore the island for food.

The work of exploring was soon over—there was not a bird, nor a quadruped, nor a single tree to be seen! All was barren and desolate. The low parts were scattered over with stones and sand, and a few stunted weeds, reeds, ferns, and other plants. The top of the mountain was found to consist of a fragment of original tableland, very marshy, and full of deep sloughs, intersected with small rills of water, pure and pellucid as crystal, and a profusion of wild parsley and celery. The prospect was one dreary scene of destitution, without a single ray of hope to relieve the misery of the desponding crew. After some days the dead cow, hams, and cheese were consumed, and from one end of the island to the other not a morsel of food could be seen. Even the celery began to fail. A few bottles of wine, which for security had been secreted under ground, only remained. Famine now began to threaten. Every stone near the sea was examined for shell-fish, but in vain.

In this dreadful extremity, and while the half-famished seamen were all night squatting in sullen dejection round their fires, a large flock of sea-birds, allured by the flames, rushed into the midst of them, and were greedily laid hold of as fast as they could be seized. For several nights in succession similar flocks came in, and by multiplying their fires a considerable supply was secured. These visits, how-ever, ceased at length, and the wretched party were exposed again to the most severe privation. When their stock of wild-fowl had been exhausted for more than two days, each began to fear they were now approaching that sad point of necessity when, between death and casting lots who should be sacrificed to serve as food for the rest, no alternative remains.

While horror at the bare contemplation of an extremity so repulsive occupied the thoughts of all, the horizon was suddenly obscured, and presently clouds of penguins alighted on the island. The low grounds were actually covered, and before the evening was dark the sand could not be seen for the numbers of eggs which, like a sheet of snow, lay on the surface of the earth. The penguins continued on the island four or five days, when, as if by a signal, the whole took their flight, and were never again seen. A few were killed, but the flesh was so extremely rank and nauseous that it could not be eaten. The eggs were collected and dressed in all manner of ways, and supplied abundance of food for upwards of three weeks.

At the expiration of that period famine seemed inevitable. The third morning began to dawn upon the unfortunate company after their stock of eggs was exhausted ; they had now been without food for more than forty hours, and were fainting and dejected, when, as though this desolate rock were really a land of miracles, a man came running up to the encampment with the unexpected and joyful tidings that*"millions of sea-crows had come on shore." The crew climbed over the ledge of rocks that flanked their tents, and the sight of a shoal of manatees immediately beneath them gladdened their hearts. These came in with the flood, and were left in the puddles between the broken rocks of the cove. This supply continued for two or three weeks. The flesh was mere blubber, and quite unfit for food, for not a man could retain it on his stomach; but the liver was excellent, and on this they subsisted.

In the meantime the carpenter had constructed a boat, and four of the men had ventured in her for Tristan d'Acunha, in hopes of ultimately extricating their fellow-sufferers from their perilous situation. Unfortunately the boat was lost—whether carried away by the violence of the currents that set in between the islands, or dashed to pieces against the breakers, was never known, for no vestige of the boat or the crew was ever seen. Before the manatees, however, began to quit the shore, a second boat was launched; and in this an officer and some seamen made a second attempt, and happily succeeded in effecting a landing, after much labour, on the island, where they were received with much cordiality and humanity by Governor Glass—a personage whom it will be necessary to describe.

Tristan d'Acunha is believed to have been uninhabited until 1811, when three Americans took up their residence upon it, for the purpose of cultivating vegetables and selling the produce, particularly potatoes, to vessels which might touch there on their way to India, the Cape, or other parts in the southern ocean. These Americans remained its only inhabitants till 1816, when, on Bonaparte being sent to St. Helena, the British government deemed it expedient to garrison the island, and sent the *Falmouth* man-of-war with a colony of forty persons, which arrived in the month of August. At this time the chief of the American settlers was dead, and two only survived; but what finally became of these we are not informed.

The British garrison was soon given up, the colony abandoned, and all returned to the Cape of Good Hope, except a person named Glass, a Scotchman, who had been corporal of artillery, and his wife, a Cape creole. Other families afterwards joined them, and thus the foundation of a nation on a small scale was formed, Mr. Glass being the chief and lawgiver of the whole. On being visited in 1824 by Mr. Augustus Earle, the little colony was found to be on the increase, a considerable number of children having been born since the period of settlement. The different families inhabited cottages thatched with the long grass of the island, and exhibited an air of comfort, cleanliness, and plenty truly English.

To this island the boat's crew of the *Blendenhall* had bent their course, and Governor Glass showed them every attention, not only on the score of humanity, but because they were his fellow-subjects; for Glass did not claim independent monarchy, but prayed publicly for King George as his lawful sovereign. On learning the situation of the crew on Inaccessible Island, he instantly launched his boat, and hastened at the risk of his life to deliver his shipwrecked countrymen. He made repeated trips, surmounted all difficulties, and succeeded in landing them on his own territory.

After being hospitably treated by Glass and his company for three months, the survivors obtained a passage to the Cape, all except a young sailor named White, who had formed an attachment to one of the servant girls on board, and who, in all the miseries which had been endured, had been her constant protector and companion; whilst gratitude on her part prevented her wishing to leave him. Both chose to remain, and were forthwith adopted as free citizens of the little community.

THE ALBION.

THIS first-class packet-ship traded between New York and Liverpool, and was of 447 tons register, with a crew, including officers, numbering twenty-five. On the occasion of her fatal voyage she set out from New York on the 1st of April 1822, carrying twenty-three cabin and six steerage passengers, making a total of fifty-four persons on board. For twenty days the voyage was prosecuted with favourable weather, and about one o'clock on the afternoon of Sunday the 21st land was made; the Fastnet Rock being then distant about three leagues. About two o'clock the ship made Cape Clear, distant about two leagues, and shortly after the atmosphere became thick and foggy, with the wind blowing fresh and heavy squalls from the southward, until the gale increased so much as to render the shortening of sail occasionally necessary. At four P.M. the vessel was running under double-reefed topsails, foresail, and mainsail, when the gale carried away the foreyard and split the fore-topsail. Some of the crew were now sent to get down the pieces of the broken yard, and to get another yard up. As the gale increased, steps were taken to enable the vessel to weather the storm by taking in the mainsail and mizzen-topsail, and setting the main-topsails. Night coming on, the decks were cleared for working the ship, and at half-past eight the wind was blowing with augmented energy, when a heavy sea was shipped which threw the *Albion* on her beam-ends and carried away the main-mast by the deck. When the officers and crew had so far recovered from the shock which this disaster had occasioned, they at once tried to grapple with the difficulties of their situation, and it was found that considerable damage had been done by the tremendous wave which had swept over the ship. The decks had been cleared of everything that had offered a barrier to the destructive force of the sea. The mizzen and foretop masts had been broken aloft; the boats, cabouse-house, binnacle, and bulwarks had been washed away; while the wave had stove-in all the hatches, state-rooms, and bulwarks in the cabin, besides deluging all the lower parts of the unfortunate packet. But unhappily the rage of the ocean had not been vented only upon the vessel and her fittings, for it was found that six of the seamen, together with a cabin passenger, had been carried overboard by the heavy sea. Personal narratives of the calamity, and of circumstances connected therewith, were afterwards given by two of the sufferers, as well as by gentlemen who resided near the coast upon which the ship was afterwards dashed.

In relating the occurrences, the mate of the *Albion*, Mr. Henry Cammyer, said :—The ship being unmanageable, and the sea making a complete breach over her, we were obliged to lash ourselves to the pumps, and being in total darkness, without correct compasses, we could not tell how the ship's head lay. The axes being swept away, we had no means of clearing the wreck. About one o'clock in the morning we made the light of the Old Head of Kinsale, but could not ascertain how it bore ; and at two we found the ship was embayed. The captain anticipated our melancholy fate, and called all the passengers up who had not before been on deck. Their state was pitiable. Many of them had received considerable injury when the sea first struck the ship, and were scarcely able to come on deck ; others had been incessantly assisting at the pumps. It is an interesting fact that Miss Powell, an amiable young lady on board, was desirous to be allowed to take her turn at the pumps. One gentleman, who had been extremely ill during the passage, Mr. William Everhart of Chester, Penn., was too feeble to crawl to the deck without assistance, but strange to say, he was the only cabin passenger who was saved.

Our situation at that moment is indescribable, and I can scarcely dwell upon, much less attempt to detail, its horrors. About three o'clock the ship struck on a reef, her upper works beat in over the rocks, and in about half-an-hour after coming in over the first reef she parted midships, and her quarter-deck drifted in on the top of the inside ledge immediately under the cliffs. Up to the period of her parting, nearly twenty persons were clinging to the wreck, among whom were two females, Mrs. Pye and Miss Powell. Captain Williams had, with several others, been swept away soon after she struck ; a circumstance which may be attributed to the very extraordinary exertions which he used to the last moment for the preservation of the lives of the unfortunate passengers and crew.

A short time before she parted, myself and six of the crew got away from the vessel. After gaining a rock in a very exhausted state, I was washed off, but by the assistance of Providence was enabled, before the return of the sea, to regain it ; and before I could attempt to climb the cliff, which was nearly perpendicular, I was obliged to lie down to regain a little of my strength, after the severe bruises and contusions I had received on the body and feet. One of the passengers, Col. Augustine J. Prevost, reached the rock with me alive, but he was, together with one of the stewards, washed off and drowned. Some of the passengers were suffocated on deck and in the fore-rigging, while others must have been destroyed by an anchor which was loose on the forecastle before the ship parted. It is scarcely possible to describe the devastation that followed. The entire cargo, consisting of cotton, rice, turpentine, and beeswax, together with a quantity of silver and gold to a large amount, was in all directions beaten to pieces by the severity of the sea, without the possibility of saving any of the merchandise or specie. Shortly after we got up the cliffs, my poor ship-mates and myself made our way to the cottage of a peasant family, who relieved our sufferings to the extent of the humble means at their command.

Mr. William Everhart of Pennsylvania, who was the only cabin passenger saved from the wreck, gave a graphic narrative of events that excited much interest at the period, and his statement, slightly condensed, is as follows:—Up to the 21st of April the voyage had been prosperous and plea-sant for the season, though I had suffered much from sea-sickness, and was almost constantly confined to my room. It was supposed that the storm of the day was over; we were near to the coast, and all hands flattered themselves that in a short time we would reach our destined harbour. But about nine o'clock in the evening a heavy sea struck the ship, swept several seamen from the deck, carried away her masts, and stove in her hatchways, so that every wave which passed over her ran into the hold without anything to stop it; the railings were carried away, as well as the wheel for steering. In short, that fatal wave left the *Albion* a wreck. She was then about twenty miles from the shore, and Captain Williams steadily and coolly gave his orders; he cheered the passengers and crew with the hope that the wind would shift, and before morning blow off the shore. The sea was very rough, and the vessel unmanageable; and the passengers were obliged to be tied to the pumps, so that they might work them. All who could do no good on deck retired below, but the water was knee-deep in the cabin, and the furniture floating about rendered the situation dangerous and dreadful.

All night long the wind blew a gale directly on shore, towards which the *Albion* was drifting at the rate of about three miles an hour. The complete hopelessness of our situation was known to few except Captain Williams. The coast was familiar to him; and he must have seen, in despair and horror, throughout the night, the certainty of our fate. At length the ocean, dashing and roaring upon the precipice of rocks, told us that our hour was come. Captain Williams summoned all on deck, and briefly told us that the ship must soon strike; it was impossible to preserve her. I was the last to leave the cabin. Some, particularly the females, expressed their terror in wild shrieks. Major Gough of the British army remarked, that "death, come as he would, was an unwelcome messenger, but we must meet him like men." Very little was said by the others; the men waited the expected shock in silence. General Lefebvre Desnouettes during the voyage had evidently wished to remain without particular observation; and to prevent his being known, besides taking passage under a feigned name, had suffered his beard to grow during the whole voyage. He had the misfortune to be much bruised before the ship struck, and one of his arms was broken, which disabled him from exertion if it could have been of any avail. It is not possible to conceive the horrors of our situation. The relentless blast impelled us towards the fatal shore; the ship was a wreck; the raging of the billows against the precipice on which we were driving, brought back from the caverns and the rocks the hoarse and melancholy warnings of destruction and death. The stoutest heart amongst us must have quaked now in utter despair, and just at the grey of dawn the *Albion* struck.

The perpendicular precipice of rocks upon which we had

been driven is nearly two hundred feet in height; the sea, beating for ages against it, has worn large caverns in its base, into which the waves rushed violently, sending back a deep and hollow sound, then running out in various directions, formed whirlpools of great violence. For a perch or two from the precipice rocks rise out of the water, broad at bottom and sharp at top; on one of these the *Albion* first struck, the next wave threw her farther on the rock, the third farther still, until, nearly balanced, she swung round, and her stern was driven against another reef near in shore. In this perilous situation every wave made a complete breach over her, and many of my fellow-passengers and the crew were drowned on deck. A woman whom I could not distinguish fell near me, and cried for help. I let go my hold and raised her, but another wave came, and as she was too far exhausted to sustain herself, she sank on the deck. At one time, fifteen or sixteen corpses lay near the bows of the ship.

As I found that the stern of the vessel was higher out of the water than the stem, and that the waves had consequently less power over the former part, I went aft, and was enabled to scrutinise our position and the damage that the *Albion* had sustained. I soon perceived that the bottom had been broken out of the ship. The heavy articles must have sunk, and the cotton and lighter articles were floating around, dashed by every wave against the rocks. Presently the ship broke in two, and all those who remained near the bow were lost. Several from the stern of the ship had got on the side of the precipice, and were hanging by the crags as well as they could. Although weakened by previous sickness and present suffering, I made an effort and got upon the rock, where I was obliged to stand upon one foot— the only hold I could obtain. I saw several of the other passengers around me, and among the rest Colonel Prevost, who, upon seeing me take my station, observed, "Here is another poor fellow." But the waves, rolling heavily against them, and often dashing the spray fifty feet above their heads, gradually swept those who had thus taken refuge one by one away: and one poor fellow, finding that he was losing his hold, grasped my leg and nearly pulled me from my place. Weak, sick, and benumbed as I was, I stood for several hours on one foot on a little crag, with the billows dashing over me. As soon as it was light, and the tide had ebbed so as to render it possible to make an effort for my rescue, the people on shore descended the rocks as far as they could, and dropped me a rope, which I fastened around my body, and was drawn up to a place of safety. Of twenty-three cabin passengers I alone escaped, and I was speedily conveyed to the hospitable residence of Mr. James B. Gibbons, where I lay for several weeks exceedingly ill from the effects of exposure to the elements upon that disastrous night. Had I been brother to my kind host I could not have been treated more tenderly.

About four in the morning information had been given to Mr. Purcell of Garretstown, to the effect that a ship had been cast upon the rocks that fringed the dairy-farms of a neighbouring proprietor, Mr. Rochfort. Mr. Purcell immediately proceeded to the spot with such assistance as he could command, and the following is his description of the scene that awaited him:—About the centre of the two farms I found a vessel on the rocks, under a very high cliff. As it was spring-tide, and approaching high-water, with a strong gale blowing, the sea ran mountains high; however, I descended with some men as far down the cliff as the dashing of the sea would permit us to go with safety, and there viewed the harrowing spectacle of five dead bodies stretched on the deck, and four fellow-creatures distractedly calling for assistance, which we were unable to render, as certain death to us would have attended the attempt. Of those we thus saw perilously situated one was a female.

Although it was impossible to hear her words of appeal, on account of the roaring of the wind and waves, yet from her supplicating gestures and outstretched arms we judged her to be calling piteously for our aid. At this time the greater portion of the ship lay upon a rock, and part of the stern where the poor creature stood projected over a narrow creek that separated the rock upon which the hull rested from another rock at a short distance. Here the sea broke over the vessel with the utmost fury, yet the hull seemed to have a secure hold of the reef, a circumstance that astonished me exceedingly. We soon discovered, however, that the *Albion's* hull had been broken across, at the point where it projected over the creek, and after a succession of tremendous waves had dashed against it, this portion of the ship rolled into the sea, and we had to witness the heart-rending spectacle of the poor woman's death, while unable to put forth an effort to save her. Towards the stern of the vessel lay three men, one of whom clung to a mast that leaned over towards the cliff. After several fruitless attempts to reach this man, we at length succeeded in throwing a rope, the end of which he secured, and we by that means brought him safely ashore. Another of the survivors we also saved, but the continuous dashing of the waves over their bodies eventually put a period to the sufferings of the others.

Mr. Marks, the American Consul, on hearing of the calamity, hastened to the spot, and immediately adopted measures for the benefit of the survivors of the crew, and the salvage of the *Albion's* cargo and specie. As the dead lay upon the beach, they were identified by the mate, and to each corpse was affixed its individual name. The consul provided a coffin for each, and all were buried in a row within the churchyard of Templetrine, four miles from Kinsale, and one from the fatal precipice at the bottom of which the *Albion* had stranded—a clergyman of the established Church of Ireland officiating at the mournful ceremony. Among the bodies washed ashore was that of a beautiful French lady, one of the passengers by the vessel. The body was first discovered by a poor Irish boy, who found it entirely nude amongst the rocks, and decently covered the inanimate form with his own coat. It was related of others of the country people that they in several instances also took off their own clothing to wrap round the shipwrecked seamen who were happily saved from a watery grave. Of the fifty-four persons on board the *Albion*, forty-two perished. The twelve survivors experienced great kindness at the hands of the Irish gentlemen and cottagers upon whose iron-bound coast the sufferers had been cast. The almost miraculous preservation of Mr. Everhart became the topic of the day, and when he repaired to Liverpool after his convalescence, the people crowded around him, to catch a glimpse of the only passenger saved from the wreck.

THE MISTICOES.

IN the earlier years of the century, the hateful profession of the pirate offered attractions to the evil-disposed and daring of all nations, on account of the lucrative rewards that were supposed to accrue from the successful prosecution of the iniquitous calling, as well as the adventurous character thereof. Of all the nationalities whose sons have from time to time been prominently identified with the nefarious trade, none have surpassed the Greek, either in the fiendish disregard of all moral and social law, or the cruelty with which the pirates of that nation have conducted their operations. To the honour of our country, large sums have been expended by us in the endeavour to sweep the seas clear of such pests to the merchantmen of the world, and the destruction of many piratical vessels, and the execution of their crews, were almost solely to be attributed to the zealous action taken by successive English governments to that end. The following narrative is from an officer on board a British man-of-war which had been specially employed in that service :—

His Majesty's ships *Seringapatam* and *Cambrian* were lying at anchor in Orcos Bay, in the island of Negropont.

About three o'clock in the afternoon of the 31st of January 1825, a vessel hove in sight, about eight or nine miles distant. The telescopes were immediately turned to that quarter, and the strange sail appeared to be an Ionian brig, with every stitch of canvas set, and coming down the channel between Negropont and the main.

Nothing occurred to excite any particular attention until the man at the mast-head called out that the brig was followed by two smaller vessels. In a few minutes we descried, emerging from a tongue of land, two Greek misticoes with every sail set, and plying their oars in chase of the brig. These craft were instantly recognised as pirates, the very gentry we were on the look-out for in that station. Although aware of this, they had the audacity to near our anchorage, and in sight of our ships still continued the chase, evidently gaining on the brig, which they, no doubt, calculated on taking under our very guns. However, they seemed to think they had carried the joke quite far enough, and, knowing that our men-of-war had pretty long arms, they at last hauled their wind, and stood back with all speed for their lurking-places. The Ionian then slackened sail.

Our men, little anticipating that any work was to be carved out for them that day, were sprawling about the main-deck, listless, and longing for something to do, when "Out boats!" sounded through the ship. The sound was electric. The boats' crews were on their feet in a moment, and the looks of the others showed how they envied them their share in the job. The men were now seen bustling up the quarter-deck for their cutlasses, which they busily buckled on, while the gunner distributed a pistol and ammunition to each man. They were in great glee; it was quite a treat to Jack.

The boats were soon lowered, and additional ammunition, provisions, and a small cask of water stowed away in each; the surgeon and his traps were not forgotten, and a party of marines completed the crew. About four o'clock P.M. the boats, eight in number, and carrying about one hundred and twenty men, pushed off from the ships, under the command of Lieutenant Marsham, of the *Cambrian.*

The afternoon was beautiful, the weather warm, with a moderate breeze. We proceeded at a rapid rate. The pirates were a long way ahead, and looked like specks on the horizon. We neared the Ionian brig in a few hours. I do not recollect if any of our boats boarded her to make any inquiries. There was no time for palavering. As evening approached we had evidently gained fast on the misticoes. Soon after the moon shone out with all her usual brilliancy in southern climes, and lit us on our chase. There was little talk; a whisper now and then, the dip of the oars, and the regular monotonous sound of the simultaneous pull in the thwarts alone broke the silence, unless when the rowers were relieved.

Six hours and a-half had elapsed since we quitted the ships. The Greeks were apparently making for the land, distant about a mile, all sails set, and pulling as hard as they could. We were coming up with them hand over hand; our boats were all close together, when a discharge of musketry was poured into us by the large mistico. One poor fellow, who had been relieved from the oars a short time before, was shot through the head. He dropped in the boat like a stone. Several others were wounded, two or three in the arms, which caused one almost to drop his oar in the water, if the man beside him had not caught it. His place was supplied in an instant. Another and another discharge followed, with many single shots. Two more fell —one hit in the shoulder, the shot passing into his body. The men were roused to fury. Our marines returned the fire. The Greeks swarmed round the sides of their vessels, taking deliberate aim at our boats. Every sinew was strained; the boats were impelled forward with redoubled

velocity. The cutlasses were drawn, the men hastily bind-
ing them round their wrists by means of a leather thong,
technically called "the becket."

Our boats swept round the misticoes on every side, the
Greeks blazing away at us, whilst the men could hardly
restrain themselves on their seats, muttering curses at the
loss they had already sustained from the impudent rascals.
One man at the head of the boat, stretching forward to pull
quicker alongside the large mistico, was struck unawares by
a Greek from the deck, and severely cut by a yataghan, a
crooked sabre, cutting like a sickle.

The men were already on their feet, the oars pulled in,
and a rush was made up the sides of the Greek, the cutlasses dangling loose from their wrists by the becket. In a
moment half-a-dozen men were on the enemy's deck, hack-
ing right and left; the rest were scrambling up like wolves,
eager for revenge, each helping and pushing up the man
that chanced to precede him, to clear the way for himself.
I was hoisted up myself in the same rough-and-ready way.
The men were cheering, not loudly, but deeply, as if
choked with fury; most of them were young hands, and
had never been in a skirmish of the sort before; but they
were willing workmen. A small party ran forward along
with me; no one ever dreamed of looking behind to see if
he was followed by the rest. No man, to my knowledge,
fired his pistol; all seemed to rely on their trusty cutlass.
The Greeks were driven to the extremity of their deck, con-
tending boldly enough with our men, who, however, to use
a pugilistic phrase, "would not be denied." The simple
checked shirts and white trousers of our sailors formed a
striking contrast to the rich-coloured garments of the
Greeks, many of whom were Albanians, all armed with
muskets, pistols, and yataghans. The latter stood no
chance with the cutlass, and its blows could be easily
parried. Many came just in time to rid a comrade of his

opponent, by lending an additional hand in cutting him down, pushing on to another quarter where the work seemed plenty, trampling on the people who lay sprawling on the deck, and slipping in the blood that already besmeared the planks. The sudden report of the muskets, the short rapid crack of pistols, the clash of steel, and the dull heavy fall of the blows, were the chief sounds heard in the scuffle, along with the sturdy stamping of the combatants, and occasional cheers of the men coming from the boats and joining their comrades.

Many Greeks sprang on the ship's sides, and then, plunging into the sea, made for the shore, distant about a quarter of a mile; others attempting the same feat were cut down by our fellows in the very act of springing overboard, whilst many were pulled back and despatched. The fury of our men knew no bounds, and it was no time to attempt to restrain them. They were mad for the moment, as men usually are in such hand-to-hand work. A tall fine-looking pirate presented a pistol at my head and fired; ere another moment elapsed he was cloven down to the left eye by one of the men, a stout muscular seaman, who always passed for an Englishman, though believed to be an Irishman. This man was very conspicuous for the power of his arm and his dexterity in the use of his weapon. The pirates attempted to guard their heads by means of their yataghans; this man broke through guard and skull at once with a single blow. Several others displayed similar strength of arm. All the men cut at the heads and shoulders of the pirates; they seldom or never stabbed. The latter manœuvre was too Frenchified and scholar-like for Jack, who hit hatchet fashion, felling the Greeks like cattle. Many of the latter, on being wounded, attempted to scramble out of the fray, and seek shelter apart from the combatants. "*Christiano! Christiano!*" they shouted; but their cry for quarter came, I fear, too late, and with a bad grace. The blood of the

sailors was on fire; the fate of their messmates stimulated
them to ample revenge; and pirates, of all others, are the
least entitled to share the mercy they scarcely ever grant.
The cries of "*Christiano!*" fell upon deaf ears at that
moment. "Too late, ye divils!" shouted some of the men,
following up their words by the *coup-de-grace.* In general
they went silently to work—the silence of a thorough-bred
bulldog.

The struggle was soor decided. The Greeks flung down
their arms, and the wrath of the men was at length, and
with difficulty, restrained by the interposition of their
officers. All the pirates who survived were wounded,
except a young lad, who had been spared. The smaller
mistico had been speedily carried. The moon, which had
shone calmly on the fray, now convoyed us back to our
ships, which we reached at two in the morning.

THE KENT.

ON the 19th of February 1825, a splendid ship of 1350 tons left the Downs on her first voyage, having on board twenty officers, three hundred and forty-four soldiers, forty-three women, and sixty-six children of the 31st Regiment of the Line. The vessel also carried twenty private passengers and a crew of one hundred and forty-eight, including the officers. Fine weather prevailing for several days after sailing, the *Kent* went swiftly on her way, and gave hope to all of a speedy arrival at Bengal, whither she was bound, before proceeding to China, her ultimate destination.

The expectations of the voyagers were doomed to disappointment however, for on the 28th a strong gale blew from the south-west, which increased in violence until the 1st of March, when the captain ordered the topgallant-yards to be struck, and the ship lay-to, under a triple-reefed maintop-sail only, with the dead-lights in. They were now in the Bay of Biscay, and much annoyance was experienced from the rolling of the vessel, aggravated by the deadweight of some hundreds tons of shot and shell that formed a part of the cargo in the hold. At each lurch of the hull the main chains were thrown under water, while the various articles of furniture in the cabin were dashed about with considerable force. Apprehensions being excited as to the security of the stowage, a descent was made into the hold by an officer and two seamen, whose movements among the cargo were directed under the light of a patent lantern, which had been taken down with them for the purpose. After a time the lantern was passed up to be trimmed, and again taken down, when the officer found that a cask of spirits had been forced adrift, and for the purpose of securing it in a safe position the sailors were told to fetch some wooden billets, the officer meanwhile steadying the cask with one of his hands, and holding the lantern in the other. But suddenly the vessel gave a heavy lurch and the light dropped from the officer's hand. In his eagerness to recover the lantern he quitted his hold of the cask, which was at once stove in, and a scene of the most terrible peril and agony immediately resulted.

Before the lantern could be recovered the spirits from the broken cask had reached the flame, and the subtle fluid was soon in a blaze; while the smoke ascending from the hatchway told but too plainly to those on deck the ominous character of the accident. Instantly the alarm was given, the captain and officers of the doomed ship were at their posts, and all that skill and prudence could suggest to arrest the progress of the fire was speedily attempted, by means of the pumps, water-buckets, and wet sails. It soon became apparent to the officers and crew, however, that the only hope that remained of overcoming the deadly enemy that had found a lodgment in the hold, lay in the thought that so long as the flames were confined to the spot where the fire had originated, a number of water-barrels stowed in the vicinity might offer an effectual barrier to the spread of the conflagration. But even that feeble ground for hopefulness was ere long to be dispelled, for the heavy columns of dusky smoke that issued from the hatchways, and hung around the shrouds and rigging, showed that the only chance of the safety of between six and seven hundred human beings was in the providential interposition of some passing vessel.

The flames having reached the cable tier, the lower decks were ordered to be scuttled, the combing of the hatches to be cut, and the lower ports to be opened for the entrance of the waves as they beat against the side of the vessel. Unfortunately, several of the sick soldiers, who had their quarters on the lower deck, together with a woman and some children, lost their lives, through their inability to reach the upper deck before the great influx of water came to check for a time the ravages of the fire. But while the danger of the explosion was considerably lessened, the ship became so water-logged that it was evident that she must speedily founder in the deep.

An awful scene was now presented on the deck of the burning ship, for death, in one or another of its most terrible forms, was now before the helpless passengers and crew. Fear-stricken and almost nude, more than six hundred persons were huddled together, in fearful expectancy of being blown into atoms, or of sinking into the remorseless waves. In tearful resignation some prepared to meet their impending doom; while others, losing their self-possession, gave vent to the wild ravings of hopeless despair. Many engaged in external acts of devotion; some falling upon their knees in prayer, while others reverently crossed themselves, as the waves dashed in fury against the hull of the *Kent,* and deluged her horrified living freight with seething foam. To add to the terrors of the hour the fastenings of the binnacle were torn asunder by the straining of the timbers upon which it had rested, and the fragments were scattered over the surging mass of men, women, and children. In the forlorn hope of discovering a friendly sail in the distance, a seaman was now sent aloft, and many eyes were eagerly directed to the foretop, as the man took up his position therein, and gazed in every direction across the expanse of angry water.

After some minutes of acute suspense to those on the deck, the sailor discerned a sail on the lee-bow, and, waving his hat in token of his discovery, shouted the cheering intelligence, which was instantly responded to by three ringing cheers from his shipmates and the soldiers, while steps were at once taken to attract the notice of the strangers. Flags of distress were speedily hoisted, and minute-guns were fired, until the distant ship showed the British ensign in answer to the appeal which had been made to the humanity of her commander, and crowding all sail she bore down upon the hapless *Kent.* The suspense on board the latter vessel now became unutterable, for each moment the peril to her passengers and crew became more imminent and deadly. The fire now raged with fury beneath the timbers upon which they stood, while the running of a tremendous sea rendered the work of extricating themselves from their horrible position difficult in the extreme, even with assistance from the barque that was now speeding onwards to their relief.

The approaching vessel proved to be the *Cambria*, of 200 tons burthen, and bound to Vera Cruz. Upon getting within hailing distance of the burning ship, the captain deemed it necessary for the safety of the *Cambria* to keep apart from the *Kent*, consequently the passage between the latter and her deliverer had to be effected by means of the boats, which were launched as quickly as possible after the *Cambria* had lain-to. To prevent any panic, or rush of the soldiers and seamen on the *Kent*, the officers of the 31st stood with their swords drawn, while all the ladies, and as many of the soldiers' wives and children as could be stowed therein, were placed in the first boat that was intended to leave for

the side of the *Cambria.* While this embarkation was proceeding in painful silence, twice was the cry raised from
the chains that the boat was swamping, but with much
difficulty she was pushed from the dangerous proximity of
the *Kent,* and was eagerly watched from the poop of that
vessel, as the tiny craft, with its crowded freight, was rowed
by willing hands in the direction of the barque.

After a heavy pull during a space of twenty minutes the
side of the *Cambria* was reached, but another and greater
difficulty had still to be overcome, as the heavy waves
threatened to stave-in the fragile boat by repeated blows
against the vessel. At length, however, all the children
were thrown on board the *Cambria,* where manly arms were
ready to receive them ; and the women, being told to seize
every favourable opportunity afforded by the heaving of the
boat, soon learnt to grasp at the proper moment the friendly
hands that were extended over the bulwarks for the purpose of assisting them also to escape from the perils which
had menaced them upon the burning ship and surging ocean.
Thus were all the women and children who left the *Kent* in
the first boat mercifully placed beyond the reach of immediate danger, the gratifying result being also accomplished
without the occurrence of a single accident.

But in the meantime the crew and remaining passengers
of the *Kent* had watched with breathless anxiety the exciting proceedings, until their own danger had been almost
wholly forgotten in the desire to see the safety of so many
feeble women and little ones happily secured. That being
accomplished, the presence of the devouring element beneath
their feet was again realised by all with terrible intensity,
and the most active measures were taken to further the
escape of other boat-loads of their number. When the first
boat returned from the *Cambria,* it was found to be impossible to come alongside the burning ship, consequently
the women and children, two at a time, were lowered by

ropes from the stern. While this proceeded many were repeatedly plunged under the waves, and three of the six boats were swamped. Some of the men in their attempts to reach the boats were drowned. One or two lost their lives, as it was surmised, through being encumbered with the weight of spoils they had thought to secure along with their own safety. A poor fellow fell through the hatchway into the flames. Another was crushed to death between the vessel and the boat that he was endeavouring to enter, while some who were unable to reach the *Cambria*, through the buffeting of the waves, also perished. Night was now rapidly approaching, the flames had fastened upon the sides of the ship, while many of the soldiers and crew were still on board, a prey to agonising pain and thirst from the raging heat, and in paralysing fear of the explosion of the magazine, which all knew could not now be long delayed.

In order to hasten the removal of the remainder, a rope was suspended from the extremity of the spanker boom, along which the men were successively urged to proceed by their officers, and then to glide down the rope into the boat beneath. But that could only be accomplished at considerable peril, for each boat was much tossed about by the action of the waves, and the poor fellows, after swinging for a time in the air, frequently found themselves plunged under the water, or dashed against the boat's side, upon letting go their hold of the rope. So many failed in this way to reach the craft in safety, that their companions chose rather to throw themselves from the stern windows on the upper deck than run the risk of being at once dashed to pieces. In the midst of the most trying circumstances, the respect that a British soldier invariably entertains for his officers was made prominently apparent. A box of oranges had been discovered, and the fruit were being shared out to the parched and blistered individuals who yet remained;

but the soldiers refused to partake until their officers had received a share of the succulent morsels.

The night was advancing, and Captain Cobb, the commander, urged the survivors on board of the *Kent* to make an effort to leave their fearful position without unnecessary delay. The wreck was now twelve feet below the usual water-mark, and the boat that was approaching from the *Cambria* appeared capable of holding all that remained. But those who stood around the captain seemed as if struck powerless with terror, and wholly unable to put forth any endeavour to save themselves. Of the officers of the 31st three only were left, and they now got into the boat that was on its last errand of mercy to the survivors. Captain Cobb refused to leave his ship until he had made another effort to persuade the fear-stricken beings to enter the boat along with him. Finding his orders and entreaties alike unavailing, the noble and humane commander swung himself, by means of a rope that hung near, over the heads of the unfortunate men, and dropped into the sea, whence he was rescued and conveyed aboard the *Cambria*, where he and all who had been saved from the burning ship were treated with the kindest consideration and care.

Having accomplished everything which it was deemed prudent under the circumstances to attempt, the captain of the *Cambria* set sail, and as that vessel receded from the ill-fated *Kent*, the men and women who had been delivered from a terrible death beheld with intense anguish the flames rising over the hull of the ship, on which too many of their friends or companions had been left, as it was thought, to certain destruction. But the fire, spreading with awful rapidity, seized the masts and rigging, and thus lighted a beacon that might be seen at a considerable distance in the surrounding darkness. The following account of the rescue of some of the sufferers who had been too paralysed to reach the *Cambria*, is condensed from the

narrative of Captain Bibby, who was attracted to the scene
of the conflagration with his vessel, and rendered all the
aid to the survivors that humanity could desire :—

About twelve o'clock at night on the 1st of March, a
bright light, proceeding apparently from a ship on fire, was
observed in the horizon by the watch of the barque *Caroline*, on her passage from Alexandria to Liverpool. As it
had blown strong on the preceding day, the *Caroline* was
at the time under double-reefed main and fore top-sails,
main-trysail, and foretop-mast staysail, close upon a wind
with a heavy sea going. Word was immediately passed to
Captain Bibby, who instantly bore up, and setting his main-
topgallant-sail, ran down towards the spot.

About two o'clock, when every eye was intensely fixed
upon the increasing brightness in the sky, a sudden jet of
vivid light darted upwards, evidently caused by an explosion,
though they were yet too far off to hear any report. In
half-an-hour the *Caroline* had approached sufficiently near
to make out the wreck of a large vessel lying head to wind,
of which nothing remained but the ribs and frame timbers,
which, marking the outlines of a double line of ports and
quarter-galleries, afforded too much reason to fear that the
burning skeleton was the remnant of a first-class East
Indiaman or line-of-battle ship. The flames, however, had
so completely consumed every other external feature, that
nothing could be ascertained with accuracy. She was burnt
nearly to the water's edge : but, becoming gradually lighter
as the internal timbers and fallen decks and spars were consumed, she still floated, pitching majestically as she rose
and fell over the long-rolling swell of the bay. Her
appearance was that of an immense cauldron or cage of
buoyant basket-work, formed of the charred and blackened
ribs, naked and stripped of every plank, encircling an un-
interrupted mass of flame, not however of uniform intensity,
as from two or three points, probably where the hatchways

13

had supplied an additional quantity of loose fuel, brighter emissions were bursting upwards. Above, and far to leeward, the atmosphere was a cloud of curling smoke, the whole sprinkled with myriads of sparks and burning flakes of lighter materials, thrown up without intermission, and scattered by the wind over the sky and waves.

As the *Caroline* bore down, part of a mast and some spars were observed rising and falling, and almost grinding under the starboard, or what might be called the weather-quarter of the wreck; for although, as has been stated, it rode nearly head to wind in the course of drifting, these spars being fast to the after-part in some degree gave the stern frame a slight cant to windward. The *Caroline* coming right down before the wind was in a few minutes brought across the bows of the wreck, and as near as was consistent with safety. At that moment, when to all appearance no human being could be supposed to retain life within the sphere of such a conflagration, a shout was heard, and almost at the same instant several figures were observed clinging to the above-mentioned mast and spars. From their low situation, almost upon a level with the water, and the rapidity of the barque's motion, she could not have been long visible before they hailed. The top-gallant-sail was taken in, the foretop-mast staysail lowered, and the ship's course continued under the top-sails and try-sail to leeward, at such a distance as to avoid the danger of falling flakes and sparks, and then the foretop-sail was braced aback and the vessel hove-to. In the meantime the jolly boat was lowered from the stern, and manned by Mr. Matthew Walker, the mate, and four seamen, who pushed off without hesitation and pulled for the wreck. Masts, spars, chests, packages, furniture, etc., were dashing about, but the men persevered, and having approached within a few yards of the stern, they caught sight of a man as he clung to a rope or portion of wreck close under the ship's counter. As the stern-frame rose with the swell, he was jerked upwards and suspended above the water, to meet a more dreadful fate, for streams of flame gushed forth through the casings of the gun-room ports and scorched the poor sufferer, whose cries of agony could be distinctly heard. The *Caroline's* men pushed at once under the stern-frame, but, when almost within their grasp, the fire severed the rope, and the man sunk to be seen no more. Efforts were then directed to save the men on the mast, when six of the nearest were secured and carried off to the *Caroline.*

The first trip occupied a space of about half-an-hour, and no sooner were the six passengers disposed of than Mr. Walker again shoved off for the wreck. No survivors having been observed on other parts, those on the mast became the exclusive objects of attention, and six more were taken aboard. For the third and last time the little jolly-boat pushed off. But when struggling against the head-sea, before they could reach the mast, the anticipated and dreaded event took place. The fiery pile was observed to settle slowly on the waves and gradually disappear. In another instant the hitherto bright and burning atmosphere was involved in utter darkness, rendered still more awful by the contrast; a dense cloud of black smoke lingered like a shroud over the spot, and to the loud crackling of burning timbers and rustling of flames a death-like silence had succeeded.

Before the burning wreck had disappeared, however, the mate of the *Caroline* had marked its position on the water by the aid of a star; but as it seemed impossible to continue the search for survivors in the darkness, especially as the floating wreckage threatened the safety of those who were engaged in the work, Mr. Walker ordered his men to hang upon their oars; and during the night they gave repeated shouts, so as to encourage any who might be riding upon spars to hope for succour at daybreak. As the first rays of light shot up from the horizon, the mast of the *Kent* again became visible. Four human forms were discerned amongst the cordage and top-work, but they were motionless. As Mr. Walker and his men approached with the boat, signs of animation were discovered in two of the bodies ; the others were dead. The still breathing men were conveyed to the *Caroline*, where, by careful attention and nursing, they were restored to life. Altogether, Captain Bibby and his crew were the means of saving fourteen sufferers by this awful calamity.

THE COMET.

O N the 21st of October 1825, a steamboat collision occurred on the Clyde, and the catastrophe sent a thrill of horror through the country, with the intelligence that in all probability the lives of seventy individuals had been sacrificed, through the carelessness or blundering of some one in charge of one of the vessels at the fatal moment. The steamboats concerned in the calamity were named respectively the *Ayr* and the *Comet.* The former was a luggage-boat of considerable power that traded between Glasgow and the town of Ayr, and was commanded by Captain MacClelland. The *Comet* carried goods and passengers to and from Glasgow and Inverness, and on the melancholy occasion was proceeding to the great port of the West of Scotland with a large number of passengers on board; although the sum total of her living freight was never accurately ascertained, by reason that the steward lost his life through the collision, and he was the only person to whom the duty had been entrusted of keeping a record of those who took a passage in the unfortunate vessel. It may reasonably be concluded, however, that at least sixty persons left Inverness in the boat, and that many

more had come on board at the various landing-places at
which she touched on her way to the Clyde.

Under the command of Captain MacInnes, the *Comet*
started from Inverness at six o'clock on the morning of the
18th of October 1825, and then went on her course by way
of the Caledonian Canal, at the western extremity of which
she arrived on the evening of the same day. Following the
customary rule, the passengers debarked at Fort William,
where they spent the night. On the following morning the
steamboat again proceeded on her journey, and arrived at
the Crinan Canal at a late hour in the evening. At Crinan,
the passengers again slept on shore at a small inn near the
entrance to the canal. Next morning, at six o'clock, the
Comet was again got under weigh ; but as the narrowness of
the canal precluded rapid progress, and a great number of
locks increased the delay, the vessel did not reach Lochgilp-
head, although only nine miles distant, till ten o'clock in the
forenoon. Owing probably to some miscalculation or interruption in passing through the canal, they had not arrived
in time to find a depth of water sufficient to float the
steamer out of the basin into the open loch ; consequently
they were compelled to wait the reflowing of the tide. At
six in the evening there was water on the bar sufficient
to float the vessel over, and they again set sail. At this
time Captain MacInnes expressed himself as confident,
wind and tide permitting, to reach Greenock at midnight.
There he proposed to stay till daybreak, and then run up to
Glasgow early next morning. From the progress which the
vessel subsequently made through Loch Fyne and the Kyles
of Bute, and her proximity to Greenock at the time of the
collision, it would appear that the captain's calculations had
been tolerably accurate. On emerging from the Kyles of Bute,
the strait that separates the island of Bute from the mainland, the wind blew freshly ; and the captain was urged by
some English gentlemen on board to touch at Rothesay, where

they wished to land. MacInnes at first showed a disinclination to do so, on account of the great leeway which he would have to make up, but at length he was prevailed upon to comply with a request that conduced in some measure to the loss of his vessel.

From Rothesay the *Comet* proceeded on her way up the Clyde. A fresh wind still blew, and there was some sea, but not so much as to impede the progress of the steamer, or demand more than usual attention from the master and his crew. During the evening, which was exceedingly cold, several of the passengers amused and warmed themselves by dancing on the deck. On the approach of morning the mirth abated, and the majority went below. Early in the night there was moonlight, but shortly before one in the morning the moon set, and the darkness gradually increased, though it never became so intense as to prevent those on board descrying the hills on both sides of the river. About two o'clock the *Comet* was off Kempoch Point, a headland on the south side of the river, between the Cloch Lighthouse and the village of Gourock, and close to which point vessels usually steer. With a culpable disregard of the commonest precaution no light was displayed on board the steamer, while a jib-sail was set, which in a great measure prevented any but the man on the look-out from seeing directly ahead. According to the most credible statement, Captain MacInnes was on the cabin-deck conversing with individuals near him. Suddenly the man forward called out "A steamboat—helm a-port!" Without further warning the *Comet* received a tremendous shock upon her bow, and before her startled crew were aware from which quarter danger was to be apprehended, she received a second blow, equally terrific, near the larboard paddle-box. The two vessels then drifted asunder, and shortly after a cry of despair from her panic-stricken passengers was heard ascending from the *Comet*. The crowd on her deck had discovered that she was sinking; and in three minutes after the concussion she went down, bow foremost, in about eighteen fathoms of water, and about one hundred and sixty-five yards from the land.

As far as could be ascertained, the two boats were doubling Kempoch Point at the same moment. The *Ayr* had her lights displayed, and the regular look-out had been kept on board. According to his own statement, Captain MacClelland had immediately before the disaster enjoined his crew to be vigilant in the performance of their duties. Both vessels were running with great speed, and for some time after the collision the consternation of the crew of the *Ayr* fully equalled that on board the *Comet*. Two seamen belonging to another vessel who happened to be on board the luggage steamer, were the only individuals who appear to have escaped the general stupefaction that prevailed. These men, with promptitude and intrepidity, instantly prepared to launch a boat with a view to succour the multitude, whose drowning cries were terrible to hear. Unhappily the efforts of the sailors were not seconded, and they found themselves impeded in their generous attempt. When the boat, with one of the men therein, had reached the water, and while the tackling was yet unloosed, the engine began to play, and boat and man were nearly lost. Finding that his vessel had suffered damage, and losing his self-possession in view of the peril to which he found himself exposed, as well as the extent of the general calamity, Captain MacClelland determined to steer from the spot without delay, and return to Greenock. In this resolution he was supported by his crew; and the *Ayr* accordingly bore away, passing in her course over the sunken steamer, and amid the death-shrieks of many of the *Comet's* passengers and crew.

The scene on board the *Comet*, during the short interval she remained above water after the collision, was described by the survivors as truly heart-rending. All who could force their way from the cabins to the deck hurried up in an extremity of terror. Many were aroused from sleep, but only to fall immediately into the sleep of death. Captain MacInnes became instantly aware of the damaged state of his vessel; but suspected that the injury was forward, and he therefore called to the passengers to come aft, trusting thereby that the steamer would be righted, while he ordered the engine to be set on ahead, so as to run the vessel ashore. Neither of these expedients availed, however, and an attempt to get out the yawl proved equally unsuccessful, for the tackling could not be unloosed. The ropes were then cut, when twenty-six or thirty people, who had crowded into the yawl, were precipitated into the water through the capsizing of the boat. The sea was now rushing into the vessel with frightful rapidity, and the water, putting out the fires, stopped the engines. The saddening calamity that ensued was heightened by the manner in which the miserable passengers clung to each other.

On the alarm being given, several wherries immediately put off from Gourock, and their crews exerted themselves to the utmost in the cause of humanity. But the majority of the passengers were soon beyond all earthly aid. The subjoined narrative by one of the survivors presents a vivid picture of the scene on board when the *Comet* went down :—

At the moment the fatal accident took place, Mr. C. A. Anderson, the only cabin-passenger saved, was below. Such of the passengers as were awake were in high spirits, narrating and listening to diverting tales. When the concussion took place, he with others instantly rushed upon deck to learn the cause. In the panic that followed, he, in obedience to the captain's orders to all on board, repaired aft. He was an excellent swimmer, and calculated upon that resource in the last extremity. While standing on the deck, holding by a rope, he was seized round the arm with a convulsive grasp by a female behind him, who was lamenting their

terrible fate. In his perilous situation he endeavoured to
shake the person off, exclaiming, "Let me go!" when,
turning round to disentangle himself, he perceived that she
who had thus seized hold of him was Mrs. Sutherland. His
heart smote him at the sight; and he immediately apologised
to her in the kindest manner for having accosted her so
roughly, being ignorant who it was that addressed him. At
that moment he perceived Captain Sutherland in the act of
throwing off his coat, or cloak, to prepare himself for swimming. Mr. Anderson, not thinking it advisable to let go
his hold of the rope, yet wishing to serve the lady, gave her
a strong shove forward in the direction of the boat astern
as her only chance of safety. What became of the unfortunate couple afterwards he saw not, as he was immediately
compelled to attend to his own safety, by finding the water
covering the deck. He retained his hold of the rope till the
water reached his middle, when a wave rolling over the
Comet carried him off his feet. The packet went down
bow-foremost; and the drowning multitude sent forth the
most appalling screams. A second wave threw his greatcoat over his head and almost suffocated him. For a time
he swam about, ignorant as to where the shore lay and
greatly exhausted. In this state he was seized by the
engineman of the *Comet*, who held him closely. They were
on the point of sinking when they fortunately came in contact with the packet's yawl, floating keel uppermost, with
several individuals clinging thereto. In consequence of
their struggles, the yawl righted, when they got into it,
though it was full of water. Without oars, they were
unable to make an effort to gain the shore. Remaining in
this situation about twenty minutes, they were discovered
by a pilot-boat, to the sides of which they clung, and in this
manner reached the shore greatly exhausted.

THE HELEN MACGREGOR.

THAT noble river, the Mississippi, has unhappily been the scene of many appalling disasters, in connection with the gigantic steamboat traffic upon its waters. Several of these calamities have been so overwhelming in the extent of the mortality which they occasioned as to have left few survivors capable of giving a circumstantial account of the events; and of the earlier boiler explosions on the father of western rivers, that on board the *Helen Macgregor* has become memorable, more by reason of the personal narrative of one of the sufferers thereby than the loss of life caused by the accident, although that was considerable. The following is the passenger's description of the fatal occurrence :—

On the morning of the 24th February 1830, the *Helen Macgregor* stopped at Memphis, on the Mississippi river, to deliver freight and land a number of passengers who resided in that section of the Tennessee. The time occupied in the debarkation could not have exceeded three-quarters of an hour. When the steamer got to the landing-stage, I went ashore to see a gentleman with whom I had some business to perform. I found him on the beach, and after a short conversation I returned to the boat. I recollect looking at my watch as I passed along the gangway. It was half-past eight o'clock. A great number of persons were standing on the boiler-deck: so called from being that part of the upper deck which is situated immediately over the boilers. It was crowded to excess, and presented one dense mass of humanity.

A few minutes after re-embarking we entered the cabin and sat down to breakfast. Although extending the whole length of the cabin, the table was crowded at every point: there being upwards of sixty cabin passengers, among whom were several ladies and children. The number of passengers on board, deck and cabin united, was between four and five hundred. I had almost finished my breakfast when the pilot rung his bell for the engineer to put the machinery in motion. The boat having just shoved off, I was in the act of raising my cup to my lips, the tingling of the pilot-bell yet in my ear, when I heard an explosion resembling the discharge of a small piece of artillery. The report was perhaps louder than usual in such cases; for an exclamation was half-uttered by me that the gun was well loaded, when the rushing sound of steam, and the rattling of glass in some of the cabin windows, checked my speech, and told me too well what had occurred. I almost involuntarily bent my head and body down to the floor—a vague idea seemed to shoot across my mind that more than one boiler might burst, and that by assuming this posture the destroying matter would pass over without touching me.

The general cry of "a boiler has burst," resounded from one end of the table to the other; and as if by a simultaneous movement, all started on their feet. Then commenced a general race to the ladies' cabin, which lay more towards the stern of the boat. All regard to order or deference to sex seemed to be lost in the struggle for which should be first and farthest removed from the dreaded boilers. The danger had already passed away. I remained standing by the chair on which I had been previously sitting. Only one or two persons stayed in the cabin with me. As yet no more than half-a-minute had elapsed since the explosion; but in that brief space how had the scene changed? In that "drop of time" what confusion, distress, and dismay! An instant before, and all were in the quiet repose of security—another, and all were overwhelmed with alarm or consternation. It is but justice to say, that in this scene of terror the ladies exhibited a degree of firmness worthy of all praise. No screaming, no fainting—their fears, when uttered, were not for themselves, but for their husbands and children.

I advanced from my position to one of the cabin doors for the purpose of inquiring who were injured, when, just as I reached it, a man entered at the opposite one, both his hands covering his face, and exclaiming, "I am ruined!" He immediately began to tear off his clothes. When stripped, he presented a most shocking spectacle. His face was entirely black; his body without a particle of skin. He had been flayed alive. He gave me his name and place of abode—then sunk in a state of exhaustion and agony on the floor. I assisted in placing him on a mattress taken from one of the berths, and covered him with blankets. He complained of heat and cold as at once oppressing him. He bore his torments with manly fortitude, yet a convulsive shriek would occasionally burst from him. His wife, his children, were his constant theme—"It was hard to die without seeing them; it was hard to go without bidding them one farewell." Oil and cotton were applied to his wounds; but he soon became insensible to earthly misery. Before I had done attending to him, the whole floor of the cabin was covered with unfortunate sufferers. Some bore up under the horrors of their situation with a degree of resolution amounting to heroism. Others were wholly overcome by the sense of pain, the suddenness of the disaster, and the near approach of death, which even to them was evident—whose pangs they already felt. Some implored us, as an act of humanity, to complete the work of destruction and free them from present suffering. One entreated the presence of a clergyman to pray by him, declaring he was not fit to die. I inquired for a minister of religion, but none could be had. On every side were heard groans and mingled exclamations of grief and despair.

To add to the confusion, persons were every moment running about to learn the fate of their friends and relatives—fathers, sons, brothers—for in this scene of unmixed calamity it was impossible to say who were saved or who had perished. The countenances of many were so much disfigured as to be past recognition. After a time, my attention was particularly drawn towards a poor fellow who lay unnoticed on the floor, without uttering a single word of complaint. He was at a little distance removed from the rest. He was not much scalded, but one of his thighs was broken, and a principal artery had been severed, from which the blood was gushing rapidly. He betrayed no displeasure at the apparent neglect with which he was treated—he was perfectly calm. I spoke to him; he said he was very weak, but felt himself going—it would soon be over. A gentleman ran for one of the physicians. He came, and declared that, if expedition were used, he might be preserved by amputating the limb; but that to effect this it would be necessary to remove him from the boat. Unfortunately the boat was not sufficiently near to run a plank ashore. We were obliged to wait until it could be close hauled. I stood by him calling for help. We placed him on a mattress, and bore him to the guards. There we were detained some time from the cause I have mentioned. Never did anything appear to me so slow as the movements of those engaged in hauling the boat.

I knew, and he knew, that delay was death—that life was fast ebbing. I could not take my gaze from his face—there all was coolness and resignation. No word or gesture indicative of impatience escaped him. He perceived by my loud, and perhaps angry tone of voice, how much I was excited by what I thought the barbarous slowness of those around : he begged me not to take so much trouble—that they were doing their best. At length we got him on shore. It was too late—he was too much exhausted ; and died immediately after the amputation.

As soon as I was relieved from attending on those in the cabin, I went to examine that part of the boat where the boiler had burst. It was a complete wreck—a picture of destruction. It bore ample testimony to the tremendous force of that power which the ingenuity of man had brought to his aid. The steam had given everything a whitish hue ; the boilers were displaced ; the deck had fallen down ; the machinery was broken and disordered. Bricks, dirt, and rubbish were scattered about. Close by the bowsprit was a large rent, through which I was told the boiler, after exploding, had passed out, carrying one or two men in its mouth. Several dead bodies were lying around. Their fate had been an enviable one compared with that of others : they could scarcely have been conscious of a pang ere they had ceased to be. On the starboard wheel-house lay a human body, in which life was not yet extinct, though apparently there was no sensibility remaining. The body must have been thrown from the boiler-deck, a distance of thirty feet. The whole of the forehead had been blown away : the brains were still beating. Tufts of hair, shreds of clothing, and splotches of blood, might be seen in every direction. A gentleman on board picked up a piece of skin which appeared to have been peeled off by the force of the steam. It extended from the middle of the arm down to the tips of the fingers, the nails adhering to it. So dreadful had been the force that not a particle of the flesh adhered thereto. The most skilful operator could scarcely have effected such a result. Several whose skin was almost un-injured died from inhaling the steam or gas.

The number of lives lost will in all probability never be accurately known. Many were seen flung into the river, most of whom sank to rise no more. Could the survivors have been kept together until the list of passengers was called, the precise loss would have been ascertained. That, however, though it had been attempted, would, under the circumstances, have been next to impossible. Judging from the crowd which I saw on the boiler-deck immediately before the explosion, and the statement which I received as to the number of those who succeeded in swimming out after they were cast into the river, I am inclined to believe that between fifty and sixty must have perished. The cabin passengers escaped owing to the peculiar construction of the boat. Just behind the boilers were several large iron posts, supporting, I think, the boiler-deck : across each post was a large circular plate of iron, between one and two inches in thickness. One of these posts was placed exactly opposite the head of the boiler which burst, being the second one on the starboard side. Against this plate the head struck, and penetrated to the depth of an inch; then broke, and flew off at an angle, entering a cotton bale to the depth of a foot. The boiler-head was in point blank range with the breakfast-table in the cabin; and had it not been obstructed by the iron post, must have made a clear sweep of those who were seated at the table.

To render any satisfactory account of the cause which produced the explosion can hardly be expected from one who possesses no scientific or practical knowledge on the subject, and who previously thereto was paying no attention to the management of the boat. The captain appeared to be very active and diligent in attending to his duty. He was on the boiler-deck when the explosion occurred, was materially injured by that event, and must have been ignorant of the mismanagement, if any existed. From the engineer alone could the true explanation be elicited ; and, if indeed it was really attributable to negligence, it can scarcely be supposed he would lay the blame upon himself. If I might venture a suggestion in relation thereto, I would assign the following causes :—That the water in the starboard boilers had become low, in consequence of that side of the boat resting on the ground during our stay at Memphis ; that, though the fires were kept up some time before we shoved off, the head that burst had been cracked for a considerable time ; that the boiler was extremely heated, and the water, being thrown in by the boat having been again set in motion, was at once converted into steam ; and the flues not being sufficiently large to carry off the steam as soon as it was generated, nor the boiler-head of a strength capable of resisting its action, the explosion was a natural result.

THE MENTOR.

THIS American whaling vessel, of New Bedford, sailed for the Indian Ocean in the year 1831, under the command of Edward C. Barnard, and with a crew of twenty-six officers and men. Having doubled the Cape of Good Hope and traversed the Indian Ocean in safety, adverse currents and winds impeded the course of the vessel, and after having been tossed about at the mercy of the elements for three days, the *Mentor* struck upon a coral reef in the night of the 21st of May. When the accident occurred the ship had been running for the Ladrones, and the rock upon which she had grounded proved to be near one of the Pelew Islands, a group lying six or seven degrees north of the equator, and in the centre of the numerous isles of the North Pacific.

Immediately the extent of their danger became apparent to the crew, ten of the men in an impulse of terror secured one of the boats, in order to effect if possible their own safety. As they were never again heard of, and the storm continued for some time after their departure from the ship, it is only too probable that all perished through the swamping of the boat. In the attempt similarly made by a second party to leave the wreck, another man was drowned, and the remainder of the ship's company, eleven in number, kept upon the wreck until the dawn, when they descried land at a distance of twenty or thirty miles. One boat now only offered a means of escape to the survivors, and having collected a few arms and a small stock of provisions, they took to sea. After sailing three or four miles, they reached a rocky islet, about sixteen rods in length, where they rested all that day and night to refresh themselves with food and sleep before making an effort to reach the land. But the stranded vessel had been observed by the natives from the shore, and twenty-two of the dusky islanders, in a canoe, paid a visit in the morning to the shipwrecked Americans.

The aspect of these savages was frightful in the extreme. Their bodies were entirely naked and fantastically tattooed, while their long and coarse black hair hung in matted locks over their shoulders. Their weapons consisted of battle-axes, spears, and tomahawks. Though not openly unfriendly in their bearing, these Pelew Islanders robbed the sailors of the greater part of the property brought away from the wreck, and then paddled off in their canoe towards the *Mentor*, meanwhile making signs to the white men to follow them. The Americans, however, desired to get rid of their suspicious visitors, and at once embraced the opportunity which the departure of the savages afforded to launch their own boat and steer in another direction to that of the nearest land. But their movements had evidently been watched by the natives, for not long after their re-embarkation the seamen's progress was intercepted by thirty canoes, which the savages had launched for that purpose. After a slight skirmish with their pursuers the survivors from the wreck left the canoes and their occupants behind, and rowing during the remaining hours of that day, throughout the night, and till the afternoon of the next day, they arrived exhausted and dispirited at another island, on which they resolved to land; but in seeking to carry out that resolution by entering a small bay on the coast, they were met by a numerous party of the natives in canoes, and forcibly taken on shore in triumph.

Baubelthouap, the largest of the Pelew Islands, is about one hundred and twenty miles in length, and at that time was supposed to contain nearly two thousand inhabitants, many of whom met together and held a solemn consultation on the case of the poor mariners whom fate or the elements had thrown into their power. The Americans were brought before the great chiefs of the community, who were seated for the occasion on a platform erected between two buildings of considerable size. These structures were composed of bamboo sticks and leaves, and appeared to form the national place for council and carousal. The deliberation concerning the ultimate disposal of the *Mentor's* men continued for the space of an hour, and was conducted in the midst of a great assemblage of the natives, male and female, young and old. Meanwhile an ominous object stood in full view of the unfortunate prisoners. A block, used for beheading their captive enemies, was in front of the platform where the chiefs sat in state, and the question under discussion obviously related to the execution or sparing of the white men now before them. At length the women set up a wailing cry, which seemed to decide the matter in favour of the captive strangers; and a cup of mercy was handed to the latter as a token that their lives would be spared. During the council the prisoners had received indifferent but not cruel treatment at the hands of the savages, and at the close of the sitting the Americans were taken to a neighbouring village, where resided a prophetess, one of the women who had been mainly instrumental in eliciting a verdict of mercy.

On the way to the sacred woman's residence a romantic

incident occurred; the party being met by a strange-look-ing old man, with long grey hair, and otherwise bearing no resemblance to the islanders, except in the tattoo-marks which had been in earlier years indelibly imprinted on his skin. As soon as the individual in question beheld the captives, he exclaimed in a tolerably good accent: "You are Englishmen!" The sound of the old man's voice, as he uttered a sentence so unexpected, excited the most lively emotions in the breasts of the Americans, and their delight could only be equalled in intensity by the surprise they felt at being thus saluted under such circumstances. The his-tory of the old man may here be briefly told. By birth an Englishman, he had been on the island twenty-nine years. His name was Charles Washington, and in early manhood he had been a hatter to trade. Then he had entered the British Navy, and had served on board the *Lion* man-of-war; but in fear of punishment for some trifling offence which he had committed, he had deserted his ship and taken up his abode with the Pelew Islanders, among whom he had attained to great celebrity, and become the sixth chief of the nation. He had adopted the habits of the natives; felt quite contented with his lot, and would not wish ever again to see his own country. Through the influence of this remarkable individual the situation of the shipwrecked men was made comparatively comfortable.

The natives, a very rude and primitive race, of a light copper complexion, seem to have been generally of a good disposition. To excess they anointed their well-tattooed bodies with cocoa-oil. The females only wore a girdle, or covering for the loins; this was made of bark, and their scarcity of clothing would appear to have been compensated in some measure, at least so far as the ladies were con-cerned, by an extreme fondness for ornaments with which to decorate their persons. One of these articles of savage female adornment consisted of a stem of the kabooa leaf, which was worn in the nose, and answered the twofold purpose of an ornament and a smelling-bottle.

After a stay of several months with these people, the Americans entered into a negotiation for their own release and departure from the island. At length consent was granted by the chiefs, upon the stipulation that in return for their freedom the mariners would send to the island three hundred muskets, ten casks of powder, with various smaller articles. Accordingly they got a canoe built, and in that and their own boat eight of the *Mentor's* crew left the island; three being kept as hostages by the natives for the due fulfilment of the contract. In the hope of returning with the promised reward the Americans were accompanied by three of the islanders, two of whom were chiefs.

One of the boats contained a crew of five, the other of six men; and never did voyagers venture upon the ocean in vessels more unseaworthy than these craft. The main hope of the sailors, as to the possibility of being rescued from their unfortunate position, lay in the chance of meeting on the open sea some ship engaged in the China trade; but they had scarcely got fairly afloat when rough weather came on, and the *Mentor's* boat was dismasted. Nor did the canoe fare much better while combating with the force of the elements; for its rudder was unshipped, and the occupants were only enabled to keep themselves afloat by constantly baling the craft, which had sprung a leak. After five days of fearful toil and danger the canoe was upset, and the crew were rescued from the waves and taken into the other boat. The stock of fresh water and provisions with which the party had started was now running low, yet they continued on their course four days more, when land unexpectedly appeared before them, together with a fleet of canoes that soon approached and surrounded the suffering men. These canoes were laden with savages, who attacked the crew of the solitary boat with the utmost ferocity, knocking some overboard with their clubs, and making meanwhile frightful grimaces, and uttering fearful yells. Nor was the rage of the savages confined to the persons of the hapless voyagers who had fallen into their power, for they used their clubs with destructive effect upon the boat, and breaking it into splinters took possession of the fragments.

While this barbarous scene was being enacted by the enemy which had so suddenly fallen upon their track, the Americans were swimming from one canoe to another and entreating their assailants to spare their lives, and allow them to get into the boats. These requests were for some time refused by the savages, who continued to beat the white men unmercifully whenever the latter caught hold of anything to save themselves from sinking. At length, however, the fury of the savages became in a measure abated, and the nearly drowning men were taken into the canoes, where they were speedily stripped of their clothing, though the sun was shining so vividly that their bodies were soon blistered by exposure to the rays. On reaching the shore they were met by a crowd of women and children, who yelled with terrific energy; then quarrelling and fighting ensued between the captors for the ownership of the several prisoners. During the continuance of this contest the latter were sadly abused, but hostilities being ended, each of the captured was claimed as the slave of one of the barbarians, and taken home by his new master.

The island upon which our unfortunate mariners had now stumbled was a low, barren rock, scarcely three-quarters of a mile in length. It has been known by seamen under the names of Lord North's, Nevil's, and Johnston's Island, and was at one time believed to be uninhabited. Its native designation is To'bee. The inhabitants resemble the Pelew Islander in the light copper tint of their skin, but there the resemblance ceases, for the former exceed the latter in the

wildness and fierceness of their appearance and disposition.
The condition of the sailors under these savages was of the
most pitiable kind.   The only vegetable cultivated on this
sandy coral rock was a species of tarrow-root, for the growth
of which proper soil had to be gathered from various
quarters.   The whole labour of gathering and mixing the
soil for that purpose was thrown upon the captives by their
indolent masters.   Nearly naked under a broiling sun, these
white slaves were kept constantly at work ; sometimes with
the scantiest supply of food, and at other times reduced to
all but the last degree of starvation.   They were also wantonly subjected to other inflictions of the most painful
character.   Captain Barnard was one of the Americans who
was thus subjected to slavery in its most degrading form.

After a painful servitude of two months upon the island
of To'bee, Captain Barnard and one of the *Mentor's* crew,
named Rollins, succeeded in getting their release, by per-
suading their masters to put them on board an English ship
which had come within hailing distance of the island.   That
act of clemency had been extorted from the savages by
promises of iron and various other articles to be given
immediately in exchange when Barnard and Rollins got
aboard the vessel.   Only a small quantity of iron was sent,
however, and the consequence was that the natives, feeling
aggrieved at that which they considered as fraudulent conduct on the part of the white men, increased their severity
towards the remaining prisoners.   Unfortunately, as he
afterwards alleged, the English commander was not in
circumstances that permitted of further exertions to obtain
the release of the remainder of the crew of the *Mentor*, and
he accordingly set sail from the locality, leaving the poor
Americans to a worse than their previous fate.

One of the cruelties inflicted upon these miserable men
by their inhuman keepers was by compelling them to
undergo the process of tattooing.   Firmly secured to the

ground, the sufferers were laid hold of by their tormentors, who then proceeded to sketch with a sharp stick the designs that were intended to be imprinted upon the skin. When the drawing had been finished to the satisfaction of the operator and the bystanders, the skin was next thickly punctured by means of a little instrument, made of sharpened fish-bones, and somewhat resembling a carpenter's adze in miniature, but having teeth instead of a plain sharp edge. This instrument was held within an inch or two of the flesh, into which it was struck rapidly with a piece of wood, applied in such a manner as to cause the instrument to rebound after every stroke. In this way the breasts and arms of the men were prepared for the application of the ink, made from the juice of a plant found on the island. The operation caused such an inflammation of the parts that only a small portion of each man's body could be done at one time. As fast as the inflammation abated, and the men could bear it, another portion was in like manner treated, until at length all the men's bodies and limbs had been tattooed. Not content with this, however, the savages were exceedingly anxious to extend the process to the countenances of their prisoners, but the spirit of the latter had been aroused to the point of resistance, and the barbarians therefore concluded to refrain from further efforts to embellish the persons of their slaves.

Of the six men left in the possession of the islanders after the escape of Barnard and Rollins, three speedily sank under their afflictions : one dying rather suddenly, and the other two, when reduced to the last extremity and unable to move, being each put into a canoe, and set adrift upon the ocean to meet a horrible death. Of the three miserable survivors two were seamen of the *Mentor*, and the third was one of the Pelew Islanders, who in the simplicity of their ignorance had set sail with the white men for an unknown land of promise. The other Pelew men, who had left their homes to receive the anticipated reward for their clemency to the Americans, had both died; one had been charged with stealing food, and turned adrift in a canoe with his hands tied together; the second had been literally starved to death.

Finding their captives were getting totally unserviceable and dying one by one, the savages began to see that it would be to their own interest to complete some bargain for the release of the men, ere the death of all rendered such a proceeding impossible. Accordingly, Holden and Nute, the two whites, received a promise that they would be placed on board the first passing vessel, on condition that their masters should get a present of iron in return. On the 24th of December 1834, the *Britannia*, an English barque bound for Canton River, passed the island, and the American seamen obtained their release. When brought on board the *Britannia* Nute was in such a deplorable condition that it was believed that two days more, under such treatment as he had received at the hands of his barbarous owner, would have ended his life. The Americans had become greatly attached to the Pelew Islander during the sufferings which they had together endured, and Holden and Nute both pleaded earnestly with the British captain for the redemption of their copper-coloured friend. But the commander of the *Britannia* did not consider it would be prudent to take the savage also on board his vessel, and the poor fellow was therefore left in his solitary servitude and misery.

In course of time the two Americans were transferred to another vessel, which conveyed them to their own country; and it is pleasing to be able to add that the Pelew Islander was also eventually released from his cruel bondage. In the year 1835, an American sloop-of-war, the *Vincennes*, took him off the island, and landed him safely among his own people. The sloop also brought home the remaining men of the *Mentor's* crew who had been left as hostages at the Pelew Isles. Unfortunately for the reputation of the white mariner among these savages, a difficulty was raised by the commander of the *Vincennes*, when the question of the promised ransom came to be debated. The chiefs naturally demanded the payment in full of the stipulated consideration. Relying upon the armament of his vessel to enforce compliance to his wishes, the American captain only handed over a portion of the reward, and in all probability left in the breasts of the natives rancorous feelings which would find expression when other white men fell into their hands.

THE ROTHESAY CASTLE.

THIS steam-packet was wrecked on Dutchman's Bank when proceeding from Liverpool to Wales with a large number of passengers, for the most part excursionists, on the 17th of August 1831. The morning previous to the disaster had been stormy, but by eleven in the forenoon the sky had cleared sufficiently to cause pleasure-seekers to avail themselves of the opportunity offered by the *Rothesay Castle* of a trip to the principality. On that fatal day when the steamer left the pier-head at Liverpool the majority of her passengers hailed from the surrounding districts, and by far the greater number on board were women and children, bent on a little relaxation from the ordinary routine of their lives by a sea-journey to Beaumaris. For an hour the vessel kept in the Mersey picking up more people, and as she cleared the lighthouse about noon the storm of the morning had passed, but the wind was blowing freshly, with a heavy sea and a strong tide running. The steamer was not suited to the service to which she had been put, for even in calm weather and on a smooth sea she had been considered infirm. Now she appeared crazy in the extreme, and her tremulous motion so alarmed those on board that efforts were made to induce the captain to abandon the journey and return to Liverpool.

As the *Rothesay Castle* went on her way, fears for their personal safety were intensified rather than abated in the minds of the passengers, and Mr. Varney of Bury, along with others, went down to the cabin, where the master of the vessel was discovered sitting at dinner, and in a state of intoxication. To the appeal made to him to return, the captain replied angrily, "I think there is a great deal of fear aboard, and very little danger. It would never do to put back with passengers, for then we would make no profit." Finding that the drunken commander could not be shaken in his purpose, Mr. Varney and those who had accompanied him in the fruitless errand went on deck, where signs of fear were now plainly visible upon almost every countenance.

The sea continued so rough, and the steamer made so little progress, that for three hours she continued within sight of the floating light. Many of the passengers became exceedingly ill from the violent motion of the vessel, and all expressed great anxiety to turn back: but the captain still refused. He was repeatedly asked to show signals of distress. That also he persistently declined to do. With all the stubbornness of an inveterate drunkard he held to his resolution to proceed, regardless of consequences, or the fate of those whose lives depended upon his decision.

Before arriving off the Great Orme's Head, and soon after nightfall, the force of the waves increased, while a strong wind blew right ahead of the steamer. This caused her to strain considerably, and take in water through her beams, and at the axle-holes inside the paddle-boxes. In the engine-room the sea water was now ankle deep, and the pumps were set agoing, but the tubes soon became choked with ashes, and much time was consumed in getting the pumps again to work. The request that the captain would make signals was renewed, but only to be again denied.

Not even a light would the infatuated madman allow to be suspended from the mast of the *Rothesay Castle*, now drifting onwards to destruction.

According to the testimony of the man who had then been at the wheel, by midnight the vessel had got far enough to windward of the Dutchman's Bank, and abreast of the tower on Priesthome Island, when the temporary stoppage of the engines caused her to lose way. She was now shipping much water and labouring heavily. The steersman had the helm aport, and the stern of the steamer struck upon the bank. When she lost way the captain was below, but he now came upon the poop and ordered the man at the wheel to starboard the helm, alleging, as a reason for the command, that otherwise the steersman would run the vessel upon the causeway on the other side; but immediately afterwards the engines were reversed, with the view of getting her into deeper water. Owing, however, to the want of sufficient steam-power, the attempt to get the boat clear of the bank proved abortive. The jib was next hoisted, but that was also ineffectual to further the desired end, and after repeatedly striking the bank and dragging along its edge for about half-a-mile, the *Rothesay Castle* came broadside upon the bank, and there remained, beyond the reach of human exertion to remove her.

Mountainous seas now kept breaking against and over the ill-starred steamboat, while ever and anon she was partly raised by the force of the waves and instantly dashed again, with tremendous violence, upon the sandbank. By this time the moon had gone down, and the sky overhead was overcast with heavy clouds. Only sufficient light was in the atmosphere to render visible the extremely pitiable scene on deck. Soon after the vessel struck the passengers made a tumultuous rush forward, but the captain ordered them aft, and seemed to consult with the mate in a suspicious manner. Noting the action, and guessing at the purport of the conversation between the two men, a gentleman cried out alarmedly, "It is all over with us, the captain and mate are preparing to leave the vessel." These words increased the terror of the miserable passengers, and almost instantly after their being uttered the intoxicated commander fell or stumbled overboard, and paid with his life the penalty of his culpable folly.

By the lurching of the hull at least fifty persons were thrown into the sea, and their drowning cries mingled with the screaming and wailing of the survivors. With few exceptions all now left on deck gave themselves up to the frenzy of despair. Parents and children, relatives and friends, were to be seen taking a last leave of each other. The women and children whose husbands and fathers were not with them in these awful moments clustered together and embraced each other, with a continuous and direful chorus of lamentation. At length, wearied with their wailing, the poor souls reclined upon each other, and lay to all appearance inanimate, as the spray from the waves which dashed against the vessel drenched their clothing with an icy coldness.

Very soon after the vessel had got with her broadside to the bank, the after-tackle of the funnel broke loose; but with great exertion it was secured and fastened to the sides, as well as the circumstances would permit. But in a few minutes after these repairs had been effected, a heavy sea brought down the chimney, together with the main-mast, both falling in a slanting direction athwart the deck to the weather-side. What number of the hapless passengers were washed overboard by that violent wave, or killed by the fall of the funnel and mast, could not be ascertained; but soon after that disaster ten or twelve persons were carried from the deck by the force of another tremendous sea. The rudder was next unshipped; and the steamer's boat having filled with water, broke from the painter and went adrift.

Many of the survivors took off their clothing, so as to combat the waves without such encumbrance, and with a faint
possibility of swimming ashore. Several threw themselves
into the sea with a wooden bench from the quarter-deck;
but all those speedily perished. On the weather-side, the
bulwarks, behind which about twenty people had sought
shelter from the anger of the elements, were next washed
away; and all who had clung to the bulwarks were buried
in the deep. About a quarter-past one the weather paddle-
box was carried off by another violent sea. Between thirty
and forty persons had been clinging about the paddle-box
just previous to its being washed adrift, and it was believed
that all who had thus sought safety must have sunk to rise
no more.

It was now apparent that the hull would, sooner or later,
go to pieces, and speedily the main-deck burst in every
direction, as well as the quarter-deck or poop. Six men,
a woman, and a boy were upon the quarter-deck, which,
after parting from its former position, was still attached to
the hull by some of the ship's tackle. Judging that the
quarter-deck, if adrift from the wreck, might be the means
of saving his own life, as well as the lives of those who
stood near, Mr. Jones, a Liverpool pilot who was on board
as a passenger, with great promptitude cut the tackle with
his pocket-knife; which timely action allowed the quarter-
deck to float clear of the wreck, and the majority of those
upon the poop were eventually and as a consequence happily
preserved.

When the quarter-deck drifted from the hull there probably remained upon the latter from forty to fifty of the
survivors. Of these some lashed themselves to planks and
jumped overboard; others were washed into the sea; about
twelve clung to the fallen main-mast, three ascended the
fore-mast, which still retained its upright position, while
two or three held on to the lower part thereof. Of all who

sought their safety by remaining with the hull of the wreck, not more than ten persons would appear to have been saved.

During one long and awful hour the straining, cracking, and rending of her timbers gave palpable indications of the fact that the final breaking-up of the hull of the *Rothesay Castle* could not be long delayed. She had struck upon the sand-bank at midnight, and about one in the morning broke across, when many more of her horror-stricken passengers were hurried into the waves. At half-past one, or shortly afterwards, the hull went into fragments, and there arose from the murky waters a terrific and deafening shriek of anguish and despair.

The escape of Mr. Edward Jones of Bangor was almost miraculous. He could not swim, but having on board found a small keg, he, with the assistance of two friends, fastened the barrel to his body by means of a piece of rope. He then seated himself with his companions in a carriage that was upon the deck. Shortly afterwards the hull broke up, and the three friends were thrown with great force into the water. The keg shifting from his breast, and getting under his left arm, it was with considerable difficulty that Mr. Jones could keep his head above water. Seeing the carriage floating past him, he laid hold of one of the wheels with his right hand; but the vehicle soon sank, and he was left without that support to battle with the ocean. An instant afterwards he observed Mr. Duckworth of Bury at a short distance, and seated upon a board, about the size of an ordinary room-door. Mr. Jones immediately relinquished his barrel, and, although he had never previously attempted to swim, by making a succession of vigorous strokes he gained the board, on one end of which he rested, while Mr. Duckworth sat upon the other. Their united weight brought the board so much under water that it was with the utmost difficulty they could keep their

15

heads sufficiently elevated to be able to breathe.   Both felt
themselves rapidly becoming exhausted, when Duckworth
contrived to divest himself of his clothing, when he quitted
the board with the intention of swimming, if possible, ashore,
and fortunately succeeded in the attempt.   Mr. Jones now
got fairly upon the wood, and putting his feet through a
hole in the centre, held on by the sides of his raft.   In that
posture he kept afloat until nearly eight o'clock, when he
was picked up by a Mr. Williamson, who had rowed towards him in a boat belonging to the schooner *Campadora*.
When thus rescued, Jones was so close to the breakers off
the Great Orme's head, that he must have perished had Mr.
Williamson been but a few minutes later in reaching him.

When the hull finally broke up a Mr. Nuttall was also
precipitated into the sea.   He was encumbered with all his
clothing and a great-coat.   In addition to the weight which
his saturated garments occasioned, his son, a fine little
fellow, took refuge upon his back.   Mr. Nuttall could not
swim, and must have sunk, had not a rope been thrown by
a kind Providence.   Eagerly seizing the line, he was able to
pull himself along, hand over hand, until he in this way
got with his burden to the floating poop, which had already
offered an asylum for eight persons.   Of those who had
secured a footing on that piece of wreckage, Mr. Nuttall
found two relatives who had been in the same party as himself on that fatal excursion—Mrs. Whittaker and her son.
In the continued presence of peril, suffering, and death,
eight of these poor creatures clung to their slippery and
limited resting-place until half-past seven in the morning.

As we have seen, seven persons were on the quarter-deck
when, with great presence of mind, it had been cut adrift
by one of the occupants, a Liverpool pilot.   Shortly afterwards they found a man floating past them upon a plank,
and were enabled to rescue the poor fellow from his
perilous situation, and give him a foothold upon the poop.

Mr. Nuttall having been also added providentially to the company on that portion of the wreck, an effort was made to gain the Carnarvon shore, by paddling with pieces of timber. Not long after daybreak people were observed upon the land, to whom Mr. Nuttall and his companions shouted, but as the distance was too far for their voices to be heard, they continued to drift before the wind, with the sea every minute dashing over them, until their terrible predicament was descried from Beaumaris Green by a Mr. Walker, who without delay procured the life-boat of that station, and the crew proceeded to the rescue of these survivors, who were now in a state of complete exhaustion. Mrs. Whittaker, whose name has been just mentioned, thus described her experiences on the fearful occasion :—

When the vessel struck I was on the quarter-deck with two boys—my own, about six-and-a-half years old, and my brother's, about eight. The first thing I noticed was the water coming over the side of the vessel. I and the boys got hold of a rope, and the seat on which we had been sitting was washed overboard. The mast then came down, and lay in such a position as to press me against the side of the vessel. The wind blew strongly, and the waves were very high. One of the boys was washed overboard, but I caught hold of his clothes and pulled him back. In the intermediate time, betwixt the overflowing and receding of the waves, I observed that the passengers were fewer in number, and some of them went with each wave, and I saw them, at a short distance, struggling in the water. At length there came a heavier wave, which broke-in the vessel's side, and swept both the boys and myself overboard, and I lost them, and saw them no more. I got hold of a rope and tried to get on deck again, but I could not; the water drove me back, and at the same time washed Selim Lamb overboard. Before this happened, some of the passengers had got upon a piece of the wreck ; it was part of

the poop, with the wheel attached to it.   Mr. Nuttall, one
of our party from Bury, was amongst them; he got hold of
the hair of my head and pulled me to them.   At this time
I was almost naked.   My garments had been torn from me
one by one, and I had only my stays and my under-petticoat
and chemise left.   I took off my petticoat, and two men
stood upon the wreck and held it in their hands as a sail.
A gentleman, whose name I did not know, said, "Don't
take her petticoat from her, poor thing;" but I preferred
that they should have it.   They then fastened a handker-
chief to a long pole.   At this time I caught hold of a gentleman, and got him upon the float.   His eyes were fixed, and
he appeared to be in a dying state.   Four of the passengers
now began to row with pieces of the vessel, and the men
who held the petticoat becoming tired, they fixed it to a
piece of wood, and we remained floating in very rough water,
until at length a boat came to our assistance, and took us to
Beaumaris.   The men of the lifeboat behaved most kindly
to me; they took off their jackets and mufflers, and in
these they wrapped me.   We were rescued nearly at the
foot of Penmaen Mawr, and conveyed to Beaumaris, where
the utmost attention was bestowed upon us by the inhabitants.   A number of ladies were also most kind to me;
they provided me with everything of which I stood in need,
and endeavoured to console me for the loss they could not
repair—that of my dear boy.

THE AMPHITRITE.

THE loss of this vessel created a profound impression of dissatisfaction in England when all the circumstances of the appalling event became known. It also gave rise to much animadversion regarding the convict system of the country, and, with other calamities of a similar character which followed not long thereafter, formed a powerful argument for the abolishment of transportation in the punishment of crime. The *Amphitrite* sailed from Woolwich on the 25th of August 1833, under the command of one of her owners, Captain Hunter; the vessel having been hired by Government for the conveyance of a hundred and eight female convicts to the settlements in New South Wales. Twelve children, whose mothers were numbered in that unfortunate though criminal gang, were also on board; the whole being in charge of a superintendent, Surgeon Forrester, whose wife had accompanied him on the fatal voyage.

When the ship arrived off Dungeness, a gale had sprung up, which increased so violently as to render the navigation extremely difficult; and the captain was obliged to heave-to for a time, finding it dangerous to carry sail. At noon on the 31st of August they made land, about three miles to the east of Boulogne harbour. In the hope of keeping her off the shore the main fore-sail and top-sail were set, but this proved ineffectual to promote the end in view. About three in the afternoon the ominous situation of the *Amphitrite* was observed by the sightseers who had been drawn towards the beach, to witness the awe-inspiring effects of a storm at sea, but without any personal inconvenience or danger to themselves.

The heavy waves that were now beating with tremendous force upon the French coast rendered it out of the question to make for the port, if Captain Hunter ever seriously entertained such an idea, which is highly improbable under the circumstances. Besides, he was to a large extent sailing under the orders of the convict-superintendent, who might be open to censure for allowing the vessel to touch land upon the voyage, and thus give an opportunity to some of the criminals to escape. Unable, however, to resist the power of the elements which were carrying them shorewards, the commander determined to run the *Amphitrite* upon the sandy beach, in the hope that when the storm had abated he might be able to float off at the succeeding high-tide. Accordingly, about half-past four, the ship came round into the harbour and struck upon the sands. In a few minutes after, multitudes of the townsfolk rushed to the beach to see the English vessel which had stranded upon their coast. That no means were adopted by the authorities of the port, either to warn the captain of his danger or to assist him in avoiding it, excited much indignation in this country. Indeed, any assistance that was proffered after the disaster came from private and individual sources. It was to be regretted that those to whom had been entrusted the lives of so many helpless women and children could not find it to be consistent with their duty to accept the aid said in two instances to be generously volunteered.

According to a popular version of the story, a pilot-boat, under the charge of François Heuret, who had upon several occasions exhibited much coolness and fortitude in the presence of danger, set out for the purpose of rendering help and succour to the voyagers in their perilous position. But from one cause or another all the gravity of the situation was not realised by those on board ; for when the French pilot and his companions reached the *Amphitrite* they were informed that their services would not be accepted upon any terms whatsoever ; and so the humane mission of Heuret ended, without his being allowed even to carry ashore some of the shipwrecked crew, who had expressed a wish to their commander to leave the ship by means of the pilot's boat, then under the bows. When Heuret was engaged in conversation with the captain and the superintendent, the greater number of the men were below tying together their personal effects, in anticipation of a speedy rescue from the danger that menaced them— the prisoners and their children were all in their berths, with the hatch over them battened down.

The bank of sand upon which the *Amphitrite* lay, exposed to the violence of the seas that were at short intervals breaking over her, was about three-quarters of an English mile from the beach—not more. At half-past five the pilot left the side of the vessel and returned to the port. Immediately after his departure, according to the statement of one of the crew, their dangerous position, together with the probabilities of the ship getting afloat, were discussed by the captain, the superintendent of the convicts, and Mrs. Forrester, each of whom dreaded the responsibility involved in being a party to the release of the prisoners from their confinement on board, without having the means or authority to lodge the women securely on shore until the re-sailing of the vessel. The wife of the surgeon was said, by the same witness, to have proposed that the convicts should be left on board, while the captain, her husband, and herself sought safety ashore in the long-boat. The suggestion is too horrible to be accepted as having been uttered by an English lady, and we would much rather entertain the opinion that the three principal individuals on board preferred to die in the faithful discharge of an onerous duty, than the alternative one that a woman could be found seriously proposing that defenceless creatures of her own sex—doubtless in many cases more sinned against than sinful—should be left to face a violent death, dishonoured and disowned.

Six o'clock came, but still no effort was being made on the sea-beaten ship to save any of the lives on board. Those in authority seemed too paralysed by the consideration of their responsibilities to take any steps towards that end. On shore, the multitude of sightseers had stood gazing in listless curiosity towards the *Amphitrite*, but no further attempt had been made to reach the ship, after the rebuff which Heuret had received, until a brave French seaman, Pierre Henin, whose name had already been honourably recorded upon the roll of the English Humane Society, addressed himself to the port-captain, saying that he had resolved to go alone to the stranded ship, in order to inform the commander that there was not a moment to lose, if any desire existed to send the crew and passengers ashore.

In fulfilment of his resolution, Henin went to the beach, stripped himself, took a line, swam for about three-quarters of an hour, and arrived at the vessel at a little after seven. On reaching the right side of the vessel, he hailed the crew, and said, "Give me a line to conduct you upon land or you are lost, as the sea is coming in." He spoke in English, plainly enough to be heard, and told them to speak to the captain. Some of the men threw two lines, one from the stern and one from the bow. The one from the stern Henin could not seize—the one from the bow he did. He then went towards the shore, but the rope was stopped. This was, it is believed, the act of the surgeon and captain. The French sailor then swam back, and told those on board to give him more rope to get on shore. The captain and surgeon would not grant his request. They then tried to haul him in, but his strength was now failing, and he returned to the beach.

The scene on the *Amphitrite* was now of the most heart-rending nature. The convicts, driven to desperation as they realised their terrible position, broke away the covering of one of the hatchways that confined them below, and rushing frantically on deck besought, with tearful entreaties, their superintendent and the captain to save them from perishing, by allowing them to go ashore in the long-boat. The miserable creatures were told, in reply, that neither the master of the ship nor the surgeon would feel authorised, under any circumstances, to liberate prisoners committed to their charge.

At seven P.M. the flood-tide began, and the crew, seeing that there were no hopes of their own rescue, clung to the rigging. Meanwhile the poor women and children remained on the deck, uttering the most piteous cries, during the space of about an hour-and-a-half, until their sufferings were ended by the waves closing over them. Finding that the vessel must soon go in pieces, the captain and some of the crew secured some spars on which they might perchance reach the beach. But their safety had been sought too late, and all on board were drowned, with the exception of three of the crew, one of whom drifted ashore upon a ladder. Just before the breaking-up of the ship, one of the sailors directed the attention of Captain Hunter to a man upon the beach, who was waving his hat, apparently as a mute invitation to come ashore. Without returning an answer to the seaman who had spoken, the commander turned away. Instantly afterwards the women and children had

dropped shrieking into the sea. The *Amphitrite* had broken
in two. The following description of this calamity was written
by one who witnessed a part of the harrowing spectacle
from the shore. It gives another colouring to the scene :—

On the 31st of August—Saturday—I walked down to
the port with a friend, and slowly advanced to the end of
the pier. Thousands have reason to remember that awful
storm ! The wind blew most furiously, drifting the sand
along with vengeance directly in our faces. Tall men and
strong men stood still at times, and turned their backs,
unable to proceed an inch, and holding fast by the railing
of the pier, to prevent their being blown over. We at
length arrived at the extremity of the pier, where there
were a dozen or twenty seamen, who seemed on the look-
out. There was a vessel about half-a-mile along the coast
northward. It appeared to us to be slowly advancing to
port. We spoke to the sailors about it. Some of them
said nothing in reply ; some said it was lying-to ; but no
one seemed in the least interested about the matter ; and
we concluded that as they must know more about sea-
matters than we did, there could not be any imminent
danger for the vessel, especially as it was so near port. We
returned home, satisfied with the answers of the Frenchmen,
and feeling that they were there waiting for the first symptoms of danger. Indeed, but for our inquiries and our
making the greatest exertion to use our eyes, while the
storm was drifting in our faces, we should have known
nothing of the matter ; for there was not the least thing in
the appearance of the sailors which could indicate that any
event of interest or alarm was going on : all was as quiet
as it could be in such a gale.

The first frightful intelligence of the wreck was brought
to me on Sunday morning, before I arose, by the children of
the amiable family I reside with, who came flocking to my
room with wonder-speaking faces : "Oh ! a convict ship has

been wrecked and all on board are drowned!" "Then how came you to know it was a convict ship, if all are drowned?" I replied, more than half suspecting that they were playfully attempting to practice on my credulity. To this they could make no satisfactory reply, but that "they had heard it from their maid." I too soon, however, found that it was almost literally true. A ship of 200 tons, laden with female convicts, bound to Australia, had been wrecked that night, and three persons only out of one hundred and thirty-six were saved! And that was the ship I had caught a glimpse of on the previous evening!

I was soon at the port. How had this terrible event come to pass? and how was it possible so near the shore? These and a hundred other questions were in every mouth; and what every one asked no one could answer. Many contradictory reports were afloat, none of which subsequently proved true. The prevailing account was, that a French sailor had gone off in a boat to the captain of the lost vessel on Saturday evening, and offered assistance, telling him of his danger: but that the captain had refused all help from ashore, saying that he would land the convicts safely in New South Wales, or perish. The greater part of this was false. One French boat only put to sea; and the man soon returned, thinking he had done enough to gain a character for bravery, and propagated this story. The three men who were saved denied that the captain refused assistance; and said, that when the boat drew near, one went to the hold for a rope, and on his return with one the boat had turned, and was making again for the shore. They added that the captain was not made aware of his danger. Another story was, that the captain was insensible, or stupified by his misfortune, from the time the ship struck. This was also denied by the sailors. These stories, however, travelled to England, and one also, which made out that the mate was saved; and information of some particulars was given on the pretended evidence of the poor man when he was drowned !

The scene which appeared in the suburbs, where the three men who swam ashore were lying in an exhausted state, was most revolting. At about ten o'clock on Sunday morning, while the dead bodies which had been washed ashore were being conveyed in carts to the hospital, these poor men were beset on every hand with questioners of every order. I shall not forget easily the horrid eagerness of different persons to get the first information. "Tell me, sir, I am the correspondent of such a newspaper, and first information is of great importance to our journal."

In the course of half-an-hour no fewer than thirty bodies of women had been washed up at the gates of Barry's Marine Hotel. Many of them were warm ; and the greatest humanity and attention were displayed by the people of the hotel and the persons there residing. But there was only *one* surgeon for fifty or more drowned women; and they had no apparatus for restoring circulation or communicating warmth—there is no such thing, they say, at Boulogne. Many might have been saved by such means; but nothing was resorted to but warm clothes, warm water, and a few such things. By eleven o'clock, no fewer than sixty-three dead women were placed in rows, in a long room of the Hospice St. Louis, in the Rue de l'Hôpital. It was a scene that might have shaken the stoutest heart. Among them there was a young mother, with her infant clasped in her arms. A great number were fine young women, and many would soon have become mothers. Two or three hours before, all were alive, and thought not even of danger ; and now the half-nude, and scarcely cold bodies, were lying one inanimate mass—the young with the old—the newly made mother with her that was about to bring forth—and these were my wretched countrywomen ! There was a dreary silence in that chamber, broken only by the mumbling voices of the attendant nuns and their busy steps; and many were gazing with heartless curiosity—and some with the accustomed air of those to whom it was a matter of business—and some were touched with pity.

Without dwelling on the apathy and cowardice of the French sailors, will it be believed, that the prefect (or mayor) was at the sea-side, and saw the distress of the *Amphitrite* on Saturday evening, and coolly went home to take his dinner, without adopting any measures for the crew! The vessel was within hailing distance, and the sailors who were saved affirmed that the water was not higher than a man's breast. Yet a hundred and thirty-three souls were lost. This could not have occurred on an English coast. Had a French vessel been wrecked at one of our ports, and had we been even at war with France, the crew would have been all rescued, and every Englishman within call would have been there to offer assistance. A dozen Englishmen would not have stood on the shore looking on!

The sum of the evidence of the three men is this: The captain, finding it impossible to get into port, intentionally ran his vessel ashore, as high up as he could, intending to wait there for the tide, which, on rising, he thought would carry him further in. His error seems to have been that he did not immediately disembark his crew, as he had a boat. But this error proceeded from his not being aware of the danger of the coast. No one on board dreamt of danger; they went to supper quite securely; and then the women, who had been dreadfully sea-sick the whole day, got into their berths; which circumstance accounts for their being nearly naked. It was about eight o'clock that the ship was driven over its anchor; and by the violence of the storm, the poop was broken off (the women's berths were below it), and in a moment the whole crew were in the waves. Even then the sailors on shore put off no boat. Still, considering so powerful a wind was blowing directly on shore, it is astonishing that so few were saved.　Many of the bodies when first cast up were warm, and the apparatus of an English Humane Society might have restored them; but they were cruelly neglected; the French guard would allow none but the authorised persons to convey the dying women from the sands.

I was standing or walking about at the sea-side from eleven o'clock to half-past one on the day of the wreck, and the scene exhibited was revolting.　The lower orders of the French people were there in droves, with carts and horses: many of them walked up to their middle into the water, to seize with a disgusting avidity the spoils of the wreck. The warm bodies were stripped for plunder, before one thought was bestowed on restoration.　The conduct of the people was more like a merrymaking than anything else. In the afternoon it was low water, and the sun came out a little.　All Boulogne flocked to the wreck.　The Sunday morning scramble for plunder had seemed a matter of business; the afternoon looked like a gala-day.　In the evening the theatre was open as usual!

THE WELLINGTON.

N the 6th of October 1833, this vessel sailed from the Cove of Cork, bound for St. Andrews, on the east of Scotland, and carrying limestone as ballast. On her passage northward the *Wellington* was driven about by contrary winds, which occasioned considerable delay; but, with the exception of the inconvenience resulting from her lengthened detention, nothing remarkable had happened either to the vessel or her crew before arriving in St. Andrews Bay. After shipping her cargo of deals, the brig again set sail, and in the North Sea encountered a hurricane which utterly disabled her, and subjected her crew to the severest privations. One who was a sufferer by the disaster has given a graphic description of the wreck of the *Wellington*, and the remarkable preservation of the majority of the persons on board. The story here reproduced is nearly in the narrator's own words:—

During a passage of sixty days, all which time we struggled against adverse winds, nothing material occurred, save the shifting of our ballast, which caused some alarm; but the promptitude and alacrity of the crew soon set it all right. On reaching the ballast-ground we discharged our ballast; and after we had repaired the rigging we took in a cargo of deals. Here four of the men left us, and we had to wait for others to supply their place. On the 23d of December we sailed on our return to Cork; mustering in all seventeen persons, including one male and one female passenger. With a fine stiff breeze down the bay, we soon lost sight of land, and nothing of note occurred till the 30th, when the wind got up from the N.W., and soon blew so heavy a gale that we were obliged to take in everything but a close-reefed maintop-sail, under which we scudded till the 5th of January. All this time it blew a hurricane, principally from the N.W., but occasionally, after a short lull, flying round to the S.W. with a fury that nothing could resist. The sea threatened to overwhelm our little craft. It was several times proposed to lay her to; but the fatal opinion prevailed that she did better in scudding. On the night of the 6th a tremendous sea struck her on the stern, stove-in all the dead-lights and washed these into the cabin, lifted the taffrail a foot or more out of its place, carried away the afterpart of the larboard bulwark, shattered the whole of the stern-frame, and washed one of the steersmen away from the wheel. The carpenter and crew with much labour secured the stern as well as they could for the night, and next morning, the wind moderating a little, new dead-lights were put in, and the damages further repaired.

Every stitch of canvas, but the maintop-sail, jib, and trysail, were split into ribbons, so that we became anxious to know how we should reach port when the gale subsided. But we were soon spared further care on that head. As the day closed in, the tempest resumed its fury, and by the following morning (the 8th) raged with such appalling violence that we laid her to. From her straining, the brig had now begun to make so much water as to require all hands in succession at the pumps till the following morning at two, when the larboard-watch went below, the watch on deck, by constant exertion, sufficing to keep her free.

At seven in the morning of the 9th, a tremendous sea broke over the starboard-bow, overwhelming all, and sweeping caboose, boats, planks, casks, everything before it to the afterpart of the deck; even the starboard-anchor was lifted on to the forecastle; and the cook, who was in the galley, washed with all his culinary apparatus into the lee-scuppers, where he remained for some time in a very perilous situation, jammed in among the loose spars and other portions of the wreck, until extricated by the watch on deck, who, being aft at the moment of the occurrence, escaped unhurt. Before we could recover from this shock, the watch below rushed on deck with the appalling intelligence that the water had found its way below, and was pouring in like a torrent. We found that the coppers, forced along the deck with irresistible violence, had, by striking a stanchion fixed firmly in the deck, split the covering-board fore and aft, and let in the water. The captain thought it time to prepare for the worst. As the ship, from her bouyant cargo, could not sink, he ordered the crew to store the top with provisions, and all exerted themselves with the energy of despair; two barrels of beef, some hams, pork, butter, cheese, and a large jar of brandy, were handed in a trice up from below, but not before the water had nearly filled the cabin, and forced those employed there to cease their operations, and with the two unfortunate passengers to fly to the deck. Fortunately for the latter, they knew not the full horror of our situation. The poor lady, whose name I have forgotten— young and delicate, already suffering from confinement below and sea-sickness, pale and shivering, but patient and resigned—had but a short time taken her seat beside her fellow-passenger on some planks near the taffrail, on which lay extended the unfortunate cook, unable to move from his bruises, when the vessel, a heavy lurch having shifted her cargo, was laid on her beam-ends, and the water rushing in carried everything off the deck. Provisions, stores, planks,

all went adrift—and with the latter the poor lady, together
with the disabled cook, floated away without the possibility
of saving either of them.   But such was the indescribable
horror of those who were left, that had we been able to
reason or reflect, we might well have envied our departed
shipmates.

A few minutes before the brig went over, two of the crew,
who were invalids, having gone to the maintop, one of them
was forced into the belly of the maintop-sail, and there
found a watery grave.   The rest of the crew, and the male
passenger, got upon the side of the vessel.   In this hopeless
situation, secured, and clinging to the channels and rigging,
the sea every instant dashing over us, and threatening
destruction, we remained some hours.   Then the hull once
more righted, and we crawled on board.   The deck having
blown up, and the stern gone the same way, we had now
the prospect of perishing with cold and hunger.   For our
ultimate preservation I conceive we were mainly indebted to
the carpenter's having providentially retained his axe.
With it the fore-mast was cut away.   While doing this, we
found a piece of pork about four pounds in weight; and
even the possession of this morsel raised our drooping
spirits.   It would at least prolong existence a few hours,
and in that interval the gale might abate, some friendly sail
heave in sight, and the elements relent.   Such were our
reflections.   Oh! how our eyes were strained, as, emerging
from the trough of the sea on the crest of a liquid mountain, we gazed on the misty horizon, until from time to
time we fancied, nay, felt assured, we saw the object of our
search, but the evening closed in, and with it hope almost
expired.   That day not a morsel passed our lips.   The
pork, our only supply, given in charge to the captain, it was
thought prudent to husband as long as possible.

Meanwhile, with a topgallant studding-sail remaining in
the top, which was stretched over the mast-head, we con-

trived to procure a partial shelter from the inclemency of the weather. Under this, drenched as we were and shivering with cold, some of us crouched for the night; but others of the crew remained during the darkness in the rigging. In the morning we all—fourteen in number— mustered on deck, and received from the mate a small piece of pork, about two ounces; the remainder being carefully put away, and reserved for the next day. This, and some water, the only article of which we had abundance—a cask had been discovered forward, well stowed away among the planks—constituted our only meal that day. Somewhat refreshed, we all went to work, and as the studding-sail afforded but a scanty shelter, we fitted the trysail for this purpose, on opening which we found the cat drowned, and much as our stomachs might have revolted against such food on ordinary occasions, yet poor puss was instantly skinned, and her carcass hung up in the maintop.

This night we were somewhat better lodged; and the following day, having received our scanty ration of pork, now nearly consumed, we got three swiftsures round the hull of the vessel, to prevent her from going to pieces. Foraging daily for food, we sought incessantly in every crevice, hole, and corner, but in vain. We were now approaching that state of suffering beyond which nature cannot carry us. With some, indeed, the horrors of our situation were already past endurance; and one individual, who had left a wife and family dependant upon him for support in London, unable any longer to bear up against these, and the almost certain prospect of starvation, went down out of the top, and we saw him no more. Having eked out the pork to the fourth day, we commenced on the cat— fortunately puss was both large and in good condition—a mouthful of which, with some water, furnished our daily allowance.

Sickness and debility had now made such ravages among

us all, that although we had a tolerable stock of water, we found great difficulty in procuring it. We had hitherto, in rotation, taken our turn to fill a small beaker at the cask, which was wedged in among the cargo of deals; but now scarcely able to keep our feet along the planks, and still less so to haul the beaker up to the top, we were in danger of even this resource being cut off from us. In this manner, incredible as it may seem, we managed to keep body and soul together till the eleventh day, our only sustenance the pork, the cat, water, and the bark of some young birch trees; which latter, in search for a keg of tamarinds, which we had hoped to find, we had latterly come athwart.

On the twelfth morning, at daybreak, the hailing of some one from the deck electrified us all. Supposing, as we had missed none of our shipmates from the top, that it must be some boat or vessel, we all eagerly made a movement to answer our supposed deliverers, and such was our excitement that it well nigh upset what little reason we had left. We soon found out our mistake. We saw that one of the party was missing; and from this individual, whom we had found without shoes, hat, or jacket, had the voice proceeded.

Despair had now taken such a complete hold of all that, suspended between life and death, a torpor had seized us, and resigned to our fate, we had scarcely sufficient energy to lift our heads, and exercise the only faculty on which depended our safety. The delirium of our unfortunate shipmate had, however, reanimated us; and by this means, through Providence, he was made instrumental to our deliverance. Not long after, one of the men suddenly exclaimed—"This is Sunday morning!—the Lord will deliver us from our distress!—at any rate I will take a look round." With this he arose, and having looked about him for a few minutes, the cheering cry of "A sail!" announced the fulfilment of this singular prophecy. "Yes," he repeated in answer to our doubts, "a sail! and bearing right down upon us!"

We all eagerly got up, and looking in the direction indicated, the welcome certainty that we would not be cheated of our hopes almost turned our brains. The vessel, which proved to be a Boston brig, bound for London, ran down across our bows, hove-to, sent her boats alongside the wreck, and by ten o'clock we were all safe on board. Singularly enough, the *Wellington*, which had since the commencement of our disasters been lying-to with her head to the northward and westward, went about the evening previous to our rescue. This we considered as another providential occurrence; for had she remained with her head to the northward, we could have seen nothing of our deliverers. From the latter we experienced all the care and attention which our deplorable condition required; and with the exception of two of our party, who were frost-bitten, and who died two days after we had quitted the wreck, all of us were soon restored to health, and reached St. Catherine's Dock, at London, on the 30th of the following month.

THE EARL OF ELDON.

THE destruction of this vessel by fire, when in the Indian Ocean and on a passage from Bombay to England, gave occasion for the exercise of all the finer qualities that are supposed to be inherent to the British seaman, and the captain and his crew proved themselves worthy representatives of their country and profession in the hour of difficulty and danger. The *Earl of Eldon* was a fine, strongly-built ship of 600 tons, and seemed in every way fitted to contend with any adverse elements she might meet with on her way. On this, her last voyage, she was laden with cotton. She also carried a few passengers. Between decks the space was filled with cotton bales, packed so tightly as to render the operation of removing the cargo from that part of the ship more difficult than stowing the same. Before shipping the cotton it had become wet through exposure during a heavy rainfall. After going through the process of drying in the warehouses, it had then been pressed into bales by means of powerful screws, and it is not unlikely that after shipment fire-damp may have been generated in the closely-stowed bales, in the same way as in a haystack, when the produce of the grass-field has been stacked in a damp condition. Including three ladies and an infant, together with the commander of the vessel, Captain Theaker, and the crew, there were forty-five persons on board the *Earl of Eldon* when she set out from Bombay on the 24th of August 1834. An officer of the Madras Artillery, who was a passenger on the occasion, has described the incidents of the conflagration, the gallantry of Captain Theaker and his seamen, and the remarkable preservation of all on board the burning ship. The following is the officer's narrative:—

On the 26th of September the trade-wind seemed to have fairly caught hold of our sails, and we anticipated a speedy arrival at the Cape. On the 27th I arose early and went on deck, where I found one of my fellow-passengers. We perceived a steam arising apparently from the fore-hatch-way. I remarked to H—— that I thought it might be caused by fire-damp, and, if not immediately checked, might become fire. The captain came on deck, and I asked him what it was. He answered, steam ; and that it was common enough in cotton-loaded ships, when the hatchways were opened. I said nothing, but the smoke becoming more dense, and assuming a different colour, I thought all was not right, and also that the captain had some idea of this kind, as the carpenter was cutting holes in the deck just above the place whence the smoke appeared to come.

I went down to dress, and about half-past six Captain Theaker knocked at my door, and told me that part of the cotton was on fire, and that he wished to see all the gentlemen passengers on deck. We assembled, and he stated the case to be this : That some part of the cargo had been spontaneously ignited, and that he wished to remove part of the bales, till he could come to the ignited ones, and throw these overboard. We of course left everything to his judgment. The hands were ordered to breakfast as quickly as possible, and set to work to discover the source of the fire. This having been done, he said there did not seem to be immediate danger, and that he hoped to avert it altogether. But at eight o'clock the smoke became much thicker, and rolled through the after-hatchway—the draught being admitted forward, to allow the men to work. Several bales were removed; but the heat from below became intolerable, the smoke rolled out in suffocating volumes, and before nine, part of the deck had caught fire; in short, the men were obliged to stop work. The hatches were battened down, to keep the fire from bursting out; the boats were hoisted out and stocked; and about half-past one, the three ladies, two sick passengers, an infant, and a female servant, were put into the long-boat, with two hundred and sixteen gallons of water, twenty of brandy, preserved meats, and biscuits for a month.

It was now two o'clock; the hatches were opened and all hands set to try to extinguish the fire. The main-hatch being lifted, and a tarpaulin removed, there was a sail underneath, which was so hot that the men could scarcely lift it; when they did, the heat and smoke came up worse than ever. The fire being found to be underneath that part of the deck, orders were given to hoist out the bales till the inflamed ones could be reached; but when the men got hold of the lashing to introduce a crane-hook, the cotton was found to be burned beneath, and the charred stuff came away in their hands.

Our case was now bad indeed. We tried to remove the cotton by handfuls, but the smoke and heat were so overpowering, that no man could stand over the hatchway, and water, in the quantities that we dared to use, only seemed to increase the fire; for had the captain ventured to pump water into the ship to extinguish the fire, the bales would have swelled so much as to have burst open the deck, and increased in weight sufficient to sink the ship; either way, destruction would have been the issue. Seeing the case to be hopeless, the captain assembled us on the poop, and asked if we knew any expedient for extinguishing the fire and saving the ship, as in that case "we will stick by her while a hope remains." All agreed that nothing could be done; the crew were all sober, and had done their best in the fearful emergency.

The heat increased so much that it became dangerous to leave the poop. The captain then requested us to get into the boats; told off, and embarked his men; and at three, himself left the ship, just as the flames burst through the quarter-deck. We put off, the two boats towing the long-boat; the ship's way having been previously stopped by backing her yards. When we were about a mile from the ship she was in one blaze, and her masts began to fall in. The sight was grand, though awful. Between eight and nine, she had burned to the water's edge; then there suddenly came a bright flash, followed by a dull, heavy explosion—the powder had caught; for a few seconds her splinters and flaming fragments were glittering in the air, then all was gloom!

Sad was the prospect now before us! In the long-boat were the captain and twenty-five of the crew and passengers, with an infant four months old; the size of the boat being twenty-three feet long by seven-and-a-half broad. The other two boats each held ten individuals, including the officer in charge. One of these had some bags of biscuits aboard, but the chief provision was in the long-boat. We were a thousand miles from Rodrigne, and four hundred and fifty from Diego Garcias, the largest of the Chagos Islands; but to get there we must brave the sea as much as in the stormy latitudes we had left, exposed alternately to squalls and calms. We therefore determined on trying for Rodrigne.

About eleven at night we rigged the boats, and got under sail. In the long-boat we carried a lantern lashed to our mast, to prevent the others from losing us during the darkness; and

at daybreak we sent them sailing in all directions to look
for ships. While the wind was light they could out-sail us,
but when it blew strongly, and the sea was high, the
difference of speed was rather in our favour, as the weight
and size of the long-boat enabled her to lay hold of the
water better. On the third day the change of the moon
approached, and the weather began to look threatening;
but as we were in the trade, we did not fear foul or contrary winds. During that night it blew freshly, with rain ;
we were without shelter, and the sea, dashing its spray over
us, drenched us and spoilt a great part of our biscuit, though
we did not discover this till we were nearly out of our
dangers. The discomfort and misery of our situation were
very great. There was a large water-puncheon in the boat,
on the top of which I slept nearly all the time we were in
the boats. The ladies were in the stern of the long-boat ;
and H——, myself, the doctor, and a Bombay lieutenant, in
the body of the craft with the men.

In the course of the next day the weather grew worse,
and one of the small boats was split by the sea. She came
alongside, and therein we put the carpenter, who made
what repairs he could, but with little hope of their ultimate
safety. Having lashed a bamboo four feet up the mast, and
fixed it on the intersection of two stanchions at the same
height above the stern, we then fastened a piece of canvas
along our weather-gunwale. The cloth was firmly lashed
along this, so as to form a kind of half-pent roof. But for
this imperfect defence we must have been swamped, and we
still shipped seas to such an extent that four men were constantly employed in baling. In the evening it blew hard,
with a tremendous sea ; and not thinking the damaged boat
safe, we took in her crew and abandoned her. Thirty-six
persons were now stowed closely in the long-boat, and we
were obliged to throw over all superfluities. We had not
more than eight inches of clear gunwale out of the water.

That miserable night I shall never forget. A single wave might have overwhelmed us. The remembrance of my past life crowded on my mind. I felt parted from this world, yet could not divest myself of a certain feeling that we would be saved. I recommended myself to Him without whose permission the waves had no power to harm us, and resigned myself to meet death. But when I thought of the short struggle that might usher us into eternity, it was no longer with calmness; there was regret at the consideration of what those would feel who awaited my return.

Wet, crushed, and miserable, the night passed away, and morning broke. Though the weather was still very bad, I again felt that hope had not entirely deserted me. A tremendous sea came rolling down, and I drew in my breath with horror: it broke right over our stern, drenched the poor women to their throats, and carried off the steersman's hat. But the captain cried out in a tone of encouragement, "That's nothing! it's all right; bale away, my boys!" He told us afterwards, however, that he did not expect we would live out the night. Although harassed in mind and body, he never let us despair. He stood on a bench the whole night, and slept none for nearly forty-eight hours. Morning again broke; and as after the change of the moon the weather moderated a little, we enjoyed comparatively some comfort. We had three small meals of biscuit and jam daily, with three half-pints of water and a little brandy. The sailors were allowed a gill of spirits each day. We had plenty of cigars, and whenever we could strike a light had a smoke, which we found to be a great luxury. The ladies were most wretched, however, for they could not move, and any little alteration in their dress could only be effected by drawing a curtain in front of them; yet they did not utter one repining word.

On the thirteenth evening after the burning of the ship we began to look out for Rodrigne; the captain telling us meanwhile not to be too sanguine, as his chronometer was not to be trusted after its late rough treatment. The night fell, and I went forward to sleep, but about twelve o'clock I was awakened by the cry that land was right ahead. Looking in that direction, I saw land looming through the mist. The boat was brought-to for an hour; we then made sail for the coast, and about half-past two the outlines thereof became more definite and clear. We now lay-to until daylight. I attempted to compose myself to sleep, but my feelings were too strong, and I betook myself to smoking.

With the first light of dawn Rodrigne appeared six miles ahead, and by eight A.M. we had all been safely landed. A fisherman, who came to show us the way through the reefs, received us into his house, and proceeded to set before us some food; meanwhile sending to the gentleman of the island information as to our arrival. Two of them came down immediately, and, having heard the story of our perils, said that our preservation was almost miraculous. We set off from the fisherman's dwelling in two parties; the married men going to the house of one of the gentlemen, and the single to that of the other. The crew were taken inland to a suitable spot, and there encamped. Our bundles were carried by negroes to the houses of our hosts, where everything needful was at once supplied to us—clean linen and a plentiful dinner. We then retired to bed, and enjoyed a luxury to which we had been strangers during a fortnight—a sound sleep.

THE NEVA.

WITHIN a period of about two years three British transport-vessels were lost, when on their way with convicts to New South Wales. By these calamities nearly five hundred persons perished. The first of the unfortunate trio was the *Amphitrite*, which, as we have seen, was run aground on the French coast, with the result that one hundred and thirty-three lives were destroyed. The second of these ships, bearing the name of *George the Third*, foundered at sea, occasioning the loss of one hundred and thirty-four lives. The third was the *Neva*, the wreck of which in the Pacific Ocean caused the destruction of not fewer than two hundred and twenty-four lives. This fearful mortality, in so short a time, among our convicts was well calculated to direct public attention to the mode of punishment then inflicted upon such as had been found guilty of felony in the United Kingdom—a punishment that seemed like death-sentences for comparatively small offences. But several years elapsed ere Justice was allowed to be tempered with Mercy when dealing with the criminal.

The *Neva*, a barque of 837 tons, and commanded by Captain Peck, sailed from Cork on the 8th of January 1835

Her destination was Sydney, as she had been chartered for the transportation of one hundred and fifty female convicts to the settlements in that part of the British possessions. Besides these felons, she had on board not fewer than fifty-five children, and nine free emigrants. A surgeon of the Royal Navy, Dr. R. Stevenson, also sailed in the ship. The convicts were in the charge of a superintendent, and the crew numbered twenty-six officers, men and boys. For several weeks the voyage was prosecuted under very favourable circumstances, until sickness broke out among the passengers and prisoners, when three of the former succumbed to their disease, and were buried at sea. A baby having been born on the way, the total number of souls on board, as the vessel sailed the last quarter of her journey, was two hundred and forty-two.

About noon on the 13th of May, according to the ship's reckoning, she was ninety miles from King's Island, at the entrance of Bass Straits. A good look-out was now kept for land, which was accordingly made on the 14th, at two o'clock in the morning. In about two hours afterwards breakers were suddenly discovered right ahead, and orders to tack were therefore given by Captain Peck, so that if possible the danger that threatened might be avoided. Without the unnecessary loss of a moment, the vessel was then put in stays, but to the consternation of all on board, she immediately struck upon a reef, unshipped her rudder, and became quite unmanageable. The wind was now blowing very strongly, and the ship was under double-reefed top-sails. Scarcely had the crew and passengers recovered from the alarm into which they had been thrown by the disaster, when the vessel again struck most violently on the larboard-bow, and instantly bilged by swinging broadside on the rock.

The consternation and alarm into which all on board had been thrown by this unexpected and melancholy event was succeeded by a panic, induced by the natural desire to secure

their personal safety. Self-preservation, indeed, now seemed
to be the one prevailing object that actuated every breast,
and the captain was loudly called upon to render what
assistance he could to rescue those who were under his care
from the perils in which they were involved. He endeavoured to soothe and console the terror-stricken people, and
earnestly besought them to restrain their feelings as much as
possible; but the imminent danger of their situation
rendered them desperate, and their cry for deliverance rose
louder and louder as the danger of the ship became every
moment more apparent.

The pinnace was now lowered, and the captain, the
surgeon, the superintendent of the convicts, and two of the
crew got into the boat, and endeavoured to make off from
the now evidently sinking vessel. The doors of the prison
being burst open by the violence with which the ship had
struck, the whole of the wretched females rushed on deck,
threw themselves over the side of the vessel, and clinging
to the boat, quickly swamped her, when all excepting the
master and the two sailors perished amidst one wild cry of
drowning agony.

With the greatest difficulty the captain contrived to
regain the ship, when he ordered the long-boat to be
launched, and that care should be taken to prevent a
similar accident to that which had just befallen them, by too
many endeavouring simultaneously to force their way into
the boat. Having taken the utmost precaution to secure
their own deliverance from death, the occupants of the
long-boat at length pushed off, but scarcely had they got
away from the ship when the craft was upset by the violence
of the surf, and the whole were precipitated into the waves.

The master and the chief mate being good swimmers,
once more succeeded in saving themselves from a death
which had appeared to be inevitable. With extreme
difficulty they managed to reach the ship, but scarcely had

they got on board when a new horror seized them by the vessel going in pieces. Every hope of preservation was now banished from their minds.

The scene was alike awful and indescribable. The vessel had been divided into four parts, each of which was covered with the terror-stricken females, all in the dress in which they had just before rushed from their beds. The remainder of the crew were clinging wildly to portions of the wreck, and screaming for help in the most piteous manner. Situated as they were, not one gleam of hope broke in to cheer or inspire them. Beneath and around them were the lashing waves, roaring aloud as if eager for their destruction. The winds howled in seeming triumph over the work of devastation and death : rocking the disjointed wreckage so that each moment seemed to the terrified creatures thereon as if it would be their last in this world. Every plank and beam creaked, as the elements beat furiously upon these slender plans of security ; but uncertain as their foothold seemed, the hearts of the poor creatures quailed lest it should sink and bury them in the water. Nor was it long before their worst apprehensions were verified. The wreck, parted as it was, soon afterwards went into a hundred pieces, the final work of destruction was completed, and the whole of the surviving people were precipitated, shrieking with horror, into the ocean.

Nearly the whole of the unfortunate sufferers were given up to an untimely death. Only two-and-twenty persons, consisting of some of the crew, and a few of the convicts, were saved, by clinging to portions of the wreck. These drifted to King's Island, situate about nine miles from the spot where this distressing catastrophe had taken place. But their struggles to gain the shore was desperate and severe, and it was not till after they had been in the water for a period exceeding eight hours, that they at last succeeded in reaching the land. Of these twenty-two sufferers, seven shortly afterwards died, from exhaustion consequent upon the excessive fatigue to which they had for so long a period been subjected.

After having buried the bodies of their unfortunate companions, and in some degree recovered from the cold and fatigue which they had themselves endured, the remaining fifteen succeeded, after considerable difficulty, in erecting a temporary tent of the articles that were occasionally washed ashore from the wreck. Nor were they suffered to perish of starvation by the Providence which had preserved them from drowning. A few provisions were washed ashore from the vessel, and upon the scanty supply thus afforded they contrived, with economy, to subsist for about fifteen days.

Fortunately for the survivors of the *Neva*, a small vessel, the *Tartar*, belonging to Hobart Town, and the property of Mr. C. Friend, had been wrecked on another part of the same island. The whole of the *Tartar's* crew had been saved, and had also erected a tent as a place of shelter, till a vessel should arrive to take them from that cheerless spot. While thus waiting for the anticipated succour, their attention was arrested and excited by numerous portions of another wreck which they found on the sea-shore.

Actuated by curiosity, and a desire to ascertain whether any of the crew of the other ill-fated vessel had escaped, the men belonging to the *Tartar* commenced a journey round the island. In this expedition they encountered perils and trials of no ordinary kind, and after a search of two or three days, arrived at the tent which had been erected by the survivors of the unfortunate *Neva*. The meeting between the two parties of shipwrecked persons was affecting. Their hearts at once warmed towards each other, and uniting in one association, they all resolved to remain together until relieved from the solitary island upon which they had been thrown.

The crew of the *Tartar* had been accompanied upon the

17

island by a passenger of that vessel, a seal hunter, who had happily saved several of his dogs. With the assistance of these sagacious animals they soon succeeded in taking a walaby, upon which all subsisted until their release from a scene of barren desolation. Each day men were placed upon the loftiest eminencies near the coast, in order to discover whether any vessels were passing within view, and in the event of a ship being seen, to hail her by whatever signals they could make. While some of the party were thus employed, others were engaged in fishing or hunting, and the remainder busied themselves in endeavouring to increase the interior comforts of the tents, which had been erected to shelter all from the inclement season now just setting in.

The mental and bodily sufferings to which these poor creatures were subjected, it would be impossible to describe. Day after day passed heavily, and still no succour came, till at last they almost began to regret that the raging elements which had destroyed so many of their companions had not involved them also in the same dreadful fate. But help came at last.

On the 15th of June, exactly one month from the time of the wreck taking place, Mr. Friend, the owner of the *Tartar*, arrived at the island, in the *Sarah Ann*, another of his vessels. It now providentially happened that Mr. Friend was passing King's Island, on his way to the whaling station at Portland Bay, and the signals made on the coast gave him reason to suppose that there were some persons there in distress. Upon landing, he was immediately surrounded by nearly the whole of the shipwrecked persons, who hailed him joyfully as their deliverer from misery and death. Mr. Friend assured them that he would do all in his power to alleviate their distress, and consoled them with the promise of landing them at Launceston as speedily as possible. They then collected together all the bodies of their unfortunate companions that they found washed ashore from the wreck, and pronouncing over them the solemn rites of Christian burial, consigned to the grave the remains of not fewer than one hundred of their fellow-beings.

This melancholy duty performed, the whole of the surviving sufferers, with the exception of two seamen and one female convict, who at the time were at the other side of the island, were got on board the *Sarah Ann*, preparatory to their departure from the island. A fair wind befriended them, and on the 27th of June they arrived in safety at Launceston, in New Holland.

As soon as the local government was made acquainted with this disastrous catastrophe, the cutter *Shamrock* was despatched to King's Island, for the purpose of taking off whatever persons might have been there left, and to pick up any portion of the wreck, or government stores, which might have floated on shore. On arriving at the island, the *Shamrock's* men found the two sailors and the female, who, on discovering that their fellow-sufferers had left the island, ad been reduced to a state of utter despair. But upon the arrival of the cutter they joyfully hastened on board. The crew then gathered all the valuable portions of the wreck and stores they could find, and having buried a few more bodies which had drifted on shore, they quitted the island and returned with the last of the survivors from the wreck of the *Neva* to Launceston.

THE FRANCIS SPAIGHT.

ON the 24th November 1835, a fine vessel of 350 tons burthen sailed from St. John's, Newfoundland. She was the *Francis Spaight*, of Limerick, and laden with timber. Her captain, mate, and crew numbered sixteen men and boys. Some of the seamen were but indifferent hands, having only been trained as boatmen on the Shannon, and had not been long enough at sea to be capable of performing efficiently the ordinary duties of men before the mast. From that cause much of the misfortune and suffering which marked her voyage on this occasion arose. The incidents here described were related by one of the sailors, and present altogether a melancholy picture of the results of incapacity and want of discipline on the part of a master-mariner and his crew :—

Nothing could be finer than the weather for the first eight or ten days of the voyage, but it afterwards came on to blow so hard that we were obliged to drive before the wind under a mizzen-topsail. At three o'clock in the morning of December the 3rd, a cry was raised on deck, speedily followed by alarm and confusion. Through the carelessness of the helmsman, who had perhaps been steering wildly, or it may be from the bad trim of the ship, she suddenly broached-to, and lay like a log in the trough of the sea. The day had not dawned; it was still very dark, and the waves broke so frightfully over her, that neither the captain nor mate could get some of the men to obey their orders. Even when the hull was filling rapidly with water, the majority of the crew refused to work the pumps, on being directed to do so by the master himself.

In less than an hour the *Francis Spaight* lay on her beam-ends, the greater part of her men endeavouring to save themselves by climbing up her side and clinging to the rigging. By this disaster the mate and two of the sailors lost their lives—the former being drowned in the after-cabin, into which he had gone only a few minutes previous to the capsizing of the vessel; the latter perishing from the same cause in the forecastle. The captain and a man named Melville now got to the fore and main masts, and cut these away; the mizzentop-mast went also over the side, and the ship almost immediately righted. The main-mast unfortunately was not perfectly free, but clung by the mainstay, and, as there was a heavy sea rolling, the waves continued beating against the side of the vessel while the gale lasted, so that it was thought sometimes she would have gone to pieces. As soon as she had righted, being already filled with water, she settled down in the sea, and there was scarcely any portion of her to be seen except the poop and bulwarks. No situation could now be more hopeless or miserable than that of the unfortunate crew, standing, as we did, ankle deep on the wreck, in the depth of a winter's night, and clinging in the darkness to whatever object was nearest, as sea after sea rolled successively over us; but we knew not the full horror of our condition until the dawn of the morning, for which all on board were now looking eastward with intense anxiety. We discovered that our provisions had been washed overboard, and as the holds were filled by the sea, we had no means of coming at any fresh water. The gale continued unabated through the morning, and the dreadful swell every now and then swept over the decks, so that for safety, as well as for shelter, we gathered into the cabin under the poop. Even here the hull lay so deep with water that a dry plank could not be found on which we might lie ; our only rest was by standing closely together, huddled up, and leaning against one another. By this means we had some shelter from the weather, and, what was of yet more consequence, some protection from the cold, which was very severe. We were, however, often driven from this wretched lodging by the seas breaking in over the ship's stern, and obliging us to rush out on the quarter-deck.

As the storm showed no diminution with the advance of the day, and the vessel lay like a log on the water, hundreds of miles from land, no one entertained even the remotest expectation of ever seeing home again, when an incident occurred which raised our hopes for a few moments, but only to leave us more forlorn and miserable than before. At about ten o'clock in the forenoon, a vessel was suddenly descried to the westward, and for some time it was thought possible her course might lie near us, but she stood far away beyond the reach of signal, and was soon out of sight. That day and the next passed away without the slightest change in the weather. On the third, it began to moderate, during the whole of which period we remained standing in the cabin, leaning against one another, or against the ship's sides, unable to take rest or sleep. We could hardly have believed beforehand that it was possible for men to hold out for so many days and nights without lying down, wholly without food, and almost without drink, yet we did not feel much exhausted, or altogether incapable of exertion.

Our greatest suffering was from hunger, or rather a sink. 'ng at the stomach, and from thirst, neither of which had we any conceivable means of allaying. There were thirteen hands alive, and of these not one had tasted a morsel of food since the wreck. For drink we had only three bottles of wine, which were found in the cabin; this was served out in wine glasses at long intervals. There was some occasional rain, which we were not prepared at first for saving, as we could get but a scanty supply by holding the cover of a tureen under the saddle of the mizzen-mast. On the fourth or fifth day after the wreck we removed a cistern from the quarter-galley, and got it under the mizzen-mast, where it was filled in two days. The periods in which little or no rain fell were, however, often long, so that we stinted ourselves to the smallest possible allowance, even when there was a sufficient supply. Some of the men when it rained held out their handkerchiefs, and when these were thoroughly soaked, squeezed the water into their mouths, or sometimes into their shoes, from which they greedily drank it; others mopped the decks, or whatever places it chanced to lodge in free from the brine. In seven days after the appearance of the first vessel, another was seen on the weather quarter, outward bound, and only four miles north. Our hopes were again revived, and for a short time the anxiety on board was intense. An ensign was hoisted on our mizzen-mast, and also part of a sail; the day was very clear, and those on the passing ship could not but see our signals—at least we thought so—but she bore away like the former one, and was soon lost to our view.

Despair was now in every countenance. How we lived through the succeeding five days it would be hard to tell, but no one tasted food; some few endeavoured to eat the horn buttons of their jackets, the only substitute for nutriment which occurred to them. There were no means of taking fish, and although birds were sometimes seen flying past, we had no means of bringing them down. Horrible as this situation was, it was made yet worse by the conduct of some of the crew towards one another. As their sufferings increased they lost all command of their temper, and became cross and selfish in the extreme—such as were strong securing a place on the cabin floor for lying down, and pushing aside those who were weak, to shift for themselves as they could in the wet and cold. There was a boy named O'Brien, especially, who seemed even before the wreck to have no friend on board, and he now endured every sort of cruelty and abuse. Most of the men now had sore legs from standing continually in the salt water, and were peevish and apprehensive of being hurt; but whatever they might have borne from others, as soon as O'Brien chanced to come near them, in search of a dry berth to lie in, he was kicked or cuffed unmercifully away, for which treatment he retaliated in curses. He had a miserable time of it—partly, perhaps, that being friendless, and the only person from Limerick on board, they could indulge their ill-humour on him with more impunity. He was the son of a poor widow at Thomondgate, Limerick, and before he joined the *Francis Spaight* used to earn a living at the quays, by rafting the timber discharged from the vessels arriving from Quebec.

On the 19th of December, the sixteenth day after the wreck, and since we had tasted food, many of the men gathered together in groups, and something seemed to be then in cogitation. The mystery was cleared up in the course of the day. When all happened to be collected together in the cabin, the captain came off deck, and addressed us about our desperate condition. He said we had been now such a length of time without sustenance that it was beyond human nature to endure any longer, that we were already on the verge of the grave, and that the only question for us to consider was whether one or all should die; that at present it seemed certain that all must die unless food could be procured, but that, if one died, the rest might live, until some ship came in sight. His opinion was that one should suffer

for the rest, and that lots should be drawn, to fix upon the
person who was to give up his life for the sake of his shipmates.
The lots, he said, ought to be drawn between the four boys,
as they had no families, and could not be considered so great
a loss to their friends as those who had wives and children
depending on them. This address was received by most of
the men with a cry of approbation—at least several voices
were heard to exclaim " 'Tis right," " Very right," " Very fit
it should be done," and none appeared to object except the
boys, who all cried out against the injustice of such a proceeding. O'Brien in particular protested against it, assert-
ing that their lives were as dear to them as if they were men
or married, and that unless the lots were drawn fairly all
round they would not submit.

The clamour for and against the limitation of the lot
continued for a short time, the second mate and a seaman
principally insisting on it, and O'Brien offering the most
determined opposition, when some mutterings were heard
amongst the men, that led O'Brien to apprehend they might
proceed in a more summary way, and at once fix upon himself. It was said, " It would be a very good deed to put
him out of the way, that he deserved it, and it would be the
right way to serve him." Friendless and forlorn as he was,
expressions like these were well calculated to terrify the
boy into acquiescence, and seeing no alternative, he at length
submitted. One of the men now prepared some sticks of
different lengths for the lots, and while the dreadful preparations were going forward, the poor boys were preparing their
minds for the result. One of them assured us afterwards
that he was almost indifferent about the whole proceeding,
having at once made up his mind for death, when he saw
the chances of escape were so few. He did not even watch
the drawing of the lot with the intense anxiety one might
suppose he would feel when life or death hung thereon, and
he awaited the decision only that if it fell upon him he

might on the moment jump overboard. A bandage was now tied over O'Brien's eyes, and he knelt down, resting his face on the knees of a sailor. The latter had the sticks in his hand, and was to hold them up one by one, demanding whose lot it was. O'Brien was to call out a name, and whatever person he named for the shortest stick was to die. The first stick was held up. The answer was, "For little Johnny Sheehan," and the lot was laid aside without announcing whether it was the fatal one or not. The next stick was held up and the demand was repeated, "On whom is this lot to fall?" O'Brien's reply was, "On myself," upon which the man who held the sticks laid these down, and said that was the death-lot—that O'Brien had called it for himself. None of the other boys could tell whether it was the right lot or not, but the men said it fell upon O'Brien, and some were heard to say that it was a good deed.

The poor fellow heard the announcement without uttering a word. He got up, took off the bandage from his eyes, and looked quietly around. His face was very pale, but not a feature of it was changed. The men now told him he must prepare for death, and the captain said it was better it should be done by bleeding him in the arm, to which O'Brien made no objection. The captain then directed the cook, John Gorman, to do it, telling him it was his duty. But Gorman strenuously refused. He was, however, threatened with death himself by the men if he continued obstinate, and he at last consented. O'Brien then took off his jacket, without waiting to be desired, and after telling the crew, if any of them ever reached home, to tell his poor mother what had happened to him, bared his right arm. The cook twice cut the veins with a small knife, but could bring no flow of blood, upon which there seemed to be some hesitation among the men as to what should be done. They were, however, relieved by the boy himself, who immediately desired the cook to give him the knive, as he could not be looking at him putting him to pain. When O'Brien got the knife and was about to cut the vein, the captain recommended him to try the left arm, which he accordingly did. He attempted to open the vein at the bend of the elbow with the point of the knife, as a surgeon would, but, like the cook, he failed in bringing blood. A dead consternation now fell upon all, but in a minute or two the captain said, "This is all of no use, 'tis better to put him out of pain by at once bleeding him in the throat," and some of them said it was good advice. At this O'Brien, for the first time, looked terrified, and begged hard that they would not do so, but give him a little time; he said he was cold and weak, but if they would let him lie down and sleep for a little, he would get warm, and then he would bleed freely, upon which some one complained that it was of no use waiting, as it was impossible the boy could sleep. The lad protested anxiously that he could, however, and told that when he was sick one night in Limerick, a doctor attempted to bleed him in the arm and failed, but after he had slept a few hours, and got warm in bed, the blood came freely. If they would now, he continued, only let him lie down on the boards for a few hours, he was sure the blood would flow. To this wish there were expressions of dissent from the men, and the captain almost immediately said to them, that it was useless leaving the boy this way in pain; it were best at once to lay hold on him, and let the cook cut his throat. O'Brien, now roused and driven to desperation, seemed working himself up for resistance, and declared he would not let them. The first man, he said, who laid hands on him would suffer; he would appear to him at another time; he would haunt him after death. He was threatening them, in short, with everything he thought at the moment might terrify, and whether influenced by the menaces, or conscience-stricken at the horrid crime they were committing, there was a general pause or hesitation among the crew. A man named Mahony was even heard to say he would have nothing to do with it, when suddenly a fellow started forward and seized the boy, exclaiming, that if the lot had fallen upon himself, he would allow his head to be cut off at once.

The die was now cast—they all rushed in upon him. O'Brien screamed and struggled violently, still threatening them, and addressing himself in particular to Sullivan, a Tarbert man. The poor youth was, however, among so many, soon got down, and the cook was once again called upon to put him to death. The man now refused more strenuously than before, and another altercation arose; but weak, irresolute, and seeing that his own life, if he persisted, would absolutely be taken instead of O'Brien's, he at length yielded to their menaces. Some one at this time brought him down a large case-knife that had been on the poop, with which, pale and trembling, the man stood over O'Brien, who was still endeavouring to free himself from those who held him. To save the blood, one of them now placed under the boy's neck the cover of the tureen, which they had before used to collect the rain, while several cried out to the cook to do his duty. The horror-stricken man, over and over again, endeavoured to summon up hardihood for the deed, but when he caught the boy's eye his heart always failed him, and he then looked supplicatingly at the men again. But their cries and threats were loud for death; he made a desperate effort—there was a short struggle, and O'Brien was no more!

As soon as this horrid act was perpetrated, the blood was served to the men, but a few of them, among whom was Mahony, refused to partake of it. They afterwards laid open the body, and separated the limbs; the latter were hung out over the stern, while a portion of the former was allotted for immediate use. Shocked as many were at the scene they had just witnessed, a gnawing hunger came upon all, when they saw even this disgusting meal laid out for them, and almost every one, even the unwilling boys, partook more or less thereof. This was the evening of the sixteenth day. They ate again late at night, and some greedily; but the thirst, which was before at least endurable, now became craving, and as there was no more blood, they slaked it with salt water. All then lay down to rest, but several were raving and talking wildly through the night, and in the morning the cook was observed to be insane. His eyes inflamed and glaring, and his speech rambling and incoherent, he threw his clothes about restlessly, and was often violent. When first the man lost his reason, one of the boys examined his clothes and found four sovereigns and five shillings in his belt, which the lad gave to the captain. It was singular that, amidst all his madness, the cook missed the money in the course of the day, and went round searching the men for it. His raving continued during the succeeding night, and in the morning, as his end seemed to be approaching, the veins of his neck were cut, and the blood drawn from him. This was the second death. On the night of that terrible day, Michael Behane was mad, and the boy George Burns on the following morning; they became so violent that they were obliged to be tied by the crew, and the latter was eventually likewise bled to death, by cutting his throat. Michael Behane died unexpectedly, otherwise he would in all probability have suffered the same fate.

Next morning the captain came off deck, and feeling too weak and exhausted to keep a look-out any longer, desired some one to take his place. Harrington and Mahony went up very soon after; the latter thought he could distinguish a sail, and raised a shout of joy, upon which those below immediately came up. A ship was clearly discernible, and apparently bearing her course towards us. Signals were hoisted with as much alacrity as our weakness would allow, and when she approached, and was almost within hail, our apprehension of her passing by, like the former vessels, was so great that we held up the hands and feet of O'Brien to excite commiseration. The vessel proved to be the *Agenora*, an American. Without hesitation, she put off a boat to our assistance, although the weather was very rough at the time, and there seemed to be a great apprehension of its swamping. The survivors of the *Francis Spaight* were all at length safely got on board the American ship, where we were treated with the utmost kindness.

THE ENGLAND.

ARLY in the year 1836, the brig *Blucher*, of Boston, when on her way to a South American port, went out of her course to perform an act of humanity, by rescuing some shipwrecked mariners from famine and death. Already had the brig picked up from the Atlantic some starving men who had abandoned their ship, and entrusted their lives to the slender security of an open boat upon the fickle ocean. The day had been cloudy, with occasional showers of rain, and just as evening was about to set in, the man on the look-out thought he could discern through the hazy atmosphere the hull of a vessel upon which were displayed signals of distress. When that intelligence had been passed along from the seamen at the bows, every eye on deck was strained in the direction of the supposed wreck, until the captain gave orders to put about the brig, in order to bear down upon the object that appeared to be drifting at the caprice of the wind and waves. In a short time the *Blucher* approached a water-logged ship, upon which were several men in the last extremity of existence, from long exposure to the elements without the means of sustaining life. The following account of the disaster, and providential relief of the famine-stricken crew was written by one who shared their sufferings :—

Having secured a passage homeward from Quebec, on board the *England*, of Newcastle, a vessel of 400 tons burden, laden with timber, and bound for Greenock, I lost no time in taking possession of my berth, and found that I was the only passenger. The vessel set sail, with a pilot on board, on the 9th of November 1835. Nothing remarkable occurred while in the river except that we had to come to anchor on account of a heavy snowstorm, and lay-to for about twenty-four hours, when we weighed anchor and set sail, our pilot leaving us the next day. On the 20th it began to blow fresh from the north-west, and up to the 23rd it increased till it amounted to a hurricane. Our ship was now obliged to run before the gale under close-reefed foretop-sails. She also laboured much, and two men were placed at the wheel. The sea had become tremendous, and our master was evidently a good deal alarmed. Being unable to go on deck himself, he was constantly calling down the mate, and asking how matters looked on deck. It was proposed to heave her to; but it was our captain's opinion that in such a heavy gale to do so would prove at once fatal; he advised them to stand firm by the wheel and keep her scudding.

The night which now closed in upon us will never be obliterated from my remembrance. I was sitting by the cabin-fire, occasionally going up the companion ladder or stair to see how things looked, the master moving up and down the cabin much discomposed, when a tremendous sea broke over the stern of the vessel, carrying destruction before it. The wheel came down with a crash through the cabin skylight in broken fragments, and in an instant we were in total darkness. The floor of our cabin was almost immediately covered with water, and a scene of horror and confusion ensued which beggars description. The two men who had been at the wheel came down the companion, having fortunately caught hold of something as the water dashed them forward on the deck. In a few minutes all hands were down in the cabin; and, having good tinder-boxes, we soon struck a light again, and getting a lantern, all went on deck except the captain.

The state of the deck was terrible to look at ; the hammocks swept overboard, with great part of the bulwarks ; the water-casks broken loose, and going to pieces. After getting the helm lashed and keeping the ship to, the wind moderating a little, we went to the pumps and found she was leaking considerably. All hands at once yoked to the duty of pumping. We wrought incessantly all night, and found that by doing so we could keep the water from gaining. We all joined in the work except the captain, who was in a bad state of health, and had so been for a considerable time before. The one-half rested while the other pumped. When the morning came, to our utter consternation we found our rudder had been broken and rendered quite useless. It only hung together, and kept flapping violently against the stern of the vessel, at every blow breaking, and opening the seams of the ship. At length the broken part detached itself, leaving nothing but a small part of the stern hanging in the rudder trunk, and the planks so shattered that the water was coming in in torrents. To stop the leak was now found to be impossible, and we discovered that all our pumping was of no avail. Our only comfort was, that we had a firm timber-laden ship under us, and of course were all aware that though she filled she would not sink. We had therefore no other alternative but to prepare with the utmost despatch for taking refuge in the rigging.

We packed up a few small bags of biscuit, a little beef and pork, and two casks of water, which we soon had in readiness ; these we hoisted up under the main-top ; then seizing our blankets, we all went aloft, some to the fore,

18

some to the main top, while our ship was filling very fast. Before going aloft we knocked out the stern and bow ports, and opened the hatches, so as to give the water ingress and egress ; without this precaution, in all likelihood our decks would have been burst by the working of the water beneath, and our timber have shifted. The shifting of a single log would have been the signal for our fate.

The ship, now thoroughly water-logged, was pitching and rolling, and we had to lash ourselves to the mast. What a prospect lay before us ! In such a cold latitude—at such a season—in the middle of the Western Ocean ! And the long winter nights ! with neither rudder nor compass, and storms and tempests to encounter ! The horrors of our situation can be imagined, but cannot be described. Our captain, a man in years, with a broken constitution, became so ill that he could take no command ; fortunately the mate and carpenter were active, and they immediately took charge, which was a fortunate circumstance. We immediately had to go upon an allowance of bread and water, which were divided to us in a most just and impartial manner during the whole period of our sufferings. For the first four days we had a moderate allowance of about one biscuit and a half, a small slice of beef or pork, and nearly two pints of water. We suffered dreadfully from cold and wet, and if we had not frequently shifted our position, would have become quite benumbed. I had the misfortune the night after I had gone to the main-top to lose both greatcoat and blankets. I happened to have on two shirts, drawers, a pair of good stockings and shoes, with a black vest, a pair of good Canadian cloth trousers, and a blue cloth jacket, and this was my all ; everything else was gone. I regretted the loss much, for although the blankets got frequently soaked with water, they still did something towards preserving the heat of the body. This unfortunate accident took place while I was asleep. Being overcome with cold and fatigue, I had fastened my greatcoat on the rigging to dry, and rolled myself in the blankets; it happened to come on to blow, and, on turning myself, the wind caught the loose clothes and swept them overboard. When I looked for my greatcoat, the rope-yarn that made it fast was there, but the coat was gone. The sleep we enjoyed in our insecure berth in the rigging was a kind of dog-sleep, and only lasted from fifteen minutes to half-an-hour at a time, and was being generally disturbed with dreams about our friends and far-distant homes, which we had little or no expectation of ever again seeing. Sometimes we awoke in a dreadful fright, dreaming we were pitched overboard, and some of the monsters of the deep ready to snatch us into their terrible maws. When we opened our eyes, it was, alas! to perceive the signs of famine or a watery grave. Most fortunately the wind began to prevail from the north-west, and we were drifted fast to a warmer and more genial climate. We then thought that, had we enough bread and water, we might survive a long time under our present circumstances; and the only immediate cause of alarm was the ship breaking up during some of the frequent and heavy squalls we had to encounter. For the purpose of standing it out as long as possible, on the sixth day after the ship was damaged we put ourselves upon just so much provisions as would preserve the spark of life: this was scarcely three ounces of bread in a very wet and mouldy condition, a small slice of beef or pork, and two or three gills of water. We were so scarce of this last article that we had to take every opportunity of securing as much as possible from the sails every time it happened to rain; this water drank very sweet; although tarry-tasted, it was to us most delicious and refreshing; and I am certain that never did the most voluptuous gourmand enjoy his most favourite beverage with better gusto than we did a drink of water squeezed from the dirty canvas. We had soon the satisfaction of getting into a milder atmosphere; how-

ever, till towards the end of December we occasionally
had very heavy weather, with a great deal of thunderstorms.
Having saved a quadrant, we found ourselves in the latitude
of the Azores ; but whether to the east or west we could
not tell, having drifted so many ways, without keeping
any reckoning.

On Christmas Day, which happened to be fine, we proposed to make a feast as well as we were able. We dared
not venture on the bread, but we got an extra slice of pork,
which some of us ate raw, others roasted. When the
weather was fine we could remain on deck, where we kindled
a fire for our cooking, but the sea was frequently breaking
over the deck with such fury that we were generally glad
to remain on the rigging. Having by this time suffered
nearly five weeks, some of us were excessively weak and
very much emaciated—so much so that we could scarcely
go up and down the shrouds. Hunger had brought on us a
kind of burning fever, and if we had had water in our power
we should have drank incessantly. Instead of heaving
overboard the rats which we caught, as we did at first, we
now flayed, roasted, and ate them, and found them delicious.
On every favourable opportunity we assembled together for
the purpose of devotion, praying with heartfelt earnestness
to Him who can make the storm a calm, and still the raging
of the mighty deep. We were constantly on the look-out
for ships, and when we saw any, hoisted signals of distress ;
they were, however, always at such a distance that they
certainly could not have seen us ; at any rate, none
approached us. We also cut pieces off our cable and made
burning torches, which we hoisted in the dark nights at the
mizzen-top, in case of any vessel passing in the night. This
was frequently done, but all was of no avail, and we
determined that the first vessel we saw, if she was on such
a tack as there might be any probability of getting to her,
we would launch the jolly-boat and chase her.

In a day or two we saw a vessel on what we thought a good tack, and, immediately launching our little boat, six brave fellows jumped into it and took to the oars, with the carpenter steering. We could afford them but a small allowance of bread and water. They gave us assurances that, should they get up with the ship, they would use all their endeavours to get its master to come after us; we, on the other hand, promised that, in the event of their missing her, we would keep large torches burning all night, so that they might find their way back again. It was about one o'clock in the afternoon when they left us, and we kept our eyes on them and the ship in breathless expectation till the shades of evening shut them from our view. About two o'clock in the morning they all returned, poor fellows! much fatigued, led by the torch-lights which we had kept blazing. They had approached within two miles of the vessel about nightfall, when, to their grief and mortification, they saw her men squaring the yards and setting off before the wind, leaving them far behind.

On the evening of the 31st of December, which chanced to be more than ordinarily placid, at a quarter to twelve o'clock we lighted up the lantern, and, having two or three Bibles, we proceeded to the quarter-deck, sang part of the 107th Psalm, read a portion of scripture, and offered up a humble prayer. When our devotions were over it was New Year's morning, and after shaking hands and wishing each other a good New Year, we retired to try if we could get a little sleep. The weather being now fine, we did enjoy some refreshing repose.

On Saturday the 2nd a vessel hove in sight. Not waiting to try signals, having so long tried them in vain, we launched our little boat with a mast and sail; some of the former crew volunteering, and some offering to go who had not gone before, there were seven ready, among whom were our first and second mates. Provided the same way as formerly, and making the same engagements to each other, they set sail, assisting the boat with their oars. There was no cheering this time when we parted ; we were in too melancholy and uncertain a state for this expression of joy and triumph so pleasing and natural to seamen. We spent that night keeping up torch-lights, expecting in the morning to see the vessel approaching us, or at least the boat in view ; but, alas ! there was not a speck seen in the horizon ; both vessel and boat were out of sight.

There was now an accurate examination into the state of the provisions which were left, and we ascertained that we could divide something for ten or twelve days longer. Our case grew more appalling. Day after day passed, and our stock of provisions was wearing to a close. Horrible feelings now took possession of us. No one gave utterance to his thoughts, but it was evident that we must either perish of famine or that one of us must be slaughtered to furnish food for the remainder. Thus we stood upon the crisis of our fate.

While in this desperate condition we were again visited by a ray of hope. On Thursday, the 7th of January, towards evening, and while trying to gather water, it being rainy, the carpenter went to the fore-top, and immediately descried a brig to leeward ; he watched her attentively and observed that she put about. He now cried out and told us she was standing towards us, for there was sufficient light for her to see us. No one can picture the joy we now felt for this prospect of deliverance ; it can be but faintly imagined. At twelve o'clock midnight the vessel was alongside of us, and we were soon taken aboard. The ship was the *Blucher*, of Boston, commanded by Captain Lourie ; she was bound with a cargo of flour, &c., from New York to Monte Video and Buenos Ayres. Our happiness was increased by finding our fellow-sufferers, with whom we had parted a few days before, and who were ready to welome us on deck !

Thus, after suffering for a period of forty-five days, we were again in the midst of comforts and safety. Captain Lourie afforded us all the humane attention which our situation required, giving us our food in very sparing quantities at first, but afterwards abundance of nourishing diet ; and we began to recruit under his care. Resolving to land us on the Azores, he proceeded towards these lonely islands, and in four days' sailing we stood off the island of Fayal. The wind proving unfavourable for landing there, and Captain Lourie being anxious to proceed on his voyage, in which he had been so much retarded by his exertions in our behalf, he desired us, the weather being fair, to get our boats launched and go ashore at St. John's, a small village on the island of Pico, where there was a landing-place for small fishing-boats among the rocks. We bade our deliverers farewell, and in about an hour we were landed at the foot of the Peak of Pico, a very lofty extinct volcanic mountain, covered nearly two-thirds of the way up with vines, orange, lemon, and fig trees, while the top, or crater, is crowned with eternal snow.

We were received at Pico by a great concourse of islanders, who belong to the Portuguese nation. We had the good fortune to meet a Portuguese gentleman here who spoke English fluently, and who immediately told our situation to the vicar, who was likewise in attendance on the beach. We were treated here with much kindness ; bread, cheese, wine, and fruit being brought to us in abundance, and a place of shelter provided. The vicar, who took the charge of us after we had got some refreshment, sent our captain's despatch over to the British vice-consul at Fayal. In two days our messenger returned with a reply, thanking the vicar for his attention to us, and also stating the British Government allowance of one shilling and sixpence per day for each individual in such cases. We remained here about a fortnight, the people all along treating us with much kindness; and we were given to understand that the vicar, after our arrival, had assembled his flock, and publicly returned thanks to Almighty God, who had so wonderfully saved us from a miserable death.

We were so much refreshed and invigorated here that in a fortnight we considered ourselves able to proceed on our way homeward. For this purpose a large boat and a Portuguese crew were provided to take us over to Fayal, a distance of about thirty miles, where we saw the British vice-consul and received every attention from him. From Fayal we were carried to St. Michael's in a coasting schooner, and thence passages homeward for the whole party were provided by the British consul-general, in different vessels which were here loading with fruit for England.

THE DEE.

THIS whaling vessel sailed from Aberdeen on the 2nd of April 1836, with a crew of thirty-three officers and men, and commanded by Captain Gamblin. Sailing northward, the *Dee* touched at Stromness, in Orkney, where sixteen additional hands were taken on board, thence she proceeded to Davis' Straits, and reached the ice on the 15th of May. Preparations were now made for capturing any whales that might show themselves, but the hopes of the crew were in this respect baffled. With unsteady weather for two or three weeks, their progress was much obstructed by loose ice and icebergs; indeed the latter became so numerous and dangerous that fears were entertained for the safety of the ship. After some delays, North-East Bay was gained, and the ship then advanced to Frow Islands. Not succeeding in an attempt made to proceed in a westerly direction, the course was changed to about east-north-east, and after sailing for several days the whaler safely reached the north water, accompanied by the *Swan* of Hull and ten other vessels.

On the 12th of August the *Dee* arrived in Pond's Bay, on the western edge of Baffin's Bay, having encountered only one heavy patch of ice on the way. On the 13th the first whale was seen, and the weather being fine, it was easily struck and secured. The fish were plentiful in Pond's Bay, and during the remainder of the month three others were killed, and three dead ones picked up. The *Dee* then moved a little to the south, but was forced to return, having met with very heavy ice, but no fish. A number of vessels were at this time in Pond's Bay, one of which had been fortunate in killing fifteen whales. Finding the fish getting scarce, and the season well advanced, Captain Gamblin thought it prudent to return homeward. He had gone but a short way when he fell in with the *Grenville Bay*, the captain of which stated that he had tried a passage to the east, and had found it blocked with ice. It was now the 13th of September, and the crew of the *Dee*, beginning to entertain serious fears, went on short allowance. The captain then resolved to try the north passage, and succeeded in getting as far as 75 degrees, in company with the *Grenville Bay* and the *Norfolk*. Cape Melville was now in sight, but the bay ice was too strong to admit of further progress, and, after a consultation, the three vessels on the 20th of September bore away to the south. On the 23rd, with heavy ice around them, they fell in with the *Thomas* and the *Advice* of Dundee, which had also made an unsuccessful attempt to find a passage along the north-east coast. On the night of the 23rd, for greater security, the five ships had to be fastened to blocks of ice, called sconce-pieces. The three following days were spent in fruitless endeavours to find an opening to the south.

Although hitherto favoured with easy weather, the ice now surrounded them on all sides. They submitted to a further reduction in food; their mess being three pounds of bread a-week, with a proportionably small quantity of other provisions. Again the five captains, after due deliberation, bore away to the north. On the 1st of October the weather was bad, with east-north-east winds, and snow, strong ice, and a heavy swell. Signals were once more hoisted for a consultation; but the Dundee vessels did not observe the call. The determination come to in the other vessels was to move as far south as possible for a wintering station.

The falling of the wind kept all the ships nearly in the same place; and on the 8th, the five vessels were fast locked in ice, within sight of each other, at the mouth of Baffin's Bay. On the 10th it was found that the drift had carried them two-and-a-half miles to the south, the wind being from the north and north-east. At this time the ice was so strong that the men could pass between the ships, but in the immediate locality of the *Dee* the swell caused frequent and dangerous disruptions.

From this time the peculiar sufferings of the crew of the *Dee* may be dated. Their allowance remained the same, but, from the scarcity of fuel, their beds became wretchedly damp. At first, to preserve their health, and to keep their shivering bodies in heat, a variety of exercise was allotted to the men, such as the unbending of the sails, unshipping the rudder, and other toils of no utility now to the ship. But the crew had not long to resort to unprofitable labours to maintain the vital warmth of their frames. Notwithstanding the increasing hardness of the frost, the ice still remained in a loose state, and a fatal crush on the ship became the subject of continued alarm. On the 16th large icebergs floated past, and the ice began to press so hard, that the vessel was crushed up till it hung by the quarter; the ice squeezing all along as high as the guard boats. Next morning at daylight all hands were called up to get out the provisions. At eight P.M. the wind fell off, but the ship still hung by the quarter. The ice, however, was at rest till eleven P.M., when there was another dreadful crush, which passed off with less harm than could have been anticipated. On the 18th the ice gave way in several places, and opened up so far that a warp had to be got out to secure the *Dee*. The other vessels meanwhile lay comparatively undisturbed. On the 20th, the ice closed again around the *Dee*. To strengthen the ship, its casks were placed in a peculiar way, and ten strong beams put in aft. This was done most seasonably, for shortly after, two successive shocks took place, of such severity that the crew fled to the ice with their bags, chests, and everything that could be lifted, under the impression that all was over with the timbers of the ship. The sufferings of the night that followed were awful. Without fire or shelter, the crew lay on the ice, while around them icebergs towering to the clouds threatened destruction to all that came in the way of their motions. Miserable as their position was, the crew could not go on board for two days, during which time the ship experienced crushes of more than former severity. On the 22nd the men went on board to take out the remaining provisions, but had again to fly for their lives. The ice, however, fell quiet on the same night, and they again took back their provisions to the ship. On the 23rd, a good many lanes opened up in the water—a most discouraging prospect, for this was always the time of greatest peril. Once more the crew took to the ice, and by cutting the nearest parts into small pieces, cleared the vessel a few feet. The men then rested for a few hours, but were aroused by another crush—the signal that their labours had been in vain. On the 24th the ice broke up to a considerable extent, and the crew managed to heave the *Dee* backwards for a hundred yards to a point where the ice seemed to be thinner. Great difficulties were experienced in conveying the chests and other articles left in the ship, but at length everything was again on board.

Warned by late dangers, and fearful of the wind, which blew from the north-east, Captain Gamblin resolved to cut a dock for the Dee. This was effected by means of heavy ice-saws, in the working of which the crew suffered terribly from the frosting of their feet. The *Dee*, when in the cut dock, seemed to be in comparative safety. From the 26th till the 29th the crew were chiefly employed in dragging ice in boats from the nearest bergs, to dissolve into water: the ice of the bergs being fresh. As the nearest berg was three miles distant, the severity of this labour may be imagined. Four bears were seen and fired at, but without effect; two of the men having a narrow escape from the animals.

Although thus subsisting, to the number of forty-nine men, on a miserable pittance of provisions—with beds freezing, and little or no fire to dispel the cold—the position of the whalers on the 1st of November was comparatively comfortable. The ice was firm around them, and the men might hope not to be overwrought, as well as under-fed. But on the 2d of the month the dock gave way, and the ice again threatened to crush the vessel to pieces. This sad reverse did not overcome Captain Gamblin's fortitude. He again got assistance from the *Grenville Bay*, and also from the *Norfolk*, and cut a new dock, in which with much difficulty the *Dee* was moored. Until the 6th, the weather was boisterous and snowy, and the sufferings of the crew very great; their supply of coals being nearly exhausted. One boat was broken up for fuel, and another soon followed. The dock again gave indications of rending, and the destruction of the hull seemed so inevitable, that the men had to leave the vessel.

A yard of canvas, given to each of the crew by the captain, and made into boots with wooden soles, proved of great advantage. Consolation also, of a higher nature, was not wanting to the distressed mariners. On Sunday the 13th, at the request of almost all on board, Mr. Littlejohn, the surgeon, began to read some sermons and prayers—a duty frequently repeated afterwards on week-days. The worship offered up by the crew was simple, sincere, and consolatory. The daylight had for some time gradually become weaker, and on the 15th the sun was not visible—a thing novel to all on board, and rendered more depressing in its influence on their spirits by the threatening appearance of the ice which the wind, and the current, called the north-east water, still continued to keep in dangerous motion. Up till the 30th nothing occurred worthy of observation, excepting the great change beginning to be visible in the health of the men. Coughs, swelled limbs, and general debility, with small red discolourations on the skin, sharp pains and stiffness, were common. On the 5th, the drifting of the ship was found to be continuing.

On the 12th, the *Thomas* of Dundee, which lay farthest of the five ships from the *Dee*, was almost heeled over by a heavy pressure of the ice, and the men were reduced to a sad condition. On the 13th, the *Thomas* was a total wreck. Two of her crew died on the ice—the first deaths that had taken place. With great toil and hardship the provisions were carried from the wreck by the men of the *Dee* and the *Advice*, and were subsequently distributed, as were also the sailors of the *Thomas*, in equal proportion among the remaining ships. Unfortunately the wrecked ship was too far off to supply firewood. Three days were spent in this labour, and the cold and wet to which the seamen were exposed in performing it laid the seeds of that disease which now began to show its fatal power. On the 18th of December, twenty-one men were affected with scurvy. To add to their distress, the ice again gave way, and threatened to crush each and all of the vessels and their crews.

The 1st of January 1837 was a day of sorrowful remembrance, it being customary for the sailors of whaling vessels to be on New-Year's day with their families. On the 4th, scurvy had made rapid strides among the *Dee's* men; fresh provisions, the only cure for the complaint, being out of the surgeon's reach. On the 5th, the men applied to Captain Gamblin for an increased allowance of provisions. This he declined to grant, expressing at the same time his hope that they knew their duty better than to use force to procure their wish. To their credit the crew disclaimed all desire to employ coercive means, and the captain rewarded their forbearance by giving each man a little additional flour. On the 6th, a brilliant sky gave hopes of the sun's speedy re-appearance, and a large sheet of water on the starboard brought anticipations of release for the ships. Next day most of the crew of the *Dee* were unable to leave their beds, which were in a deplorable state from the intense cold, and also from vermin. On the 11th, the first death occurred in the *Dee*, the sufferer being William Curryall, a seaman. The funeral-prayer was read by Mr. Littlejohn, and the crew then, with sad hearts, carried the body to a distant opening in the ice, where it was consigned to the deep.

Daylight was now showing signs of return, and on the 16th the sun again appeared in the heavens. Captain Gamblin, unhappily, did not long enjoy the light, as his health began to fail, and he was unable to take the usual observations. Under these depressing circumstances, the mate, finding the crew becoming weaker day by day, resolved to take in two reefs of the topsails, from the fear that all hands would be ineffective, if the vessel got out to sea, and a gale came on. Only fifteen men were found able to go aloft on this duty. The drift still continued southward. Four of the men died between the 19th of the month and the 1st of February, and two days after, the heaviest stroke of all befell the *Dee*, in the death of its commander. At the desire of his friend Captain Taylor of the *Grenville Bay*, Captain Gamblin's body was placed in a coffin, to be carried home. The other bodies were laid beneath the polar ice.

Though the whalers were now three or four degrees farther south, the frost was felt to be more severe. Every liquid was frozen; icicles were hanging on the water-cask, at the distance of six feet from the fire. The beds were

covered with solid ice ; the pillows frozen in every part but
where the head lay ; the men all the while bowed down
with mortal sickness. So scarce was fuel, that it could only
be used for the melting of ice and cooking of victuals. By
the 12th of February, six others of the crew had sunk under
their hardships. On the 13th, a stretch of water was seen
not far off, but the bay ice continued strong. The *Dee* was
still moving rapidly to the south. The other vessels were
advancing more slowly, the *Advice* being at this time not
less than twenty miles farther north than the *Dee*. Between the 23d and 27th, six of the survivors of the latter
vessel died, and, by the 7th of March, other five had followed
their departed shipmates. These deaths enabled the remainder to enjoy full allowance of provisions. Six hands
only were able at this time to do duty, and the ship was in
great danger of a fatal squeeze from the ice, which was
loose, and rapidly breaking up. It was still so entire, however, as to allow the mate of the *Dee* to go over to the
Grenville Bay, and ask assistance, should the *Dee* get out
into the open sea. Twenty of his men being sick, Captain
Taylor could not promise help. The *Norfolk* and *Advice*
were about seven miles distant from the *Dee* on the 9th,
and on the 11th the whaler of Dundee was seen with sails
set, going into the open sea. Between the 11th and 15th,
three more of the *Dee's* crew died. On the 16th, after being
locked up for five months and eight days, the *Dee* got fairly
into open water, to the great joy of all on board.

Favourable winds attended the whaler on her homeward
passage, but owing to the fearful scourge which had attacked
them, few of the men were able to go about their duties.
But for the good weather they now experienced, probably
neither the ship nor any of the men would have reached
land. The scurvy was so deadly, that in six weeks, twenty
more of the crew fell victims to the disease. On the 27th
of April 1837, the *Dee* was towed into the harbour of

Stromness, by the *Washington* of Dundee. When Captain Barnett of the latter vessel bore down upon the disabled whale-ship, only three of the crew were able to go aloft. Two days before, the survivors had hailed a fishing boat, when off the Butt of Lewis, but the fishermen, thinking perhaps that the *Dee* was plague-stricken, cruelly refused to render the desired aid. When Aberdeen was reached on the 5th of May, the quay was crowded with the weeping relatives of forty-six seamen, who had died during a voyage of thirteen months to and from the Arctic regions.

THE KILLARNEY.

ON the morning of Friday the 19th of January 1838, the steamboat *Killarney* left Cork for Bristol with forty-two persons on board, twenty of whom were passengers. With the wind blowing stiffly from the north-east she passed the lighthouse, and when fairly at sea the vessel dipped considerably, on account of the heavy freight she carried, part of which consisted of a large number of pigs. Having shipped several seas, the passengers became alarmed, and asked the captain to return to the harbour rather than risk the dangers of the Irish Channel. To that request the crew and engineers added another of like import, and the commander, thus solicited, ordered the packet to be put about for the purpose of returning to the Cove, which was accordingly done : the vessel reaching the harbour about six hours after setting out. At six P.M. the wind had moderated to some extent, but otherwise the weather still continued to wear a threatening aspect. Shortly after dinner, the cabin passengers had the information conveyed to them that the captain was ordering preparations to be made for again starting the steamboat, when they jointly requested that he would go down to the cabin and hear their united protest against such a proceeding. The only answer returned to that appeal was the splashing of the paddle-blades in the water, indicating that the steam-packet was under weigh once more.

As the *Killarney* quitted the harbour for the second time on that fatal trip, it was about eight P.M., and she stood in the direction of Ballycotton, but going very slowly, while the wind momentarily increased until it blew a gale. This continued until midnight, the steamboat meanwhile rolling fearfully, with the pigs bearing her down to leeward, and every third wave breaking over her deck and causing her to ship much water, which poured down into the forehold, as the hatches had been left open on account of the animals stowed therein, to the number of three hundred. The pigs on deck numbered three hundred and fifty, and the commander found that his only hope of saving his vessel and the human lives on board lay in the lightening of the former, by throwing the quadrupeds into the sea. Accordingly, all the available hands were thus employed until four in the morning, but the task was then only partially accomplished, for the pigs clung to the vessel as if destined to be the agents for her destruction.

Till now the crew had managed, by means of the engine-pumps, to work the hold tolerably clear of the water that was shipped, but about the last-mentioned hour some small coal got into and choked the pumps. The water then rose rapidly to the level of the engine-fires, which it extinguished. The engines no longer moved, and all hope of being able to proceed without assistance vanished from the mind of the commander. Some of the sailors even seemed completely paralysed; but others held out bravely, and the captain did all that man could to encourage and stimulate his subordinates of every grade.

With one exception all in the cabin were now silent and despairing. But one voice was to be heard—that of a woman. The passengers had quitted their beds, and congregated in the ladies' cabin, and thence a woman's accents ascended to Heaven for help and succour in their dire necessity. Mrs. Lawe also endeavoured to cheer her companions in misfortune with her counsel and example, as well as by her prayers. The sailors who went down to the cabin she specially exhorted not be daunted, but to put their trust in God, who could protect them on the sea as well as on the land. While engaged in supplicating the Divine clemency, the deck and cabin passengers assembled around her; meanwhile she held one of her husband's hands clasped in her own. Thus she continued until the steward appeared in the group, and called on all to go on deck, as the *Killarney* was nearing the fatal rock.

To add to the horror of their disabled condition, a dense fog hung around the vessel and prevented an accurate idea of her position to be formed. During several hours a number of the crew, assisted by some of the deck passengers, had been engaged in endeavouring to lighten the steamboat by drawing water from the hold with the aid of buckets. These efforts were so far successful as to enable them to get up steam by noon on Saturday, but not in sufficient strength to propel the packet. About three in the afternoon the fog cleared away before a strong wind that speedily increased to a hurricane. But the lifting of that dense curtain, which had for several hours obscured surrounding objects, revealed to those on board best able to realise the situation, the awful certainty that the *Killarney* would ere long strike upon one or another of the numerous rocks that lay about the coast towards which she was drifting. It was when her destruction was seen to be inevitable that the steward entered the cabin and gave notice to its occupants of their approaching fate.

Warned of their danger, but powerless to avert it, the cabin passengers hurried upon deck, to find that a heavy sea had broken over the vessel, carrying away a portion of the bulwarks, together with a number of the deck passengers who had thereto been clinging. The same tremendous wave had also swept away the taffrail, binnacle, breakwater, and the wheel, and cleared the deck of all the pigs that had been stowed thereon. That destructive wave was quickly followed by another, which separated Mr. Lawe from his amiable wife, and hurried him overboard. But Mrs. Lawe soon followed her husband into eternity, for while an effort was being made by the steward to save her, the rope to which she was clinging slipt from her hands, and her body disappeared beneath the surface of the turbulent water.

Between four and five P.M., after several blows against the rock, the *Killarney* was carried upon it by an irresistible sea, when efforts were at once made by the crew to save themselves and the remainder of the unfortunate passengers. Some of the seamen, together with the captain and the mate, secured their own safety by leaping upon a rocky ledge near to which the steamboat had been thrown. But their leap for life had been a dangerous one, and only fitted to be undertaken by men of hardihood and nerve. The less daring men and timid women had to spring into the waves and be dragged therefrom one by one, by means of a rope, right on to that part of the rock upon which the others had landed. It was while endeavouring to reach the shore in this way that Mrs. Lawe lost her life. Altogether, about twenty persons were rescued from the wreck, by being drawn through the breakers, besides those who had saved themselves for a time in the manner indicated.

But the position of the survivors was still dangerous in the extreme, for their rocky asylum was about two hundred yards from the shore, and there was no beach from which assistance might be extended to the drenched and cheerless creatures. A perpendicular cliff, rising three hundred yards above the sea, seemed to oppose a barrier to all hope of rescue from the land. The sailors had contrived to clamber to the sheltered side of the rock; the position of the passengers was not quite so enviable. One of the latter, who wore but a shirt and waistcoat, was seated astride a projection with his face towards the sea. Another clung by his fingers to a crevice, with his toes resting upon a narrow ledge. He lay upon his face and hands, with every sea washing over him; all were exposed more or less to the combined action of wind and sea.

The persons on the side next the land, observing some country people on the rock, shouted to them, hoping to attract their attention, but no answer. The shout may never have reached the land, but some of the countrymen subsequently descended, and carried off some of the pigs that had been washed ashore. Night then came on. About eleven o'clock the wind blew terrifically, but amid the raging of the storm a startling shriek was heard. One of the passengers had lost his hold, and, tumbling headlong, his neck was heard to crack on the hard rock, and he fell into the sea. The engineer some time previously had called to his companions that he was unable to hold on any longer. Putting his hands into his pockets to warm them, a sea washed him from his slender footing. Finding himself falling, he contrived to catch hold of the rock, about twenty feet lower down, by which he held on for some time, every sea washing over him, and eventually succeeded in regaining the position he had lost. Soon after, another who had been dropping asleep was heard to fall into the sea.

When morning broke, some of the country people appeared on the cliff and resumed the work of plunder. They were followed by a number of the neighbouring gentry and some ladies, and then were put into execution some plans for the deliverance of the sufferers. The great difficulty was to get a rope to reach the rock. On Sunday, ducks with the ends of ropes fastened to them were sent out—one only reached, and that the survivors were not able to catch. Wire was attached to bullets, and rope to the wire, and sundry shots were fired, but without the rope being sent to the unfortunate people.

On Sunday, when all efforts to relieve them by the above-mentioned means were found to be in vain, Mr. Hull, brother to the officer of the coast-guard, suggested the fastening of a long rope to one part of the promontory, and carrying it along the beach to the other side, until another dependent from the middle was brought within reach of the survivors. This was effected, but the dependent rope was so weak, and it was then so late, that it was necessary to give over further exertions for that evening, and, direful as was the alternative, leave the unfortunate sufferers exposed to the fury of another night. The night, however, was not so tempestuous as the preceding one, and at daylight many were on the spot to give their assistance, Lady Roberts among the first. On going away at night-fall, the rope was left extended as described, and ready for operations in the morning ; but during the darkness some inhuman wretches cut the hawser and carried it off !

On Monday morning, Captain Manby's life-preserving apparatus was brought from Kinsale, but the same diffi-culty was again experienced. Shots were fired from guns and small cannon brought for the purpose, but without success, and resort was again had to Mr. Hull's plan. This succeeded. Captain Manby's apparatus was affixed to the centre rope, and about eleven o'clock two loaves of bread and a little wine and spirits were lowered to them ; the first they had partaken of for two days. After refreshing themselves they were hauled up in the cradle, one by one.

Their agony it would be impossible to describe, when they on Sunday saw the attempt to rescue them abandoned— when darkness settled down upon the deep, and they could no longer distinguish the figures of the persons on the cliff above.

Their sole sustenance during these two tedious days and nights were a little salt water, and the few scraps of sea-weed that they gathered from one of the bleakest and most barren rocks on the Irish coast. The number rescued from the rock was fourteen, one of whom (the carpenter) died soon after. Two others were lost from the breaking of the rope, and one, a sailor, was drowned in the attempt to swim ashore. When landed, they all seemed in a state of collapse ; their feet were swollen, and the circulation was scarcely perceptible. The following particulars are from Mr. Collis, one of the survivors :—

I went on the deck about fifteen minutes before the vessel struck the rock, in consequence of a heavy sea coming into the cabin. I had been very sick, and lay quiet till then. The vessel drifted stern-foremost against the rock. I saw the rush towards the bulwarks, and an intention of getting over them on the rock. I joined the rush, and being fresh, I think I was the second or third who got thereon. Poor Foster, who had been at the pump, and was nearly naked, got over also. I saw him next me to my left as I faced the rock. Next him was the carpenter, and on the outside of him one of the engineers. To my right stood an engineer ; next him Dr. Spolasco, and next him a woman. Where the rest of the people were I did not see. Some stood on narrow ledges of the rock, and held on by their hands. Poor Foster and myself had very bad footing. Our toes were thrust into holes and we held hard with our hands or we should have fallen. I think this was about four o'clock, and from that time till dusk Foster and I exchanged but one or two words. Just then he complained much of cold—his teeth and mine were chattering dreadfully. He asked me if I had two coats on. I said no, but that if I had, he would have had one of them long before. I gave him my muffler, which he tied round his waist, and I gave him my pocket-handker-chief. and helped him to tie it round his head, as he had no hat on—nor had he a coat or trousers. At daybreak I spoke to Foster, but he did not answer me. I looked at him—his eyes were fixed and staring, but he kept his position. I took him by the hand and tried to open it: in vain—he was stiff and dead. In a moment or two he fell head-foremost and was dashed against the rock below. In about four hours after, the engineer to my left was evidently dead. Dr. Spolasco moved round to the leeward of the rock, next the land. I followed him, and found great benefit from the exertion. On Sunday, the captain was near me on my left; next him was a sailor, and on the upper part above me Dr. Spolasco, in a fissure of the rock. So we remained all day. Towards night, I shifted into a small split about two feet wide, with a bottom to it, in which a sailor and I sat. We remained so all night, and in some degree assisted to keep each other warm. The second night was more calm, and being placed on the leeward side of the rock we were not so extremely cold; every sea drenched us all the first night, and I plainly felt the water running down my back, and out at the legs of my trousers. My feet were completely dead and cold up to my knees, and my hands not much better; another night must have frozen us all to death. When it came to my turn I was taken to land in the cradle. I scrambled up part of the cliff, which was perpendicular and slippery. Some countrymen carried me to the top. I there met a friend, who took me on his back to the next house, where I met Lady Roberts, whose kindness and attention to myself and the rest of the poor fellows soon restored us.

THE ITALIAN SLOOP.

ABOUT fifty years ago, an English merchant was induced to charter a small vessel in order to convey a miscellaneous cargo to Alexandria. By what he considered as a piece of good fortune, an Italian sloop lay in the Mersey, after having discharged her freight, and only awaited the chance of a fresh loading, so that she might return to the Mediterranean. The merchant having agreed to the moderate terms demanded by the master of the vessel for the use thereof, the new cargo was speedily got aboard, and preparations were made for sailing by the master and his crew of seven men, all Italians. Accompanied by a younger brother, Mr. Kerr, the owner of the cargo, stepped on board, and the sloop left the Mersey with a fair wind for her destination. The only persons on the vessel were the eight Italians and the two Englishmen. One of the latter having detailed his adventures during the voyage, the truthfulness of the narrative has been vouched for by the late editors of *Chambers's Journal*. The following is a slightly condensed version of Kerr's story:—

For a time our vogage· was a pleasant one. But before we entered the Straits of Gibraltar, the wind changed, and with it came changes of another and more alarming kind. The master of the sloop, who was a middle-aged man, of sallow complexion, though with features not otherwise unpleasing, suddenly dropped the obsequiousness of his manners, and appeared to shun all intercourse with my brother and myself. As the weather became increasingly squally on our entering the Mediterranean, the man's behaviour became more distant and repulsive, and the expression of his eye at times was such as to excite the most unpleasant sensations in the mind of the two persons who felt themselves wholly in his power. At length the thoughts brooding in the master's mind found vent in words. One day, as I stood on deck, the ship chanced to give a heavy lurch, and the Italian cried out, "I am ruined, and that accursed fellow is the cause of it!" At the same moment he pointed to me, and cast on me a look full of hate and menace, which was reflected from the countenance of more than one of the crew. Similar expressions fell in mutterings from his lips day after day, until I became seriously alarmed, and for the first time consulted with my brother as to my awakening fears. He had observed all that had passed, however, as closely and clearly as myself. Both of us were inclined at first to think that the fears of the master and the crew regarding the weather had only temporarily drowned their better feelings and reason, seeing that the storm came not at our bidding. This explanation of their conduct proved but a pleasing illusion. The weather improved, but this was far from producing any favourable alteration in the master and the crew. Their looks became more and more lowering, and, finally, open threats of murder were vented against us by the master of the sloop!

My brother and myself had long been guarded in our movements, but this menace brought on a crisis. It was now but too plain that our destruction had been meditated by the Italian, and that he had been hitherto merely lashing himself into the proper pitch of fury, and gradually preparing the minds of his men for the execution of the diabolical purpose. How dreadful was the condition in which we now found ourselves ! In the centre of a vast sea, cribbed up in a small vessel in the midst of wretches ready and willing to destroy us—these enemies, eight in number, while we were but two, and one of these two a youth of eighteen—our feelings can be but faintly conceived by those who have never confronted danger in so terrible a form. Though feeling, however, the full horror of our position, we did not permit ourselves to be overcome with despair. The cabin appropriated to us fortunately contained our own stores of provision ; and in this place, after the master's murderous threat, we shut ourselves, barricading the door with all the heavy articles of furniture contained in the room. This proceeding was taken as a declaration of open war ; it was an avowal of our knowledge of the purposes entertained against us ; but it was the only step that could render us even for a moment secure.

Above me I heard the tread of assassins, whose thirst for my blood would not permit them to rest ; beside me lay a beloved brother, entrusted to my charge by a doating mother far away ; a sense of fearful danger and a feeling of deep anxiety were kept graven on my mind from these two causes, independently of all considerations of peril to myself, and yet I did not feel sickened or depressed at the prospect before me. On the contrary, I felt an energetic vigour, both of mind and body, which can only be ascribed to the exciting nature of the circumstances in which we were placed. As I painted to myself the possibility of a death-grapple with the men by whom we were surrounded, I felt my muscles become as hard in every limb as a cable rope, and was conscious of possessing such capabilities of exertion as would render my death no easy matter for even eight foes to accomplish.

The excited spirit did not forsake me. In the afternoon of the day following that on which we shut ourselves up, my brother and I found it impossible to endure any longer the close confinement of the cabin without enjoying a mouthful of fresh air; and after another consultation, we came to the resolution of going together upon deck. Determined to sell our lives as dearly as possible, we armed ourselves with two large carving-knives with which the room was fortunately provided, and took with us every other defensive weapon which we possessed. Thus equipped, we stepped upon the deck, locking the cabin-door behind us. Glaring eyes, like those of hungry tigers, were fixed on us by the master and the crew, but the fire of watchful determination lit up the glances that were returned for theirs, and the villains quailed at the thought of attacking two resolute men, or more probably they calculated upon having a future opportunity of taking us off our guard. We were allowed to return to our cabin unmolested. But no man had spoken to us; no one had bid us good-morrow; every countenance was sullen, dark, and lowering.

For many consecutive days a similar scene was daily repeated. During each of these visits to the open air, every motion made by us was performed with such caution as became those whose movements were watched by demons, ready to spring upon their victims on the slightest show of incaution. But although it seems impossible that they could have been unsuccessful in a combined attack, their hearts uniformly failed them; for they saw well that some of them must have fallen—that we would not die alone!

Matters were in this situation when, by my calculation of time, it seemed to me that we should be approaching the eastern Mediterranean coasts, as our course had not been changed, as far as I could observe. An alarming confirmation of this conjecture was presented to me one night as I sat alone in the cabin, my brother having laid himself

down to sleep. The night was calm, and all was silent as
my own brooding and voiceless thoughts, excepting the tramp
of two men walking upon the deck. These were the master
and his mate—worthy and inseparable associates! Either
they spoke louder, or the evening was stiller, than usual;
for I distinctly heard the murmur of their voices, which in
the like situation I had frequently endeavoured to catch in
vain. I placed myself in the most favourable position for
hearing, but my ear could gather sound only, not sense.
At last, however, the voices increased in loudness—a violent
stamp was made upon the cabin roof—and I heard the
master's voice exclaim, with a curse which I shall not repeat,
and in tones which showed that passion had for the moment
got the better of prudence, "It must be done to-morrow,
Antoine! Cowards! to think that we should have so long
shrunk from two men! But, to-morrow they must die, or we
lose our chance. We are close on shore, and will be boarded
by some one immediately!" The mate appeared to have
reminded him of his imprudence in making this loud
exclamation as they recommenced their walk, and their
conversation sank to the same murmuring tone as before.

On that momentous night I closed not my eyes. The
sentence which I had overheard, although in one sense a
death-knell, was in another a signal of hope. We were
approaching the neighbourhood of human beings who were
not our enemies—of those who might rescue us from the
fangs of these murderous harpies. To be ready for whatever
might happen, I packed up all our most valuable articles,
partly in a small box, and partly about my person. I
resolved also not to acquaint my brother with the words of
the master, but to go upon deck by myself on the following
day, and bear the brunt of the anticipated assault alone.
That I should go on deck I was determined, as there only
could the means of emancipation be found.

But my brother had not been asleep; he had heard the

words of the master distinctly, and he insisted in the
morning upon going with me upon deck and sharing my
peril, whatever it might be. As I stepped on deck, I felt
that the scowl which was cast upon me by the master was
returned by a glare of as tiger-like a character as his own.
My glance rolled keenly from side to side as I observed
some more suspicious movements than usual on the part of
the master and mate, and I prepared to buckler my dear
brother's body with my own, and die like a brave man!
The fatal moment was evidently drawing nigh, and I silently
but fervently commended my soul to my Maker, when
suddenly—"A ship! a ship in the offing!" was the cry
from one of the crew. The master and the rest all ran to
the farther end of the sloop, and gazed towards the vessel.
I also would fain have gone and made signals to it, but
dared not move from the spot. Things remained in this
position for some minutes, the crew being still busy with
the ship in the distance, when my brother touched me on
the arm, and whispered hurriedly, "A boat! a boat close
under us!" It was so. A small boat, with four men therein,
had come near us unobserved. I made eager signs for it to
lie-to, and at the same time motioned to my brother to bring
the box from the cabin. He did so, noiselessly; in one moment
it was into the boat, and in another we had sprung into it
also, with all the energy of desperation. "Row! row! for
our lives and for your own; and for this," was my earnest
whisper to the boatmen, showing a purse well-filled with
gold. They seemed at once to comprehend that it was a case
of peril, and pulled swiftly in the direction to which I
pointed, which was, the reader may be assured, the opposite
one to that in which the Italians still gazed. All this was
the work of a moment, for it was work done by men whose
faculties for exertion were indescribably aroused. When
the crew of the sloop did observe our departure, we had
made a considerable way from them, and all that they could

do in their impotent rage and vexation was to send an un-offending shot after us. They did not attempt to follow. It may be that, on consideration, they congratulated themselves on the possession of the cargo, which must have been the main object of their desires, and trusted never to see us again.

The first thought, it may be supposed, of my brother and myself on finding ourselves fairly free of the Italian sloop, was one of gratitude to heaven for our deliverance from that awful bondage. Our rescuers proved to be fishermen of the Delta, dwelling near the mouth of the Western Nile. Once safely ashore, and the personal jeopardy of my brother and myself ended, my mind reverted to my property, and I resolved not to let the treacherous Italians off, without making some attempt to reclaim what was my own. Calculating, from the point at which I was landed, that they would probably run for the port of Alexandria, I hired a boat to carry us across the Bay of Aboukir, and through Lake Mareotis to that city. My conjecture was correct; the Italian sloop was in the harbour. The authorities were applied to, and so strong were my proofs of a right to the cargo that the greater part of it was yielded up to me; but a due consideration of the scanty chances of justice there, and a deficiency of evidence, made me depart from my purpose of charging the wretches with their perfidious intent to murder.

Printed by WALTER SCOTT, "*The Kenilworth Press,*" *Felling, Newcastle.*